GUILT
and the
CHRISTIAN
a new perspective

GUILT
and the
CHRISTIAN
a new perspective

by
Jeffrey G. Sobosan

THE THOMAS MORE PRESS
Chicago, Illinois

ISBN 0-88347-140-X

Contents

"And human love needs human meriting;
    How hast thou merited—
Of all man's clotted clay the dingiest clot?
    Alack, thou knowest not
How little worthy of any love thou art!
Whom wilt thou find to love ignoble thee,
    Save Me, save only Me?
All which I took from thee I did but take,
    Not for thy harms,
But just that thou might'st seek it in My arms.
    All which thy child's mistake
Fancies as lost, I have stored for thee at home—
    Rise, clasp My hand, and come!"

Francis Thompson
The Hound of Heaven

Preface

THIS book gives me the opportunity to examine at length the experience of guilt. For this I am deeply grateful to the kind invitation to write it from Joel Wells, editor at Thomas More Press. Unhesitatingly he also permitted what initially was to be a very small book to grow into its present size as I became more involved with the permutations the experience of guilt can take in Christian living.

The following pages are meant to be what I like to call a "spiritual entertainment." By this, however, I do not mean that I want the book to entertain the reader so much as I want the reader to entertain the book—to take what I say into himself in a personal and persuasive way. For only then can I be certain that my time and effort in constructing it have been worthwhile. Some writers, we know, exercise their craft for themselves; it gives them a tremendous feeling of contentment. But I do not; it is too much work for mere self-satisfaction. I exercise it for you.

I would also like to acknowledge now for their unqualified attentiveness to the needs of a working author two administrators here at the University of Portland, Rev. Richard Berg, C.S.C., Dean of the College of Arts and Sciences, and Rev. Richard Rutherford, C.S.C., Chairman of the Department of Theology. Finally, as in my other books, I need to acknowledge the wit, patience, and understanding of my good friend and colleague, Rev. Thomas E. Hosinski, C.S.C., who is like a safe harbor in often turbulent weather. To him this book is gratefully dedicated.

Introductory Words

MANY of our experiences are outright sources of joy for us; many are sources of pain. Of those experiences that cause us pain, however, some can be used so that their final result is not a negative but a positive one. I am going to be suggesting throughout this book that guilt is one of these experiences. Left alone, unused for any further purpose, the experience of guilt is pain-producing. It can cause frustration and embarrassment; or more seriously, self-comtempt, even self-hatred; or more seriously still, despair, a paralyzing sense of one's worthlessness. When the experience of guilt does not break its own confines, when it is not set within a larger context of experiences, it can only generate forms of pain in our minds and hearts. Drawing meaning solely from itself, guilt always leaves behind a damaged, aching human spirit.

The spiritual life always requires a certain delicacy of perception if the individual is to see the less obvious currents of meaning in his experiences.

Otherwise he can too easily succumb to what I call "the seduction of the immediate." By this I mean that on the basis of the immediate or unreflected effects an experience has on him he concludes that these are the *only* effects that experience can have. He commits, in other words, the classic error of all inductive logic: he tries to make the particular universally applicable. And so it never dawns on him that guilt can be more than pain-producing because he has never gone beyond its immediate effects in a thoughtful way. He remains stuck in his pain and his sole task becomes the discovery of a way to live with it. This is a situation of pathos, pity, wherein guilt is approached as one might an enduring and debilitating cancer. The concentration of the individual is on his pain rather than on how he can make it serve the purpose he intends for his life. Guilt, in short, has become an end in itself.

What we will be doing in the following pages, then, is suggesting a wider frame of reference in which guilt can cease being only a source of pain for the individual and become a constructive element in shaping the meaning he wants his life to possess. More specifically our suggestion will be that this wider frame of reference is provided by the individual's commitment to Christian living, his conviction that the witness of Jesus is the "way" he must follow in guiding his existence. Why have I selected this particular frame of reference in which to place the following discussion of guilt? The reason is basically two-fold.

First, I am aware that most if not all of the readers of this book will be professing Christians. More than that, they will be Christians with an active interest in pursuing their appreciation of experiences they judge pertinent to their commitment as Christians—in this case the experience of guilt. The very fact that they are reading this book seems to me a sufficient demonstration of this point. An indifferent Christian, after all, would be spending his time in other pursuits. I have therefore written the book for the concerned rather than the unconcerned Christian, and its abiding frame of reference will be my understanding of guilt as it relates to Christian commitment. On the other hand, I will be suggesting in chapter one that the experience of guilt *in itself* is not specifically Christian or even religious; that it only becomes such when *intentionally* placed within the context of Christian or religious commitment. Otherwise it remains a bald human experience accessible to anyone. What interests the Christian, in other words, is the *gestalt,* the configuration of meaning that his experiences of guilt take on when they are qualified by fidelity to the witness of Jesus. It is the same interest, for example, that a Buddhist would have when he qualifies his own experiences of guilt by fidelity to the teachings of Gautama, or a Moslem to the teachings of Mohammed, a Marxist to the teachings of Marx, and so on.

Secondly, I have set this book in a Christian framework as a reaction to the research I did before I began writing. In addition to the obvious study of books and articles, this research also included personal interviews with countless people. During its course, however, I became increasingly alarmed at the ease (and rapidity) with which many people assigned to "religion," particularly Christianity, a perverse complicity in creating the guilt they experienced. It was as if they would live guilt-free were it not for this complicity, as if Christianity is clearly the culprit who has invaded human consciousness with guilt. An excellent example of this stance can be found in Paula and Richard McDonald's popular book, *Guilt-Free*. Not only is the title itself an immediate deception—no one can eliminate the experience of guilt from his life, like he might a bad cold—the treatment of Christianity (particularly Catholicism) is condescendingly simplistic and misleading. Witch-hunts are always unpleasant to read about, especially when the hunters have foolishly, or worse, deliberately misrepresented their prey. As opposed to the above book, therefore, I would recommend the much more profound and perceptive analysis of guilt you will find in a book like Paul Ricoeur's *The Symbolism of Evil*. It is far from easy reading, but a close and attentive pursuit of the book will draw from you a more thorough and

sympathetic appreciation of the relationship between Christian commitment and the experience of
guilt. Needless to say, I am hoping that this book
too will have a similar effect. Its intent is not only
to tap characteristics of guilt with which the reader
is already presumably familiar (feelings of irresponsibility, defilement, the need to be forgiven, etc.)
but to offer him perspectives on the meaning of
guilt which he may not have yet considered.

We cannot be naive here. There is no doubt that
along the course of its history the Christian community has developed strains of piety that have encouraged what I will call in the following chapters
an "illegitimate" guilt. Christians are only human
beings, after all, trying to teach each other what it
means to follow their Lord. And sometimes this
teaching has gone awry and distortions of the witness of Jesus have occurred. In chapter one we will
see that Jesus himself faced similarly distorted
teachings in the religious community of his own
day as represented in the Pharisees. In chapter
three, we will home in even more closely on this experience of an illegitimate guilt when discussing the
motives and manifestations of scrupulosity. Our
suggestion throughout these pages will be that
while Christian piety has sometimes encouraged an
illegitimate guilt, the teachings of Jesus not only do
not encourage it but are clearly involved in an argument with any piety that does.

Guilt, as we said, is an experience from which we

are never entirely free. And anyone who denies this is deceiving himself and/or you. We are creatures of consciousness, valuing beings who are placed in a world where guilt is an undying possibility. It is our recognition of this point that will underlie the discussion of temptation and evil in chapter two. We will describe temptation as the experience which continually keeps guilt around the everyday corners of our lives; we will say that evil, *doing* evil, is the actual cause of guilt. Both these phenomena, temptation and evil, are embedded deeply within the tradition of Christian spirituality, and within any trained Christian conscience. Our discussion of each will rely on this tradition and training, as well as on the analysis of convictions and responsibility offered in chapter one.

Again, however, the intent of our remarks will be to suggest that while guilt in itself is a negative experience, it can be employed in positive and beneficial ways toward developing the meaning of Christian commitment. The individual, of course, always has the option of stopping with the negative experience and allowing this to determine his understanding to Christian living. But then he brings pain into his life which he need not. More seriously, he does a disservice to the witness of Jesus. For while the interior Master clearly recognizes that the lives of his followers will be hard and difficult, he also teaches that true commitment to him ends in the abiding presence of a spirit of tranquility, not the pain and peacelessness of guilt. I have suggested in another book, *The Ascent to God,* that certain humor is required to understand this teaching, an awareness of one's limits no matter how strong or heart-felt one's commitments. In this regard I might also note that the very word "humor" may in fact share the same root as the word "humility" (*humus,* earth, soil). In that case, like humility, it would require an act of self-abasement indicating an ability to assess accurately one's limits without despairing in pride or self-pity over this assessment.

The movement of guilt in human minds and hearts is typicially *centripetal* (if I may borrow a term from physics). By this I mean that the direction of the experience is inward; it concentrates the attention of the individual on himself. He becomes occupied with his own life, the failures and inconsistencies he finds there, and seeks to amend these for his own sake, for the "clearing" of his conscience and peace of mind. What I will suggest in chapter three, however, is that this centripetal (or inward-directed) movement is only the first of two movements in the individual's consciousness of his guilt. The second movement following it must be *centrifugal,* or outward-directed. Then the individual's attention is concentrated no longer on himself, the guilty effect on his own life of the evil he has done, but its effect on others. Our discussion will center specifically on the experiences of forgiveness and repentance in Christian life and their relationship to guilt. We will be recommending that the movement of guilt in our minds and hearts is always cut short whenever it does not turn outward, away from ourselves, in consideration of others.

The experience of guilt can run away with us. It can become obsessive in our lives and begin to affect how we think and feel across the board. Thus when we begin to examine our own personal history (or more widely, the history of the race) we see only reasons for an enduring, irremovable guilt. Our own lives become a repeating tale of the same faults, the same sins, the same evil deeds. And the wider history of the race reveals only a story of racks, guillotines, all the depraved tortures of which human beings are capable. We conclude that reasons for guilt characterize human life like open, unhealable wounds. There is no lasting grace, no final blessing in human endeavor, nothing that redeems us from the malevolence which is the final line, the summation of our history. At this point we have slipped into the spirit of pessimism we will describe in chapter four. And in the process we have abdicated the profound realism we will also describe as the viewpoint represented in the witness of Jesus. Within the context of Christian commitment there can be no such thing as an irremovable guilt nor the spirit of pessimism which it breeds. There can be only a realistic vision of human endeavor which acknowledges the causes for both guilt *and* blessing in our lives.

Let me conclude with some dictionary definitions. Their merit is that they presumably represent
the commonplace understanding of a word. Webster's defines guilt as: "1. The fact of having committed a breach of conduct, especially as violates
law and involves a penalty. 2. Guilty conduct; sin.
3. Guiltiness; culpability." The reader can see,
however, that by itself this definition does not aid
very much in understanding the experience of guilt.
To achieve a fuller understanding we must isolate
for further investigation the two key words "law"
and "culpability." Webster's defines the former in
this way: "The binding custom or practice of a
community; rules of conduct enforced by a control-
ling authority; also, any single rule of conduct so
enforced." The latter, culpability, is defined as:
"The state of deserving censure or blame." Working with these two additional definitions we may
then offer as our own definition of guilt something
like this: *The experience which occurs from vio-
lating without excuse the laws or customs of your
community when you are convinced these derive
from an authority greater than yourself.* The community that will concern us in this book is the
Christian community; the remainder of these pages
will be devoted to understanding what our definition of guilt might mean for its members.

I

Convictions and Responsibility

THERE are a number of starting points I could have selected to initiate these reflections. But since my principal intent is to offer suggestions regarding the religious, specifically Christian understanding of the experience of guilt, I would like to locate my starting point in the same place Christian tradition locates the beginning of all human experiences. That place is the story of the Fall and exile of humankind recorded in the third chapter of the book of Genesis. We know it as the story of Adam and Eve. In a vocabulary perhaps many of you find comfortable, we may look upon it as the classic "case study" describing the source of the guilt we feel—a case study whose general outline has the added merit of being familiar to us all. It is embedded at the very beginning of scripture because an appreciation of its meaning will affect the way the rest of scripture is read.

The story, however, can function not only as a case study; it also functions as a myth. By this I mean that it provides us with a conceptual framework, a *rubric* if you will, for understanding experiences we have—for our interests, the experience of guilt. The words of the story, I am saying, are not to be taken literally, as if the truth the story is teaching us is immediately apparent upon a first reading. It is not; and to think it is denies the subtlty and genius of the authors. The truth, rather, is not the words themselves, as writing, but is contained *in* the words. And it is our task to draw this truth out. Let us engage this task through the following series of observations.

1. *Fallenness and Exile*

1. The story is meant to apply to all human beings, represented in the two individuals Adam and Eve. And to the extent it does not, it fails. Each of us must see himself in Adam, each in Eve—which means that the story, while admittedly set within a religious context, intends to offer not just a religious but also an anthropological statement. That this is indeed the intent of the authors is clearly conveyed in the very names they chose for the representative couple. "Adam" derives from the Hebrew word of the same spelling and means "ruddy" or "rough," as in "ruddy complexion." What the reader must keep in mind here is that for the originators of the myth, living on the eastern swing of the Mediterranean where the heat of the sun, the dryness of the air, the lack of effective

emollients, and simple aging tend to roughen human skin, the word is being used as a term describing the general appearance of all human beings. (Adam, in fact, is typically used as the generic word for "man" and "mankind.") "Eve," on the other hand, derives from the Hebrew word, *hehweh,* which means "to live." When you combine it with "Adam," then, you know that in the story of these two individuals the true intent is to tell the story of all living human beings. Or if you prefer: The story is a case study not just of two people but of all of us.

2. The locale of the story is a garden situated in the east (Eden) where nourishment is readily available and harmony defines the relationships among creatures. We are all familiar with the pictoriography of Paradise. Yet the foremost characteristic of the locale is not the pleasant environment it provides but the fact that here the man and woman "walk with God in the cool of the day," meaning that they enjoy direct discourse with him. I mention this characteristic now because it will become important to us later on when discussing the meaning of the exile from the garden subsequent to the man and woman's sin.

3. The antagonist in the story is the serpent. He is clearly superior not only to the other animals but even to the man and woman. He is described as the most clever and subtle of all creatures, so that as soon as he is introduced into the story we know that

the man and woman will be unable to resist the persuasiveness of his suggestions and taunts. Given the general function of serpent figures in archaic myths —as symbols of chaos—we also know from his first appearance in the story that things will start going awry. This character of the serpent will become critically important when we try to locate the deed we traditionally call the "original sin" and try to understand the nature of the feeling of guilt following upon it.

4. With the trial put to the man and woman we come to the heart of the story. Its specific context is God's mandate that they not eat of the tree of good and evil knowledge. They submit until the serpent becomes active, confronting the woman with the inquiry, "Why may you eat of all that grows in the garden save this tree?" The woman responds with the only answer she can, "We may not because God has forbidden it." The answer is clearly sufficient for the woman. But the serpent persists, "Why has God forbidden it?" To this inquiry Eve simply rehearses the reason given by God himself, "Because God has said that on the day we eat of the tree we will surely die." All during this exchange, of course, we know that the serpent is going to emerge the convincing partner, demonstrating a cogency in argument before which the woman appears only naive and gullible. We already know of his superior cleverness and wit. We know that the woman does not stand a chance and will suc-

cumb eventually. And so she does with the serpent's very next statement. He denies the reason given the woman by God for not eating of the tree, arguing instead that God's mandate is based on the knowledge that to eat of the tree would make the man and woman themselves "like unto Gods." It is too much; it is irresistible. The authors of the story know that there can be no greater temptation than the thought that there is a way for God's creatures to become like God himself; that the characteristics of divinity are accessible to human beings. And so the woman succumbs, eating of the forbidden tree; and the man too, under the influence of the woman's recital of the serpent's words.

5. Traditional piety has usually located the commission of the "original sin" in the above deed. And the guilt that follows is consequently seen as the effect of disobedience to God's command. But we now know that this cannot be. The character of the serpent prevents this viewpoint—unless we say that God judges the man and woman on the basis of a temptation they are clearly incapable of resisting. This idea, however, would have been abhorrent to the authors of the story, since it requires the image of a God who relates maliciously to us. No; if we wish to locate the sin that causes the man and woman's guilt we must look further into the story, to what they do after their disobedient act.

6. The man and woman try to hide. In shame over what they have done (they have, after all, dis-

obeyed God) they seek to avoid his presence. But who can hide from God? A person might hide from himself, burying his awareness of those portions of his life that bring him shame. He might even hide from others, keeping secret from them whatever he wishes. But no one can hide from God; the idea would have struck the authors of the story as irrelevant or just plain silly. Thus the man and woman are found, and we come at last to the scenario describing the true test that God wished to set for them. He knows they have been disobedient, but their disobedience is only the preliminary act needed for the confrontation that now occurs. To God's question about how they know they are naked, they confess they have eaten of the tree. *But neither one of them stops there;* neither is satisfied with the simple confession. Each goes on to relate *why* he and she has eaten of the tree. And what is the reason each offers?—this is what interests God far more than their disobedient deed. "It was not my fault," says the man, "the woman seduced me into the deed." "It is not my fault," says the woman, "the serpent seduced me into the deed." It is these further words they speak, these words of blame and the refusal of responsibility for what they have done, that causes the anger of God, his disappointment and rightful judgment. For all along it was precisely this confrontation that would provide the trial of their faith, the test of their integrity in relating to each other and to God. And their failure here, their mutual blaming and irresponsibility, is where in fact we must locate their sin, the original sin.

7. The feeling of guilt that goes hand in hand with this sin thus derives from an awareness of irresponsibility: the individual has not accepted accountability for his deeds but has tried to attribute it to others. If we are to believe the story, guilt is at root always born from the consciousness that the individual has illegitimately refused responsibility for what he has done; guilt is the result of a denial of integrity. And if we accept the intent of the story—that it is not conveying a truth about just two people but about every living human being —we know that this intent has been adequately acquitted. Every human being who has ever lived has committed the "original sin"; we have all repeatedly refused responsibility for what we have done, seeking to place it on others. We have all engaged in mutual blaming; we have all suffered the guilt this produces. Each of us is indeed Adam; each is Eve.

We cannot end our discussion of the Fall, however, with only an interpretation of the sin committed. We must also recognize that the sin produces a certain result, and that this result, like the sin itself, has a role to play in our understanding of guilt.

Genetic Ignorance

What is this result? I want to suggest that it is ignorance, and that this suggestion is supported in the story in two different ways. First it is supported in the saying that after the Fall the man and woman are exiled from the garden. Why is this exile important? Traditional piety has tended to answer this question by pointing to the harshness of the life the man and woman must now lead outside the garden —the toil for food, the antagonism of other creatures, subjection to aging and diseases finally leading to death, and so on. But this answer is obviously insufficient, since it presumes that the man and woman knew nothing of these experiences prior to their sin. To take this stance, however, begins to make demands on our intelligence that we cannot meet. It requires that we consent to the idea that the sin altered the very being, the very nature of the man and woman so that now they will undergo experiences they previously did not. But how can we accept this and understand them as human from the very moment of their creation? We cannot. No—to understand the true effect of the exile we must look elsewhere in the story, and only then raise the issue of why life outside the garden is described as being so harsh.

I would suggest that this true effect is expressed in the saying that after the exile the man and woman no longer walk with God or see God face to face—expressions which I view as euphemisms for the idea that they no longer enjoy direct discourse with God. The presumption being made in the story is that the lack of such discourse issues in ignorance, that is, an inaccessibility to God's will and providence and thus to the "truth of things." It is because of this inaccessibility, in other words, that the experiences in life we previously mentioned are in fact harsh. If the man and woman could only know for certain why they must toil for their food, why conflict emerges among the creatures of God, why they must age and grow sick, what awaits them at death—if they could only know for certain the meaning of these experiences, if they had direct access to God's will in them, their harshness would dissolve. Yet it is precisely because they do not have this access, because they no longer "walk with God," that these experiences are sources of pain for them.

The second way the story suggests ignorance as the result of the Fall is expressed in the idea that the knowledge gained from the forbidden tree is of good *and* evil. Why this is another way of describing the emergence of ignorance in human consciousness reflects a simple psychological logic which I would outline as follows. If a person believes without qualification that everything is good—all people, events, situations—then his certainty regarding this goodness dismisses from the outset the possibility of ignorance. From the beginning his evaluation of his experiences is premised on the unquestioned presumption that they are all good. So, too, with the person who believes oppositely that without qualification everything is evil;

he also has dismissed from the outset the possibility of ignorance in evaluating the people, events, and situations that populate his life. It is only when an individual knows both good *and* evil he becomes ignorant. It is only when he can ask regarding some experience, "Is it good *or* evil?" that he can find himself speaking with his next breath the classic confession of all ignorance, "I don't know."

It is exactly to this confession, of course, that all conscientious parents (whether they like it or not) must bring their children. For as a child's reflective abilities begin to emerge he will tend to conclude, under the pervading influence of his parents' benevolence, that all people behave benevolently. But then he begins to experience the malevolence of which human beings are also capable. And so he now tends to conclude just the opposite from what he did at the first stage—namely, that all people behave malevolently. His response to this conclusion can take any one of several turns. He can become frightened and withdrawn; he can become increasingly, even neurotically dependent on his parents (whom he still sees as completely benevolent and protective); he can become aggressive and mean-spirited, absorbing into his behaviour the malevolence he believes everyone possesses; and so on.

I know a boy, Timmy, who has recently entered this second stage of development and has chosen the aggressive/mean-spirited response. Needless to say, his parents are both concerned and confused as to what their own proper response to Timmy's present behaviour should be. From a trusting son he has become a suspicious one; from a receptive, affectionate child he has become a recalcitrant, cold, and bullying one. My suggestion to the parents has been that Timmy has undergone a yet unidentified trauma that has initiated him into the human capacity for evil, and that this experience has temporarily diminished or repressed his awareness of the human capacity for good (even as he continually experiences this goodness in them). My advice to the parents has been to encourage in Timmy an awareness of both the good and evil in human beings; to teach him to live with the mature satisfaction that the question of human goodness or evil cannot be answered without qualification one way or the other.

In analyzing the result of the Fall in the above way (as ignorance) we see that the story in Genesis again presents us with a truth about all living human beings, not just the two named Adam and Eve. Just as we repeatedly commit in our own lives the sin committed in the story—the sin of claiming irresponsibility—so we are all prey to the ignorance which derives from no longer "walking with God." Left on our own we are plagued with the knowledge of good and evil, the inability to answer *with compelling certainty* any inquiry regarding right and wrong behaviour.

But within the religious context of the story in Genesis (a context that Christians, too, must recognize), the point is precisely that we are *not* alone; that despite the exile from the garden we still do have access to God's will; and that this access gives us a compelling certainty regarding questions of right and wrong behaviour. Only now the access no longer derives from "walking with God" but from faith. It is no longer produced from the external activity described in the metaphor but from an internal activity of the mind and heart.

For the religious consciousness, of course, this faith, this internal activity is not something indifferently approached, as if it were simply a "take it or leave it" option. It is not something that makes little difference but all the difference in the world —specifically in appreciating how the experience of guilt is to be understood. It is premised, as we said, on the conviction that God does not abandon us completely in our ignorance but sufficiently "intrudes" into the course of human development to reveal his will regarding the meaning of right and wrong behaviour. That is why we noted at the beginning of this chapter that a proper understanding of the myth of the Fall is essential to an appreciation of why the rest of scripture is written. Scripture is in essence a "lifting" of our ignorance regarding God's will for us; it is the record providing the framework in which we can determine what is right and wrong behaviour. Religiously speaking, in other words, guilt can arise only within the context of the conviction that God's will is in fact known—but that we are nonetheless capable of going against it. Yet since this knowledge is in turn based on the personal conviction that God has indeed revealed his will to us, we must conclude that the experience of guilt derives even more basically from a going against ourselves, that is, from any deed, any thought or action, that expresses infidelity to the convictions we have shaped. Though we have only touched on it here, this relationship between guilt and personal conviction will have to be kept in mind throughout the remaining pages. *The experience of guilt is born from an act of disloyalty toward oneself; it emerges whenever an individual contradicts his convictions.*

So far we have kept our remarks within a specifically religious context. This simply reflects what will be our basic approach throughout this book. We should note, however, that they could be applied just as legitimately in a non-religious context. There are countless surrogates for God's will that can function as the sources of convictions we shape. In later pages, for example, we will suggest that one of these for a small child is his parents. His relationship with his parents is the principle indication to the child that he is not alone but has access to a will that provides him with compelling certainty—conviction—regarding right and wrong behaviour. His parents are the little child's god and goddess whose words are always presumed to be true. The child, of course, in what is often a traumatic process, discovers in time that this presumption can no longer be blindly affirmed but must be approached with discretion; that he need not feel guilt in all situations when he transgresses the parental will; that he has developed convictions apart from, possibly contrary to, those provided by his parents. Again, however, these differing convictions need hardly be religious. They can derive from quarters that either ignore or are openly hostile to the idea that God's will is accessible to us. An individual might become convinced, for example, that the writings of Marx provide the most persuasive basis for determining right and wrong behaviour, or the writings of Buddha or Epicurus or Freud or Nietzsche. Or he might become convinced that peer pressure provides this persuasive basis, or the pursuit of personal pleasure. In all cases convictions are shaped without appeal to the accessibility of God's will. But the convictions are still just as influential over the individual's behaviour and still can cause guilt when betrayed.

Unhealing Guilt

We should also acknowledge at this point not only the possiblity of a "profane" but of an unhealing sense of guilt—that is, the seemingly permanent feeling of broken convictions that many people experience. Let us look at this feeling a bit more closely, seeking to identify its source. And to give direction to our seeking let us use as our specific guide, appropriately enough, the witness of Jesus. For one of the more remarkable merits of this witness, I think, though it is commonly ignored or overlooked, is that it can instruct us in general psychological truths about our behaviour as well as the specific interests of the religious consciousness.

I would like to begin with an act of the imagination. I would like the reader to place himself back in time to the religious community in which Jesus lived, Judea of the first century. And I would like him to ask: What is the heart of this community, the source of its living relationship with God? He must answer: The Law, the patterns of right and wrong behaviour that had developed throughout the previous history of Judaism.

Yet even the slightest reading of the New Testament indicates that Jesus found this heart cold, not life-giving but killing. He had a quarrel with the Law (or at least with its teachers, the Pharisees) that was relentless. It caused the hatred of many toward him, and contributed to their desire to be rid of him. Why; what was Jesus' quarrel with the Law, the patterns of behaviour he found within his community? To answer this question we must trace, even if very briefly, the understanding of the Law as it was received by those with whom Jesus lived and prayed.

The Law was initially meant to be a consolation

to the people. *It was intended to provide them with the assurance that certain patterns of behaviour were pleasing to God, while others were not.* As Israel became religiously mature, however, or at least more morally sensitive, it became obvious —and this is the critical thought—that the great law codes of the Old Testament were not entirely effective in fulfilling this intention. The primary code, for example, the Decalogue of Ten Commandments, dealt for the most part with borderline situations in life, extreme behaviour that made it somewhat irrelevant to everyday life. Most people, after all, did not ordinarily commit murder, perjure themselves, steal, commit adultery, blaspheme God by idolatry or profanity. The remaining major codes (the so-called Jahwist Ritual, Deuteronomic Code, Holiness Code, Code of the Covenant, and Priestly Code) were able to maintain greater relevance, particularly in their ritual prescriptions (the laws of atonement, cleanliness, filial respect, etc.). But again, a large portion of these laws were pertinent only to the priests and did not touch the everyday lives and concerns of ordinary people, who still wanted the security of knowing what to do in order to please God.

It was to answer this question (in large part, I believe, under the influence of "wisdom" teachings) that there developed in Judaism that almost obsessive interest in interpreting the Law which culminates in pharisaism. These interpretations were often exquisite in their detail. To the question a common man might ask, for example, "How do I obey the third command, keep holy the Lord's day?," the response might come back, "Among many things here is one you must not do: you must not walk more than fifty cubits" (a cubit is the length between a man's fingers and his elbow). Anyone can easily see what has happened here. The Law which originally was meant to serve the people, telling them how to please God, has become a burden. In the detail and complexity of its interpretations, *which in common piety possessed the authority of God's revealed will,* it had become impossible to fulfill. Far from creating a feeling of consolation in people, it only created a permanent sense of guilt, the constant feeling of being disloyal to one's convictions regarding right and wrong behaviour. No matter how hard an individual tried to follow the Law, he was always aware of points in his life where he was breaking it; he was continually experiencing guilt.

It was into this situation that Jesus came preaching his message of the fulfillment of the Law. What does this mean? What is the "fulfillment" Jesus preaches? To answer this question I would like to draw an example from science. Everyone is familiar by sight with the mass/energy conversion theory of Einstein: $e = mc^2$. It is a simple formula expressing the idea that energy is equal to mass multiplied by the speed of light squared. But how many people are familiar with the overwhelming amount of work that produced this formula, the mathematical detail and intricacy that undergirds it? Very few are, and very few are expected to be. But that is not what's important. All that matters, rather, is whether the work is fulfilled in the formula, that is, whether the formula represents *and* justifies the work.

A similar analysis, I think, can also be applied to the question of Jesus' fulfilling the Law. What he does is to take the mountain of interpretive details in the Law which were thought to express God's will and simplify them into a few set formulas. In the process, of course, just as with the procedure Einstein would have followed, extraneous or contradictory interpretations had to be identified and eliminated from consideration. This Jesus obviously did, as the gospels amply indicate.

Now it is my position, shared by other theologians, that this whole process of fulfillment (simplification, reduction) is represented in two major formulary stages in the New Testament. The first stage is represented in the blessing of the Sermon on the Mount (Matthew 5) and in the Mandates of the Kingdom (Matthew 25). We may understand the first half of this first stage, the so-called Beatitudes, as characteristics of the frame of mind the individual must develop in order to express God's will, God's law in the world. We may understand the second half of this first stage, the Mandates, as characteristics of the behaviour that is born from this frame of mind. The two, the attitude and the activity, must go together; they are inseparable. The first without the second is sterile; the second without the first is blind.

The second stage is represented in the command of the double love. It fulfills (simplifies) the Law even further than the Beatitudes and Mandates.

> When the Pharisees heard that Jesus had silenced the Sadducees they got together and, to disconcert him, one of them put a question, "Master, which is the greatest commandment of the Law?" Jesus said, "You must love the Lord your God with all your heart, with all your soul, and with all your mind. This is the greatest and the first commandment. The second is like it: You must love your neighbor as yourself. *On these two commandments hang the whole Law,* and the Prophets also" (Matthew 22:34-40; see also Mark 12:28-31, Luke 10:25-28).

The first point to note about this command is that neither of its two loves is given priority *in importance,* though Jesus does appear to give the first love priority *in sequence.* He seems to be saying that you must first love God before you will know how to love your neighbor. Presumably he means that you will indeed love God as soon as you become aware of the fact that God has first loved you (by giving you life, by offering you redemption, etc.).

The second point to note is that "neighbor" is a generic term meaning everyone. That Jesus intends this meaning is perhaps brought home most clearly in the parable of the Good Samaritan (Luke 10: 29-37). The individual who proved himself a neighbor to the wounded man is defined not as the person who is near him geographically (the wounded man had been traveling) nor "spiritually" (the priest and levite passed him by) but the man who showed him love.

The third point to note is that there is actually a third love embedded in the command: You must love your neighbor *as* (you love) yourself. The presumption here is that you do indeed love yourself; in fact, that unless you love yourself you will scarcely be able to love others, let alone God. You cherish your desires and goals, for example, and wish to make yourself lovable to others. The requirement in the command is that you extend this love of self to others by cherishing *their* desires and goals, by making *them* lovable to others.

The fourth and for our interests most important point to note is that while the mandate of Jesus requires *that* we love, it offers no explicit details on *how* we love. To be sure, when the rest of his witness is taken into account there is some detailing of this *how* (we have already mentioned the Beatitudes and Mandates of the Kingdom); love always exists within certain behavioural confines. But when compared with the strictures present in the Jewish Law the command of Jesus, as Paul confesses in his letter to the Romans, could only be experienced as liberating. For it is now the individual himself who defines the specific patterns of behaviour he must adopt *in his own life* to express fidelity to Jesus' mandate. They are not defined for him by others in ways that do not (or cannot) consider his limits. While the experience of guilt consequently remains a possibility for him, it is no longer something forced upon him by others who require behaviour that gives recognition to the confines of his own particular existence (his education, talents, etc.). No—because his specific patterns of behaviour are now self-determined on the basis of his conviction regarding the truth of Jesus' mandate, his experiences of guilt are also self-determined. The law that guides him, in short, is now a personal law; it is the object of his free decision within the context of the specific circumstances that describe his life. Or differently said: His experiences of guilt are now something he brings upon himself.

We may note that experiences of unhealing guilt, like the convictions that guide our behaviour, need not emerge only within a religious context. There are guilt-ridden people who seldom if ever exercise their religious consciousness. Impossibly precise and demanding patterns of behaviour based on peer pressure, for example, can cause a permanent sense of guilt. The advertising media know this very well, of course, and continually suggest that the refusal to purchase a certain product somehow diminishes your humanity or respectability (or, very commonly, your beauty and attractiveness) in the eyes of others. For a person convinced that status before peers (other businessmen, other housewives, etc.) is the determining influence shaping criteria for right and wrong behaviour, this relentless pressure from the media (among other sources) can issue in a constant feeling of guilt: I am always failing in something I should be or have to maintain my status. What may at root be a legitimate conviction (I should behave so as to gain the respect of others) has, like the sanctity given all the laws of the Pharisees, gone to an extreme in its demands. And thus the conviction is turned into the source of a permanent and burdening guilt. In this situation the individual may, of course, remain guilt-ridden. But then he leaves himself open to the damaging, sometimes killing effects that an unending guilt always produces in the mind and heart.

One of these effects that we might touch on here is an unremitting sense of loneliness. It is this loneliness, for example, that describes the life of a woman I know whom I will call Beth. She sees herself as existing in a world requiring so many expectations of her—expectations she is convinced she must meet, but which she consistently doesn't—

that her guilt issues in a constant feeling of alienation, "foreignness," "unacceptability" in the
world surrounding her. Beth is never "at home"
with the people and events that populate her life because she is never at home with herself. She feels
that she is always under scrutiny regarding her behaviour, a steady watchfulness to see if she acquits
the demands made of her, and that she is always
failing this scrutiny. Her life has become like a hall
of mirrors; everywhere she turns she sees only reasons for experiencing guilt. Gradually her feeling
of unacceptability in the world around her has become more acute, and this in turn has produced her
heart-rending loneliness. Beth has allowed her
world and what she believes to be its legitimate
but overwhelming demands on her to become the
source not only of an unhealing guilt but an iso-
lating guilt.

An individual in Beth's situation may, as we
said, remain there, forever prey to the loneliness
that an unhealing guilt can generate. Or she may
opt to follow the procedure recommended by Jesus. She may affirm his basic conviction, but then
determine on her own discretion its specific applications in her behaviour. In that case whatever guilt
she experiences will be neither forced upon her nor
unhealing. Within the limits of her own life, guilt
will emerge whenever she breaks the patterns of behaviour she herself has determined are appropriate
expressions of her conviction. But just as she can

now blame no one else when she breaks these patterns of behaviour (without committing, as we have suggested, the "original" or basic sin), so she now has it within her power to heal this breach, and with it the source of her guilt. Just how she might go about this healing process will occupy us at considerable length in chapter three when discussing forgiveness.

2. *Obedience and the Shaping of Convictions*

Convictions, of course, do not fall out of the sky; they do not enter our lives willy-nilly. There is a process, a pedagogy that leads to them. And St. Paul, I believe, is as apt as anyone in describing what this process is. He calls it "obedience;" and it would be worth our while to examine at some length what he means by this word. Our suggestion will be that if the root cause of guilt is disloyalty to our convictions, then guilt must be understood within the context of obedience.

The word obedience is a conflation of two Latin words: the prefix *ob-*, and the main root, *audire*. The prefix almost always functions in Latin as a preposition meaning "on account of" or "because of" or "through (the agency of)." But in some instances it also functions as an intensive, that is, it indicates that the meaning of the word following is to be emphasized. In these instances the word is always used as a prefix to a verb, never as a preposition (so far as I can discover). It functions in the same way, in other words, as the much more common prefix *con-,* as in the word "confess." To confess is not only to admit or acknowledge (from the Latin root, *fiteri*), but to do so openly, without reservation. The same function could also be traced out in the derivation of other *con-* words, such as I have done elsewhere with the word "contrition" (See Jeffrey G. Sobosan, *Act of Contrition,* Notre Dame: Ave Maria Press, 1979, pp. 16–19).

Our concern, then, when studying the meaning of "obedience," must center on the word that follows the intensive prefix. In its Latin form this word is *audire,* meaning "to hear" or "to listen." Obedience (*ob* + *audire*) thus means not only to hear or listen, but to do so intensely, thoroughly, with full attention. It is the type of hearing, for example, that would describe prayer or reflection or study when you engage in these without distraction. It is not a half-hearted hearing, a minimal or indifferent listening to what is being heard. It is full-hearted devotion, a single-mindedness toward what is being heard, an experience, in a sense, of rapture. Obedience centers the thoughts and feelings of the individual on the object of its concern. It gives direction to the wanderings of a fragmented mind and a divided heart.

Our understanding of obedience, however, cannot stop simply with this description of the type of hearing it involves. Then it would be little more than a recognition of the human capacity for prolonged, concentrated, and controlled attention. What we must do, rather, is go on and draw a conclusion from this description. And the conclusion, I think, is this: that what the individual has heard thoroughly, intensely, fully, what he has studied, prayed about, reflected on, *will become the source of a conviction he forms.* He does not remain indifferent to what he has heard, the object of his obedience. He does not stand away from it as a disinterested observer, a mere analyst. No—because of this study, reflection, prayer, because of the time and energy he has expended, he has become involved in what he has heard in a personal fashion. And this involvement, precisely because it has been intense, issues in a conviction, a judgment regarding the object of his obedience.

We must obviously be careful here. For there is a demonic element that can also emerge in this whole process. This occurs whenever convictions cease to grow and develop; or whenever the continuing prayer, study, and reflection required by obedience are no longer practiced; or whenever there is little or no awareness that people with other convictions might teach the individual something that could refine or even alter completely his own convictions. It is an awareness of this element, I think, that underlies Jesus' several observations about the obstinacy of the Pharisees, their hardheartedness and refusal to tolerate convictions other than their own. Similar observations, of course, could also be made (to greater or lesser degrees) about each of us. Demonic convictions are paralyzed convictions. They express a conceit and self-asertiveness about the utter rightness of the way one thinks or feels that makes them far more suitably the forerunners of sin than the children of obedience.

The relationship I wish to draw between obedience and guilt is now transparent and may be captured briefly in the following definition: *Obedience is fundamentally an act of personal loyalty.* It is loyalty to your convictions, just as disobedience now becomes an act of personal disloyalty, a refusal to acknowledge in your behaviour what you affirm as true in your mind and heart. Disobedience, in other words, is primarily a going against yourself, and as such is the fundamental act that issues in the experience of guilt. It is not primarily a refusal of some authority outside yourself—as the commonplace understanding suggests—just as obedience is not primarily subjection to this authority's will.

Obedience and disobedience are first of all internal qualities of the individual's character. They define the fidelity or infidelity with which he approaches some truth of which he is convinced. That is why the ancient feeling commonly associated with guilt, the feeling of defilement, describes so accurately the effect guilt can have on an individual. He feels "dirty," unclean, because by his disobedience he has soiled with contempt something (his conviction) he has judged true and worthy of attentive care. He has defiled himself.

A classic illustration here is Shakespeare's Lady Macbeth. In a sleepwalking trance she continually wrings her hands in a cleansing motion because of the blood she feels there from her complicity in murder. The intent is clear: she is trying to wash herself of the defiling guilt she has experienced because of her crime. On a more ordinary level it is this very same image—"washing away" the feeling of defilement that comes from guilt—that describes the piety surrounding many Christian penitential rites (for example, Catholic "confessional" practice). I can adequately substantiate this from my own experience as a Catholic priest. To my frequent inquiry of penitents, "Why have you come to confession?," I often receive the reply, "Because it makes me *feel clean* inside."

From the above observations we will thus conclude that whenever it is engaged *only* on the external level—the level on which the criterion of judgment is solely the alignment of one's will with someone else's—the question of obedience has been incorrectly reduced to political or sociological considerations in which the more serious issue of personal integrity has been sidestepped. Then the experience of guilt becomes centered on the external relationships the individual has with others (and so becomes more readily susceptible to that feeling of unhealing guilt we described in the previous section) rather than on the internal relationship he has with himself.

Training in Guilt

The experience of guilt that is centered on the external relationships one has with others is typically characteristic of the child. When a child experiences guilt it is not usually because he has offended some personal conviction (he is not generally capable of the obedience that leads to convictions) but because he has offended the will of a superior authority, a parent or teacher or peer group. The feeling of alienation that guilt produces in a child is other-directed more than self-directed; he feels estranged more from those around him than from himself. And consequently it is to these external relations that he will look to heal his feelings of guilt. He believes, for example, that behaving in extraordinarily pleasing ways toward his parents will provide an adequate "salve" healing the guilt and estrangement his previously displeasing behaviour has produced. He tries to make up for his misdeeds and their consequences in good deeds. We will see in chapter three that this simple perception of the child (that wrong behaviour can be healed in its effects by subsequent right behaviour), when understood with a greater sophistication, also provides an important basis for the healing of guilt in adults.

It is this very perception, for example, that under-girds the spirituality of the *mitzvah* (good deed) which plays so dominant a role in what both Testaments have to say about the experience of being forgiven.

I would now like to suggest that the pedagogy which leads from the child's concentration on his relationships with others as the source of his guilt to a concentration centered on his personal convictions goes through three basic steps. I would describe them as: 1. the stage of the simple imperative; 2. the stage of the *quid pro quo* contract; and 3. the stage of singlemindedness. Each, I think, also finds a parallel expression in the pedagogy of the religious community that develops from the Old to the New Testament.

1. The stage of the simple imperative. In this stage, right and wrong behaviour is determined on the basis of a simple mandate from a superior authority. It is enough here to be told, "do this; don't do that," without explanation or promises. Pedagogically this is the stage of the little child who will understand a simple imperative but not a rationale accompanying it. When a two-year old toddler crawls over to a wall and you can see that he has every intention of inserting the handle of his spoon into an electrical outlet, you do not try to explain to him why he should forsake his intention. You do not lecture him on the neurological damage it will cause his body; you do not promise that he

will be deprived dessert at the evening meal. The child is not going to understand anything you say in explanation. Instead you go up to him and issue the simple imperative "No!," perhaps repeatedly and with some harshness in your voice. If the child nonetheless persists in his intention you may need to support your imperative with some subsidiary act, perhaps a light slap on his hand. The point is that your simple imperative must create in the child (for the child's own good) an inarticulate feeling of guilt regarding the particular activity under consideration. He must learn that somehow he is displeasing you, the superior authority, by engaging in this activity, and that avoiding your displeasure is of more worth than doing what he desires.

In the biblical record, this stage of human development is represented in the Decalogue, the code of the ten commandments. These also are formulated as simple imperatives without explanation or promise. The superior authority, of course, is Jahweh, and the presumption is that his simple command is a sufficient motive for determining behaviour. The decalogue represents the first stage in the community's growth toward singlemindedness. Here guilt is also experienced as the result of an offense against the will of an acknowledged authority (God); and its healing again occurs as this offense is followed by appropriate acts overcoming the estrangement the offense has produced. Everyone is familiar with the exquisite detail these atoning acts frequently involved in Old Testament piety. The important point to remember about them, however, is the demand that they be *relevant and proportionate* to the offense committed. I mention this now because it will influence our remarks later on about the relationship between guilt and contrition. For, in Christian piety, the idea that atoning acts can heal guilt has frequently ignored the idea that these acts must be relevant and proportionate to the offense committed. When they are not, the experience of guilt tends to linger on; the individual remains unpersuaded that he has sufficiently acquitted his responsibility to overcome his wrong behaviour by corresponding good behaviour.

2. The stage of the *quid pro quo* contract. In this stage right and wrong behaviour is determined on the basis of an agreement with a superior authority. Once a child reaches a certain level of consciousness it becomes increasingly difficult to issue simple imperatives regarding his behaviour, or at least to do so effectively. For, faced by these imperatives there will eventually emerge the question "Why?" It is in response to this question that the superior authority—let us say the child's parents—begins to form a *quid pro quo* relationship with him. This typically follows a punishment/reward scheme and is captured in a statement like: "If you do this, then I will do that." Guilt at this stage of development is thus experienced in the context of a lack of integrity: the individual has contracted with a superior authority regarding appropriate behaviour, and

then has broken this contract. If the contract also happens to be set within a reward/punishment scheme, then the guilt he experiences will likely be compounded by fear. It is a fearful or frightening guilt that he now feels. Oppositely, when he fulfills his part of the contract it is not just contentment that he feels over his practice of integrity but also the joy of receiving the agreed upon reward.

The parallel to this stage of human development occurs in the two Testaments in the great law codes that evolve subsequent to the Decalogue. For the most part these are clearly premised on a contractural (or fealty) relationship with God that recognizes mutual obligations between the agreeing partners. In fact a preliminary indication of the format of these codes can already be found in the edited version of the fourth command that appears in the Decalogue: "Honor your mother and father so that you may live long in the land." Long life is clearly being presented here as the reward for filial respect —an approach that is taken in none of the other nine commands. Guilt in the context of these codes thus emerges for the same reason as it does in the second stage of the behavioural training of children. It emerges from a lack of integrity: the individual has contracted with a superior authority (God) regarding appropriate behaviour, and then has broken this contract. Moreover, since it is almost universally presumed in the codes that to break an agreement (a covenant or testament) with God is a fearful thing, the *quid pro quo* contract underlying the codes is typically set within a reward/punishment scheme. You cannot deny your fealty to God with impunity; his justice will be swift and appropriate.

3. The stage of singlemindedness. In this stage right or wrong behaviour is determined on the basis of a conviction the individual has formed. As a child's consciousness continues to develop and he begins to exercise greater critical ability, it becomes increasingly plain to him that the *quid pro quo* contract undergirding his patterns of behaviour is frequently transgressed in ways that make him feel cheated. He does the good, and no reward follows; he observes others being wicked, and they are rewarded for it. If experiences like these occur often enough, the question "Why?" will again emerge. Only now its context will be, "Why should I do the good when it issues in no reward; why should I avoid evil if evil can bring me joy?" The questions, of course, are rhetorical; his experiences have already provided the answer, "I should not." And with this answer the guilt he previously experienced from a lack of integrity in fulfilling the contract determining his behaviour begins to dissolve. He cannot feel guilt while he simultaneously feels cheated. It is too unfair. Consequently he moves away from fidelity to the contract, more often than not toward behaviour in which the determining criterion for right and wrong is the question, "What is best for me?"

When the above question emerges in the course of a child's development the task of pedagogy is to encourage singlemindedness. By this I mean that the superior authority—again, let us say the child's parents—must abandon the *quid pro quo* relationship they have so far used for his instruction in right and wrong behaviour. In its place they must now engage the difficult task of encouraging within the child a fidelity to the good *precisely because it is good*. His own experiences have already taught him that to practice this fidelity for the sake of a reward is often frustrating, even maddening. The parents must tap this negative experience. They must use it delicately to move the child toward an appreciation of good behaviour for no other reason than that it is good. In the process they must obviously encourage in him as well the realization that fidelity to the good will indeed often hold no reward; in fact, it may often cause him pain. In other words, what they must initiate in the child is the obedience we previously described, the personal involvement in questions of right and wrong that will issue in a conviction which, suspending questions of reward and punishment, becomes the basis of his behaviour.

Purity of Heart

In the two Testaments this third stage of human development is paralleled in the teachings of Jesus, specifically in the sixth beatitude taught in the

Sermon on the Mount, "Blessed are the pure in
heart." Purity of heart is singlemindedness. In
Kierkegaard's telling phrase, it is to will one thing.
This is opposed to the doublemindedness that underlies the *quid pro quo* approach to one's behaviour, wherein the good is done not for its own sake
but for the sake of a reward. The good is willed
only because a more basic willing is focused on its
corresponding reward. What Jesus is trying to
teach in his sixth beatitude is that this doublemindedness will always be caught up short by experiences like those previously described, when the
good we do is not only not rewarded but even punished. He is trying to encourage us to suspend all
such considerations and, on the basis of our convictions, to do the good anyway, no matter what the
results. It is clearly a hard, difficult doctrine that
Jesus is here teaching, all the more so whenever
considerations of ease in determining our behaviour have become a paramount concern. The example of Job comes to mind here (an example we will
recall more than once in succeeding pages). He is
the perfectly good and faithful man whose life has
nonetheless become a tale of monstrous suffering.
Yet it is his friends, not Job, who seek ease—the
easy explanation, the easy solution—in dealing
with his situation. Their words are a blight upon
Job's mind, a distraction and temptation away
from the only stance that he believes possible, the

stance of singlemindedness. He must remain a good and faithful man for no other reason than his conviction that this is the way he must be. And while it causes incomprehension, a hostile confusion that prohibits peace of mind, his undeserved pain cannot kill his conviction. Jesus in Gethsemane, suffering the same incomprehension, the same hostile confusion that turns his sweat to blood, would have embraced Job as a brother.

The scenario of Gethsemane is written differently in each of our lives. We are all repeatedly confronted by the fact that the good we do is greeted with indifference, mockery, contempt, even outright hatred. The thought that continually intrudes upon us in these situations takes the form of an inquiry, "Why bother to do the good?" Until an individual reaches the third stage of development we have described, the stage of singlemindedness, he will be unable to offer a convincing response to this inquiry. Should he continue to do the good, then, it will typically be because he fears the response of a superior authority should he refuse. But this is only an *external* response to his inquiry, premised on his relationship to others more than on his relationship to himself. For all the while he is doing the good he may in fact wish he were doing evil. But his fear holds him back. Only when he becomes singleminded does this fear dissolve, because now his response is an *internal* one premised on his relationship with himself, that is, his convictions. But while fear may dissolved at this stage when he fails to do the good, the experience of guilt still remains a possibility. And again it emerges as the result of an act of disloyalty—directed now, however, not toward a giver of simple imperatives or toward a contract made with others, but toward himself.

II

Temptation and Evil

THE ideal of Christian living is to exist without offense against our convictions, to be singlemindedly obedient to the revelation of God's will in Jesus. It is an ideal in the sense that we can approximate but never completely enact it. Or differently, it is an ideal because while it is not achievable it is nonetheless *workable,* that is, capable of being pursued in life. It is within the context of this ideality of Christian living that we wish to examine in this chapter the experiences of temptation—specifically temptation against the way of life proposed to us in the life of Jesus—and evil. In the process, our intent is also to gain a more thorough appreciation of the experience of guilt. Temptation, we will suggest, may be legitimately and fruitfully understood as the setting in which guilt becomes a possibility; evil, we will say, is the actual cause of guilt.

1. *The Experience of Temptation*

Let us start our reflections with a dictionary definition. Webster's defines "temptation" as:

"1. Act of tempting; seduction. 2. State of being tempted, or enticed to evil. 3. That which tempts, especially to evil." To understand the meaning of temptation, therefore, we have to go back to the meaning of "tempt." This word derives from the Latin, *temptare* or *tentare,* which means to handle, attack, test, urge. Webster's definition consequently reads: "1. *Archaic.* To put to trial; to test. 2. To endeavor to persuade; to induce; incite. 3. To lead, or endeavor to lead, into evil; to entice to what is wrong by promise of pleasure or gain. 4. To provoke, as anger, or a person to anger." The merit of these dictionary definitions lies in their conciseness. As we noted in the Introduction, they provide a starting-point for reflection on what is presumably the common understanding of a word.

Whenever we admit that we are subject to temptation we are acknowledging the weakness that is laced throughout some conviction we possess. Weakness can here be described as a lack of energy either to do something or to resist something being done to us. It is the awareness of this weakness within us that causes both the uncertainty that we can withstand a temptation, and the preference to avoid any situation where this uncertainty is resolved. Our suspicion is that the persuasion or enticement that constitutes the temptation can overcome our will to resist it. Temptation always involves the question of conviction—more specifically, the strength of a conviction in the face of an inducement to abandon it.

Awareness of our weakness before temptation thus has a direct bearing on our commitment to Christian living. Conscious of the fact that we can only approximate in our lives the witness of Jesus, we are simultaneously conscious of the existence and strength of those factors that seduce us away from this witness. We are caught between our conviction regarding the revelation in Jesus and our weakness in maintaining fidelity to it. In other words, we are not at peace with our goals. They conflict with each other, and this conflict is what we call temptation. And so, while we strive to be generous, while we assert this as a goal for our behaviour, we still find delight in greed. Or while we strive to be forgiving, we still take satisfaction in spite. Or while we seek humility, pride always stands in our way. It is a conflict of *wants* in which we are here engaged. We want to be generous, forgiving, humble; yet we also want to be possessive, spiteful, and self-assertive. This is the bifurcation in our desires—the truth that we are not singleminded creatures—that tempts our pursuit of Christlikeness and makes guilt a possibility.

The experience of such conflict can be harrowing. If we presume that an individual's conviction regarding a certain ideal is sincere, if we say that it has "captured" him as a guide for living, then all serious temptation against it will be disturbing, disorienting. The conflict will have a tendency to freeze or paralyze the individual. He will experience decisional difficulty, a lack of willfulness, an inability to re-affirm or deny his conviction. He will be caught between the conviction and the temptation, finding neither stronger than the other—like a hungry animal caught equidistant between two sources of food and unable to decide which direction to take. We find such conflict expressed, for example, in the individual standing before a piece of merchandise he is being tempted to steal from a store. He is like a statue, just staring at the merchandise, letting it fill his mind. But his outward immobility belies the inward conflict he is experiencing. He wants the merchandise while also wanting to remain faithful to his conviction that thievery is wrong.

In situations like this we have just one of many concrete illustrations of the ambiguity in our convictions. Without a conviction we could hardly view the conflict of options before us in terms like "fidelity" and "temptation," "weakness" and "strength." Instead, the options would be simply that—options—and choosing one or the other would derive from considerations other than a conviction regarding right and wrong patterns of behaviour. In this case the man who is considering the theft of the merchandise would now be hesitating not because the theft conflicts with his behavioural ideals, but because he is weighing the possibilities of being apprehended. This is what defines the nature of his paralysis as he stands before the merchandise, as opposed to the paralysis of the first man. The difference between them is that the second man sees each of his options amorally, whereas the first sees one option as good, re-affirming his conviction regarding an ideal, and the other as evil, denying this conviction. Each is frozen before the decision to commit the theft, but their reasons are worlds apart.

We can put the above distinction differently by saying that the second man does not *wonder* why he is being tempted toward the theft, whereas the first man does. For the second man the temptation represents a congruence of circumstances that has brought him to a point where theft is a feasible act for him. Perhaps these circumstances were arranged through his manipulation; perhaps they are the result of mere chance. In either case, however, he does not wonder *why* he is considering the theft, but only that it is a possibility now before him. In following this line of thought, of course, he shows himself a good pragmatist, concerned only with the obvious, concrete results of his behaviour. He does not ask himself what results this behaviour might have beyond its specific context; what it indicates about his character; what it says of his values.

The situation of the first man is quite different. His thoughts are centered not on the chances of success or failure in the theft, but on why he is considering the theft at all. It is a disturbing wonder that occupies his mind—how his conviction can so easily be placed in jeopardy; how the discipline with which he has nurtured his conviction can so easily be weakened. In a sense, he is amazed at the temptation now before him, because it raises doubts about a conviction that he believed was definite. And he is disoriented by his amazement because it presents him with an awareness that his convictions are easily affirmed in an armchair, but not so easily when put to an actual test.

Testing Our Commitment to Christian Living

With the last remark we come to what Webster's defines as the first, though archaic, meaning of the word "tempt." I am not sure why this meaning is termed "archaic." If the term intends to indicate that the meaning is an ancient and respected one, then I have no quarrel with it. But if it intends to indicate that the meaning is no longer used, then obviously I do, since it is precisely the meaning I employed above. As there described, a temptation is a test or trial of some conviction the individual possesses; it is what makes the experience of guilt a possibility. It is the proof demonstrating the sincerity of his conviction, the verification that his conviction is not mere bravado, an empty bragging, a convenient posture. To offer a concrete example: it is the meaning of temptation that underlies a man's view of a beautiful woman as a "temptress" against his conviction regarding marital fidelity or religious celibacy. She presents him with a trial of this conviction, all the more difficult if she is agreeable to a sexual liaison or is actively pursuing it. She is a living option against which his marriage or religious vows are tested. Her seduction is an opportunity that demonstrates the strength or weakness of his conviction.

The outstanding scriptural case study of the above meaning of the word "tempt" occurs in the book of Job. This is not meant to disparage other examples, such as Abraham's temptation on Mount Moriah when he is asked to sacrifice Isaac, or Moses' temptation in the desert when he is asked by his followers to deny his faith in Jahweh. But whereas these temptations form a part of the stories about Abraham and Moses, the *entire* story of Job, all we know of Job, is a record of the testing of his faith in God. From the very first verses of the Book of Job this purpose is set forth. The prologue in heaven tells of a bickering Satan's point that Job is faithful to Jahweh only because his faith has never been tried. Job is blessed with wealth, children, a good wife, power. Why shouldn't he manifest a praising fidelity toward Jahweh, since he has no reason for cursing him? Jahweh is irritated by the argument—it has too much the ring of truth—

and so agrees to Satan's suggestion of tormenting Job to discover if his faith is as easily lost as it has been easily won. The intention of the book to record a trial or test is further justified by the very meaning of the word "Satan," which best translates as "adversary" or "prosecutor," as in a courtroom. That this is the meaning of the word, however, is not entirely unexpected. For of the five principal angelic functions described in the Old Testament—revelation, healing, consoling, reprimanding, testing or trying faith—the last (after revelation) is by far the most common. It is premised on the idea that an individual's words, his promises or protests of faith in God, mean nothing until they are proven true before an attractive opportunity to deny them.

In the New Testament the outstanding example of this same meaning of "tempt" occurs when Jesus is assailed on the mountain with doubts of his mission. Again Satan is cast as the adversary or prosecutor whose purpose is to test Jesus' conviction regarding God's will for him. Lesser examples, without the figure of Satan, also occur in Gethsamane and on the cross when Jesus cries out his words of despair. In each instance Jesus is in a conflict situation where he must decide to re-affirm or deny his conviction to submit always to his Father's will. And in each instance, we may be sure, he undergoes a harrowing, disorienting experience. The anger on the mountain, the sweat of blood in Gethsemane, the agonizing cry on the cross—all these indicate that the temptations of Jesus were profound trials of his faith in God.

The temptations that Christians face are similar in kind, though not usually in degree, to those of Jesus. What shapes the behavioural patterns of a Christian is his conviction regarding the rightness of Christlike living. It is this conviction, for example, that causes his indecision before the temptation to steal. He cannot picture Jesus as a thief. Yet there he is, a Christian professing the desire to be Christlike while contemplating theft. His profession is at odds with his contemplation, his conviction with the opportunity now before him. And he is disturbed and disoriented, much like Jesus was on the mountain, in Gethsemane, on the cross. Unlike Jesus, however, every Christian knows how easily he has given way to these temptations in the past, how seductively they have lured him despite all his discipline in attempting to live as Christ. His past is a list of failures in this attempt. And he asks for deliverance from temptation out of concern for failing even more in the present and future.

In older days the source of temptation against Christlikeness was laid squarely at the doors of Satan or one of his cohorts, the lesser demons. It was a primitive psychology that reigned, and the prevailing image was that the demon created the tempting situation and/or planted the tempting thought in your mind. The demon is still the adversary. But whereas in the book of Job he was still at the service of God and could only tempt by God's will, later on, at least in popular spirituality, he was thought to be an all but autonomous power, able to tempt without the consent of God. From being the servant of God, even if an irritating, somewhat unmanageable one, he became the enemy of God. No longer an angel in the court of heaven, he became the lord of hell.

Nowadays, of course, most educated people do not understand the source of their temptations in such a personalized fashion. They do not imagine the temptations as coming from the whispering of a demon in their minds, or the demon's power to manipulate situations and events. They do not think that save for the existence of the malevolent power of these demons they would otherwise not be tempted away from Christlikeness. The demonic is not a personal entity whose absence would allow us an unswerving obedience to God's will in Jesus. Rather, the demonic is a part of our very world, our existence, the existence of others. Jesus himself seems to suggest this very idea in that harsh and condemning rebuke of his disciple Peter, "Get behind me, Satan" (Matthew 16:23). It is not some other entity that Jesus is addressing, but the man Peter himself, the close friend, the favored follower tempting him away from obedience to his mission.

Peter is himself the tempter, Peter's words the temptation that Jesus sees as satanic, adverse to the will of his Father.

The modern sophistication that has dismissed the idea of personal demons, therefore, should not dismiss at the same time the idea of the demonic in existence. The demonic may be understood as all those factors that lure us away from expressing in our lives the witness of Jesus. We need not picture the demonic as a three-headed beast, as with Dante, or a clever-witted and rational being, as with Goethe. But we can picture it as an influence or quality in existence that deflects us from the goal of Christlikeness. The notion of a demonic tempter can be ignored, in other words, but the notion of demonic temptation cannot. For every professing Christian lives with this temptation without respite. It awakes with him in the morning and retires with him at night. It wears the masks of people he knows, situations he encounters, events that befall him—all the elements that describe his life in the course of a day.

The above understanding takes something of the spectacular out of the demonic. The literature of previous ages could record in epic language the warfare between Christian and demon. The lines of battle were clearly drawn, the issue clearly stated, the victor the one who proved the more committed to his position. It was a view of the demonic that elicited heroic images of both tempter and tempted.

Today, as we said, the demonic is much more familiar, unremarkable, prosaic. It is not a spectacular intrusion into a life that is otherwise quite ordinary. It is not so unusual, so out of proportion or out of place, that it is immediately perceived as the demonic. Rather, it resides precisely in the ordinariness of life, so much so that its temptation becomes all the more insidious. Beaudelaire was right when he said that the neatest trick of the devil is to convince us that he does not exist. The easiest way this can be done is when the demonic becomes so intertwined with our ordinary existence that it goes unseen. Having become so close a part of our lives, we become blind to its presence.

A Community of Tempters

The above remarks lead us into the second point we wish to make about temptation. We will take the cue for our reflections from the sixth request of the Lord's Prayer—"lead us not into temptation" —and emphasize the single word "us."

It would be easy to read this request as implying that temptation comes from outside us, that is, like the demons of old, as an intruding force upon our lives. And in one sense, of course, this reading has merit. We have all had experiences of events and situations that happen to us autonomously. We are suddenly "thrown" into a situation, or an event is suddenly "thrown" at us, that is in clear conflict with our convictions. We have had no influence over the situation or event. We have not manipulated it into existence. We have done nothing to incite or encourage it. Yet there it is, an undeniable presence in our lives. Our example of the man contemplating theft would again be a case in point. He is walking through a store, and suddenly he is tempted to steal a piece of merchandise. He has not planned the theft; he has not been meditating on thievery. But there, suddenly before his mind's eye, attached to the particular piece of merchandise, is the thought of stealing it. It is this type of experience that allows us to understand the derivation of the metaphor of demons "whispering" in our ears. A thought has come so spontaneously, so uncontrollably, that its source seems a personal power beyond our control. We can picture the invisible demon standing beside us and suddenly asking, "Why not steal it?" The temptation has been thrown at us, unrehearsed, unbidden, undesired. Yet there it is, present in our minds, and dismissed not nearly so quickly as it came.

As I said, this understanding of the request has merit. Where I believe the individual goes wrong is when he judges it the only understanding, or even the preeminent one. For I would argue that the source of temptation that first besets the individual is not something that confronts him in this sudden, unexpected fashion, but something with which he lives every day. It is we ourselves, "us," who are this source. Let me explain this in the following way.

There is never a single reason that can explain the evolution of a culture's values. There is no single point in time, no single event or person, from which cultural values derive their complete existence. To be sure, there may be an initial catalyst —a Buddha, Jesus, Mohammed—for these values, a single individual who is thought to have originated or best taught these values. But the fact that the values come to define a culture (more or less, or in a selective fashion) is the result of a whole congruence of circumstances that cannot be isolated from each other. It is these circumstances, for instance, that explain our description of European culture as "Christian" and Levantine culture as "Islamic." It is not that Europeans have never heard of Mohammed or Moslems of Jesus: they have heard of each other since the seventh century with the founding of Islam. What explains their separate cultures, as it might European and Chinese culture until the late Middle Ages, is not mere ignorance of each other, but that circumstances —political, social, economic, let alone the conviction of possessing religious truth—permitted the growth of Islam in the Levant but not Europe (save for southern Spain), and vice versa. A similar situation also prevails in explaining the differences in American culture premised on expressing Lockian principles of democracy and a Chinese culture premised on expressing Maoist principles of communism. Again, it is not ignorance but the varying way historical circumstances have shaped each culture that has allowed the growth of Lockian values in one and Maoist values in the other.

It is also a truism that each of us is an acculturated being. By this I mean that each of us is born and bred into a cultural context where values already exist. We inherit these values as the basis for the behavioural patterns in which we are trained. The strongest influences exercised on us during the formative years of childhood teach us to cherish or condemn certain ways of thinking and acting. We are deluged with a pedagogy designed to create in us an acceptance of this teaching with little if any concern for different viewpoints. The way we are taught to act is cloaked in rightness. Any other way is dismissed as unworkable, held suspect, or vilified outrightly.

When I say, therefore, that it is ourselves who are the foremost source of temptation against the practice of Christlikeness, I say this insofar as we are acculturated beings. It is the values we absorb by the simple fact that we are located within a particular culture which create the demonic forces hindering our practice of Christian living. A cultural context as found in America, for example, that emphasizes economic competition and the spirit of greed, will not provide a setting for the easy practice of Christian generosity. Yet precisely because this competition and greed is so interwoven into the culture many individuals may not perceive its inherent contradiction to the spirit of generosity that Jesus taught. The message of Jesus has either faded away or its interpretation has been shaped to fit the culture's values. On the other hand, some individuals may indeed see the contradiction but simply ignore it, preferring to isolate for attention other Christian attitudes that find greater welcome within the culture: the regular worship of God, devotion to family and friends, honesty, etc. A similar but more recent conflict exists between Christian attitudes and the increasing sense of sexual freedom in American culture. To some extent this freedom is obviously a healthy development, considering the sexual straight-jacket in which generations of Americans lived. But when this sense of freedom is excessive, when it reaches the point of uninhibited indulgence without respect for oneself or others, then it is in obvious conflict with the witness of Jesus. It is the same type of conflict we find in an uninhibited indulgence in alcohol or food, where respect for oneself, if not for others, has also been clearly abandoned.

Values like the above, encouraged or tolerated within his culture, are the primary sources, I think, of the individual's temptations against Christlikeness. But these values do not exist of themselves.

They do not float free in the atmosphere, waiting to be absorbed like a breath of air. They exist within people. It is because people have accepted the spirit of competition and its corresponding greed; it is because people have practiced their freedom to excesses of disrespect for themselves and others, that people are the sources of temptation against Christian living—you and I and everyone else—and hence the source of guilt when temptation succeeds. We should be wary of personifying the demonic as a power or authority outside ourselves. This leads too easily to excuse-making, self-justification, and a refusal to accept responsibility; in short, to a repetition of the "original sin."

Additionally, of course, we must acknowledge that chronic temptation against our convictions can be self-generated not only by our acceptance (or at least entertainment) of the cultural values surrounding us, but also by personality traits that may be peculiarly our own. A young man I know, whom I will call Michael, would be a case in point. He is a deeply committed Christian yet also a homosexual. And while his understanding of Christianity permits homosexual orientation, it does not permit its practice. As a result Michael lives in an almost constant state of temptation—guilt is always around the corner—and his life is often tortuous in the confrontation between his commitment and the persistent attraction (and opportunities) to break it.

What Michael experiences as self-generated temptation because of his sexual preference, however, other people I know experience just as severely because of their unremitting inclination toward blind anger, laziness, self-pity, and so on. In all cases it would be satisfying to say that their commitment has invariably won out, but it hasn't. Yet at least the steady temptation they experience from within themselves, and the guilt when it triumphs, indicates that their commitment still exercises a persuasive influence over their lives. In one way or another self-generated temptations like these obviously characterize us all. They may not be as chronic or encompassing as in the above cases, but they emerge with a regularity keeping us aware that our commitments continually co-exist with temptations to deny them.

Let us say, therefore, that when the individual requests, "lead us not into temptation," he is in effect asking, "let us not be a temptation to each other and to ourselves." He is recognizing that the tempter he has to face is not a two-horned and tailed beast, but his next-door neighbor, his friends, his business and professional associates, his family, his own thoughts and feelings. To some this might sound too misanthropic, too concentrated on the ambiguity in our own and others' convictions. But better this seeming misanthropism than that naive optimism which views humanity as a congregate of virtuous beings whose vice is solely due to the wicked scheming of outside "powers," influences beyond their control. This optimism has too much the flavor of an alibi—sometimes pathetic, sometimes comical, sometimes infuriating— ignoring the demonic in each of us, the anti-Christ that ever strives for victory no matter how strong our commitment to Christlikeness.

A Change of Character?

There are some who would disagree with the above remarks on the basis of what they understand to be the redeeming activity of Jesus. They point out the biblical assertion that we are "new men" or "new creatures" because of Jesus' redeeming work, blessed by God, and God's sons and daughters. This is a legitimate and indisputable reference to the New Testament. The Pauline epistles especially make repeated use of the idea that because of Jesus our existence is transformed. In 2 Corinthians 5:17, for example, we read: "If anyone is in Christ, he is a new creature; the old has passed away and the new has come." Our disagreement, however, is with the way the reference is interpreted. For we cannot approach such passages as indicating a change in the very structure of human character, as if because of Jesus human beings no longer behave except in a redeemed fashion. What they indicate, rather, is not a change in human character but a change in human possibilities—and then only within the context of the conviction that Jesus revealed God's will. The point is not that we are compelled to behave more virtuously because Jesus lived. Obviously we are not. The point is that our virtuous behaviour can now be understood as the will of God, to the extent that it reflects the behaviour of Jesus himself. The possibilities for wickedness that marked human existence *before* Jesus lived are not destroyed because he lived. They are not even diminished. To take a quick look at the history of this century they even seem to have increased, or at least to have become more sophisticated and effective. The possibilities that have changed are not located in human character as such, but derive from faith in the truth of what occurred in Jesus. Pre-eminent among these we must name the possibility that death greets with new life any individual who has done his best to approximate on earth the witness of Jesus. But this possibility in turn is premised on the yet more basic possibility that in his words and deeds Jesus revealed the will of God.

We must say, therefore, that it is in the possibilities it sets before us that the life of Jesus is redemptive for us. But whether or not we become convinced of these possibilities always remains a personal decision. There is no such thing, in other words, as irresistible grace—when this means an activity of God that willy-nilly leads us to Christ-likeness. Not having been changed in character by the activity of Jesus, any change we undergo can only occur by our own free choice. Our transformation is our own doing, guided by the witness of Jesus; it is not something done to us. We are not forced to Christlikeness, we choose it. We are not bound to witness to Jesus, we commit ourselves to it. We are not constrained into Christian living, we must work at it. What God does in Jesus is to show us the way to live, not destine us to it. Jesus is the manifestation, the *epiphany* of God's will, so that if there is irresistible grace here it is the grace that makes this way of life something that in itself is pleasing to God and blessed. But it is not irresistible in the sense that we cannot refuse this way of life. We can and frequently we do. And when we do we experience guilt.

It is the possibility of the above refusal that is the temptation from which we ask deliverance when we pray, "lead us not into temptation." In the first instance we are asking that the source of this temptation as it exists in other human beings not deflect us from our commitment to Christlikeness. We are asking that their acculturated values, when these conflict with the example of Jesus, not weaken our witness to Christian living. Our request is a confession of the influence that others have over us and our weakness before this influence. It is a recognition that we do not live alone, isolated in our convictions, but in a community of mutually relating individuals.

But we must also acknowledge a second meaning to the request. Whereas with the first meaning we are asking that others not be a source of temptation *for us,* with the second meaning we are asking that we not be a source of temptation *for them.* From being self-oriented, our request is now other-oriented. It is an acknowledgement that just as others manifest values that conflict with Christlikeness, so do we. The result is that whenever we pray, "lead us not into temptation," we are praying for ourselves in a double sense. In the first sense we are praying for ourselves as the passive recipients of temptation; in the second we are praying for ourselves as the active source of temptation. Neither side of the request has priority over the other; they are both joined in a single prayer that must not be broken. We are recognizing that if we are habitually deflected by others from witnessing to Jesus, we ourselves will tend to deflect others in turn. This is what psychologists call "the power of mutual influence," or more technically, the symbiotic structure of the human psyche. To the extent, therefore, that we acknowledge the weakness that pervades even the strongest conviction regarding the rightness of Christlike living, we are recognizing this weakness in both others and ourselves. We offer no exemptions from the "us," but let it stand as it is, inclusive of all who pray to the Father.

Responsibility and Personal Example

The issue the above remarks raise is that of personal responsibility, or more exactly, personal example. We are admitting that by the model of our lives we must provide for others a pedagogy toward Christlikeness—that is, an effective pattern of instruction whereby they might learn the meaning of Christian living. After all, plain common sense indicates that to the degree we become Christlike, to that degree we provide a decreasing temptation against Christlikeness for others. Yet it is an example we ourselves must set—as we said above, no one makes us Christlike. We become Christlike by our own volition, through a responsible commitment to the witness of God's will given in the words and deeds of Jesus.

This responsibility is first described as *responsiveness*. By this I mean that our witness to Christlikeness finds its primary expression in the way we "answer" our experiences of others. This was also the intention of our remarks in the last chapter on the commandment of Jesus requiring us to love our neighbor as we love ourselves. Confronted, for example, with the pride or cruelty in others, our responsibility demands that we reply not with our own pride or cruelty but in a fashion demonstrating the Beatitudes Jesus taught (Matthew 5). Or confronted with the homelessness or illness or hunger or others, our responsibility requires not indifference or neglect but a reply expressing fidelity to his teaching on the Mandates of the Kingdom (Matthew 25). We must also stress, however, that this responsiveness is not just passive; it is also active. It does not wait until opportunities for its expression come knocking at the door; it seeks them out.

The motive for this responsiveness is our conviction regarding the rightness of the way of life Jesus taught. The conviction is the cause, the reason determining our conduct. And it is this in the double sense of being both the *terminus a quo* (the source) and the *terminus ad quem* (the purpose) describing our behaviour. When we express the beatitudes or mandates in how we act, we do so as an act of fidelity to God's will as expressed in these teachings. Conversely, when we do not express these teachings in our activity we do so as an act of infidelity to God's will. In either case, however, our judgment is premised on our conviction regarding these teachings as expressive of God's will. Without this conviction we would make no such judgment. At the root of all Christian awareness that we have been faithful or unfaithful to God's will lies the conviction that this will has been demonstrated in Jesus.

To pray to be delivered from temptation, therefore, is fundamentally a God-centered act. In fact, the irreducible context of all Christian prayer is our relationship to the Father, as this is mediated through the revelation in Jesus. But if this is so—if prayer indeed indicates our relationship to the Father—then the question of our fidelity or infidelity is directed not first toward the man Jesus but toward God himself. As we are faithful or unfaithful in our commitment to be Christlike, we are being faithful or unfaithful not just to another man's will—as if we were striving to be like Buddha or Socrates or Confucius—but to the very will of God. This is the initial and enduring perspective of all Christian faith. And it is what sets this faith, this conviction worlds apart from the fidelity or infidelity we express toward something like the ethics of Socrates, or the constitution grounding American civil government, or the expectations of a spouse. We would say that in the first case our fidelity or infidelity is a religious act, while in the second it is a profane one. In the first case we are engaged in a relationship with our Creator, in the second with our creations.

If an individual greets with indifference the events that occurred in the life of Jesus—what he said and did—or if these events are of no more importance to him than those which define the life of any other great man, then his option of fidelity or infidelity to the Father's will remains an open question. By this I mean that the option is determined by the individual's own particular needs, hopes, whims, and so on. The "way" of Jesus is then just one of many ways to live, with a certain attractiveness and unattractiveness. To some it may be attractive, for example, in many of its promises, but unattractive in its demands, the moral task it sets for every individual. To others it may be a "way" that is aesthetically beautiful in its expression but quite impractical in its exercise. Jesus is holy, pure, one of the best products of human generation, but quite unrealistic, even naive in the pattern of life he followed and taught. As long as either of the above viewpoints determines the individual's approach to what happened in Jesus, the pursuit of Christlikeness remains a bald option, chosen or denied without further consideration. But when the individual's viewpoint is determined not by the attractiveness or unattractiveness of what Jesus did and said, not by aesthetic judgment regarding his person, but by the conviction that in him God's will was revealed, then there is no option. The choice is clear from the beginning: in following or ignoring the example of Jesus the individual is expressing his relationship to God. There are no options for a committed Christian faith; there are no options before God's will. The New Testament witness to Jesus is not judged as it stands, with no prior conviction. It is judged with the faith that in this witness God is speaking to us, and that our own response can be to submit.

Our central concern in this section has been with the above phrase, "a committed Christian faith." We have argued that despite the strength of this faith (or conviction), our pursuit of Christlikeness is not inevitable, drawn to certain success. For while there are no options for a committed Christian faith save to follow the witness of Jesus, this option is not one which is *always* applied in the Christian's life. Laced throughout his existence are factors that habitually deflect him from this application. We have been calling these factors "temptations," so that when we say the Christian "gives into" temptation we do not mean that he is denying the option he has made for faith in Jesus but rather its faithful application in his life. And we have been suggesting that his experience of guilt is the clearest indication to him of this denial.

I have always found it inexact, therefore, and somewhat insensitive, to say that an individual has denied his convictions as a Christian when what he has actually done is erred from their proper enactment. It is distressing to witness a universal condemnation of any individual's convictions on the basis of the infidelities, even the frequent infidelities, he commits against them. Where our attention should be located is not here but in the opposite direction, the fidelity he demonstrates toward his convictions. Only when this fidelity becomes increasingly the shadow of his infidelity should we begin to doubt his convictions. Only when he more often betrays than affirms the example of Christ should we begin to hesitate calling him a Christian. For then we may fairly wonder whether he has prayed to the Father, and sought to demonstrate the sincereity of his prayer by how he lives, "lead us not into temptation."

2. *The Meaning of Evil*

Of itself, temptation against our convictions is not evil. As we said, temptation resides in the posing of possibilities before us, when one of the possibilities is an affirmation of a conviction we possess and the other is its denial. It is the state prior to the choice—yet demanding the choice—of one of these possibilities over the other. It is a state of tension, in other words, wherein the individual is confronted by two opposing desires of more or less equal influence. It is an experience of trial, testing, decision-making—sometimes easily resolved, sometimes issuing in a paralyzing uncertainty. Evil, on the other hand, we will broadly define as the result of this trial when the possibility chosen is the one in conflict with the conviction the individual possesses. Of course, he may not initially understand (or admit) this choice as evil. By wit and argument, for example, he may see it as entirely appropriate to the commitment he has made. This is the response of sophistry, the subtle interpretation of the choice in order to accommodate it to the con-

viction. Or he may simply set it outside the context
of the conviction altogether, saying the choice has
no particular pertinence to it. This is the response
of irrelevance, the outright dismissal of the relationship between the choice and the conviction. In
all such instances judgment on the choice's evil, if it
is made, can only be made subsequent to further reflection, that is, with the realization that the initial
response justifying the choice was inadequate. We
will call this realization the "moment of humility"
—when the individual confesses that what he has
done was wrong, without excuse or justification. It
is the moment when evil becomes a personal reality
and guilt is experienced.

It is the above understanding of evil as the result of personal choice that governs our response to
the temptation that precedes it. We desire that in
the face of temptation we always choose re-affir-
mation over denial of the commitment we have
made (based on the conviction we possess) toward
the witness of Jesus. Simultaneously, however, we
are also aware that this request will never be completely met; that it represents an indication of the
sincerity of our commitment but not of all our
future behaviour. For we recognize that the freedom which grounds our commitment to Christlikeness, and the difficulty of the commitment itself,
prohibits an absolute fidelity to it. Or as we noted
in the last chapter: we can approximate but never
fully demonstrate in our lives the witness of Jesus.

The tradition of Christian spirituality recognizes the above point when it says that we are both good and evil beings. I take this recognition to mean that there is never a point during life when evil (keeping in mind the description we have given it) becomes an impossibility for the individual. Not only does it remain a possibility, it remains one which is more or less frequently enacted. As a result, we cannot ask God to forbid our performance of evil, in the sense of making it an impossibility. For to do so would be to request that God intrude into our existence in an extraordinary fashion and so involve us, I think, in two difficulties that must at all costs be avoided.

The first difficulty is the implied presumption that God can and *will* alter human character at our request. In the present context the implication would be that the proper response to our request would be a suspension by God of our ability to commit evil. Yet this would directly offend both the phenomenon of our freedom and the related idea that commitment to Christlikeness is not blindly but willfully engaged, with difficulty and discipline. We are clearly no longer free if, through an intervention by God, our ability to choose for or against Jesus is suspended. This would call for a radical change in human character, which inerrantly demonstrates that we are free to choose *pro* or *con* before any option accessible to us. Even in its most reduced state, as men like Frankl and

Camus suggest, when we are subject to the influence of enormous political or social or emotional pressure, this freedom still exists in our irreducible ability to affirm or deny, to say yes or no—if not out loud then at least to ourselves. Furthermore, if we also assert that this freedom is a gift from God, the design of his providence in the shaping of human character, then any request that this gift be retracted would again not make sense. The undeniable experience we have of our freedom, and the faith that this freedom is a quality of our character intended by God, prohibits the intelligibility of any petition seeking its dissolution. Without freedom, the ability to commit evil, our commitment to Jesus would not be chosen but predestined. It would not be a commitment engaged by our fee will but a destiny over which we have no control. In short, it would not be a commitment at all, but a *fait accompli*. And the result would be an image of ourselves as pawns or playthings in the hands of God, free to do no one's bidding but his.

The second difficulty centers on the psychological response that any expectation of a direct intervention in our lives might elicit. If we request that God deliver us from evil, and yet find that we still commit evil, there may arise a tendency to blame God for it. The argument would be that we asked not to commit evil, but that God chose to ignore our request. Hence the final responsibility for the evil we have done is not ours but God's. The logic

of this position, however, is based on a clear misunderstanding of the individual's dependence on
God. Like the individual who thinks he has no responsibility to cure his illness but can rely solely on
God's intervention, so here the individual thinks he
can acquit himself of responsibility for his evil
deeds by asserting that what he does is done by the
will of God; that otherwise he would be unable to
do it. Correspondingly, of course, and conveniently, he has also shut himself off from the possibility
of experiencing guilt.

This is a type of argument we often find in children. In seeking to avoid responsibility for some
wrong he has done, the child will frequently explain
the action as the result of an external cause that exercised an uncontrollable influence over him. Nor-
mally this cause will be another child, a friend or
sibling. "So-and-so *made* me do it; I asked him not
to, but he made me do it." This is the child's repeated line of argument. By stating that he asked
his friend or sibling not to make him do the wrong,
the child believes that he has sufficiently protested
his own innocence and transferred responsibility
away from himself. In his own mind, of course, his
position is airtight—or at least adequately convincing to absolve him from the wrong he has committed. His parents, however, are perceptive enough to
see through the excuse. Through patient explanation they will attempt to encourage him to accept

the responsibility that is rightly his for the wrong he has done. They will teach him that while he should seek to avoid evil, there is virtue in admitting responsibility for evil once done. This admission, they will say, is a key ingredient in avoiding evil in the future. Until the child admits that he is capable of committing evil he will have no cause for confronting it. Until he experiences guilt he will refuse responsibility.

Sometimes the above pedagogy is not successful. More rarely, in the case of disinterested parents, it is not even employed. When this happens the child who blames others for the evil he commits grows into an adult who does the same—repeating over and over again the original sin recorded in Genesis. The child is father to the man. In an adult, however, the attitude is far more distressing because we expect adults to behave in a more responsible fashion than children, with a greater willingness to accept responsibility for their misbehaviour and the guilt accompanying it. Whenever an individual carries into adulthood attitudes derived from childhood, without modification or critical judgment, he has grown in years but not maturity. In extreme cases, of course, where the "pruning" process involved in mature development has been grossly neglected, the result may be an individual who is totally incapable of relating to the world around him save in childish patterns of behaviour. This would obviously indicate severe psychic maladjustment and require for its relief close and extended care.

Sometimes, however, a curious twist occurs in the above development. While he might willingly and maturely accept responsibility before other human beings for the evil he commits, the individual still retains a childish attitude toward God. While he admits his wrong before family or friends or associates, in his heart he is secretly blaming God for it. This inward stance is often petulant and complaining, expressing irritation or disappointment with God for permitting him to commit the evil. "Why did you let me do it? Why didn't you prevent it? Why did you guide me in that direction?" He is too proud or clever to express this petulance before other human beings. For he is aware that they would judge it for precisely what it is—an immature refusal of responsibility. But he is not too proud or mature to express it before God. God is a made-to-order scapegoat for him. If he does not have the satisfaction of publicly blaming his evil on someone else, at least he has the private satisfaction of doing so. After all, God does not confront him face to face, questioning or cross-examining his refusal of responsibility.

Monstrous Evil — Everyday Evil

As I mentioned in the Introduction, I undertook a series of personal interviews while writing this book to determine what a more or less commonsense understanding of guilt might be. The basis of many of my reflections throughout these pages is provided by my interpretations of this understanding. While interviewing people on the specific concern now under consideration, I made an especially curious and enlightening discovery. To my question, "What is evil to you?," I found that without exception all of them described evil in what I would call "monstrous" terms, that is, extreme terms of wickedness, malevolence, brutality, criminality, and so on. This was expressed most pointedly when I asked them to offer some examples of what they meant by evil. All of them responded by listing particular acts, the standard litany of murder, rape, child-abuse, sadism, and so on. Some even responded by attaching specific names to these acts: "Well, the types of things Hitler (or Stalin or Charles Manson) did . . ." Evil was clearly understood by these people as an *act,* something an individual did. Without exception it was also understood as an act whose result was violent physical harm to another human being. There was nothing subtle in their understanding of evil; their responses to my question were immediate, unhesitating, and all of a kind. It was the type of response one might receive if he asked for reactions to the word "holocaust." With rare if any exception these reactions would include descriptions of the maniacal cruelty that drove a dictator to the systematic extermination of a people. They would perhaps detail the horrors of human vivisection, showers where people did not wash but were poisoned to death, ovens where men, women, and children were incinerated like so much rotted meat. Very few if any individuals would offer as a response the meaning of the word in the Old Testament, as when it says "to offer a holocaust to the Lord."

What amazed me about the above responses was their apparent indifference to the subtlety and everydayness that can also characterize evil. I was likewise struck by the fact that evil was consistently understood as an act, always of physical violence, directed against another. Not one person mentioned such psychological phenomena as pride, deceitfulness, greed, or such psychological violence as unrelenting criticism. While reflecting on these responses I began to find my amazement turning into distress. What application could I give to the idea of evil if it was understood as an act but not an attitude, as unusual but not commonplace? How could I relate it to every Christian's commitment to the "way" of Jesus if it pertained only to deeds that most men and women never commit?

My resolution of this question was a simple judgment: the responses were inadequate, indicating only an awareness of gross evil. I even wondered if there was not an unconscious motive behind these responses, a type of defense mechanism directing attention away from the behaviour of those being questioned. For my own experience told me while gross evil certainly existed, it hardly represented all that evil was. There were other forms of evil, commonly present and manifest in human behaviour. They represented not a spectacular but a quite ordinary evil, deriving from attitudes comfortably at home in all of us. But compared with such monstrously evil acts as murder, rape, child-abuse it was easy to see how their consideration could disappear from consciousness. After all, the pride which drives a wife to browbeat her husband on a daily basis loses its seriousness when compared with the pride that drives a dictator to exterminate thousands of Jews on a daily basis. The anger which causes a student to fling a piece of chalk at his teacher pales before the anger which causes a murderer to fling a knife at his victim. Commonplace evil tends to be forgotten, or excused, in our awareness of the extraordinary evil of which human beings are capable.

But I think it is exactly this commonplace evil from which we must first seek deliverance in our lives—as when we ask of the Father, for example, "deliver us from evil." And I say this principally out of recognition that it is from commonplace evil that gross evil most frequently derives. This is what we strikingly call a "snowballing effect." The individual who tends to think his petty deceits are not really evil or are readily excused, who experiences no guilt over them, may soon find his tolerance for deceit extending to an ever broader application. Or the individual who tends to think that his petty thefts are not really evil, may soon find himself justifying grand larceny. The evil that we permit ourselves, just like the virtue we practice, has a tendency to feed on itself, growing larger in the process. This is the commonsense insight that underlies the psychology of habit formation. A habit is a pattern, a gestalt that increasingly describes an individual's behaviour—or in Webster's definition, "an aptitude or inclination for some action, acquired by repetition and showing itself in facility of performance or in decreased power of resistance." We find in the train of habit that the little white lie we told in childhood has become with adolescence and adulthood a clever and complex practice of deception; or that the stealing we allowed ourselves in childhood has with passing years become neatly professional. We discover, in short, that the commonplace evil we ignored or excused has ceased being so commonplace. It is something like this development, I think, to which Jesus is alluding when he offers this strikingly concrete and familiar example: "Every man who looks at a woman lustfully has already committed adultery with her in his heart" (Matthew 5:28). This is one of the "harsh" sayings of Jesus. It is made *in extremis* in order to drive home the point he wishes to make. That point is that evil begins in our most ordinary activities, and that a failure of diligence here can lead to increasingly serious consequences.

Examination of Conscience

It is acceptance of the above idea that underlies the minuteness which Christian spirituality has often encouraged in the individual's "examination of conscience." In the past, this encouragement sometimes went to distressing extremes in its concern for detail. The individual was taught not only to recall the basic fault, but the number of times it was committed and the specific expressions it took. Frequently this had the adverse effect of producing in him an attitude of scrupulosity (we will examine this attitude more closely in the next chapter). Or worse, it encouraged in him a type of distorted pride in acknowledging the evil he had done: If I confessed to more or greater evil than you, the honesty and humility of my confession implied a greater sanctity; if my *mea culpa* rang out louder than yours, so much the more did my holiness. Yet the motive for this encouragement was, in principle, justifiable: if the individual remained sharply conscious of the commonplace evil he committed, it was unlikely that he would be tempted to greater evil.

I myself shared in this encouragement in the specific context of seminary training. Every day a time was set aside for the practice of *particular examen*. This was a period for recollecting the ways in which the individual had been unfaithful for that day in his commitment to Christian living within the world of the seminary. Additionally, there was a longer period set aside each week for what was called "the chapter of accusation." At this time individuals would publicly confess these infidelities to all gathered, and receive from the religious superior a penance meant to provide retribution for them. In neither ritual was the individual ever encouraged to examine the positive expressions of his commitment to seminary life, his fidelity to the rules and regulations guiding his particular community. Both were designed, rather, to emphasize his reasons for feeling guilt about his behaviour. In a similar way this same emphasis often prevailed in Catholic confessional practice, though here again (as with the seminary rituals) it is far less common than in past years.

We must also note that while Christian spirituality has emphasized a specificity of detail in the individual's recollection of the evil he has *committed,* it has also encouraged an examination of the psychological *attitude* that has issued in the evil activity. The question is not only *what* the individual has done, but *why* he did it. The fact that a woman I know habitually browbeats her husband is only half the evil she must admit. The other half regards the attitude that is the source of her browbeating. It is just this attitude, fact, that must receive the greatest attention whenever an individual is con-

templating the evil he has committed. For to concentrate solely on a list of deeds, with little or no
reflection on their psychological motives, will not
produce the amendment of behaviour the individual presumably desires. He will find that however
many lists he makes they all basically relate to each
other, if not in specific content, then certainly in
overarching traits or characteristics. He will discover that from the changing details of the evil he
does and the the guilt he subsequently feels there
emerges a pattern of behaviour based on particular
motives or attitudes. And he will realize that it is
these motives or attitudes that must first receive his
attention if his deeds are to be amended.

The browbeating wife, therefore, whose attention is directed only toward the specific expressions
of her browbeating—her private and public humil-
iations of her husband—and not the pride that
motivates it, will find it impossible to amend her
behaviour. As long as the motive goes unattended it
will provide a recurring source for her behaviour.
What she must do is ask herself not *"How* do I
browbeat my husband?,"* but *"Why* do I browbeat
my husband?"* Once she discovers the answer in
her pride, she will then be able to correct its specific
expressions. She will have learned that it is the attitude from which her actions spring that is the
source of the evil she does; that the actions, while
evil, are only the flesh and bones of this attitude,
the way it is revealed.

This double character of the evil that marks our existence is clearly indicated, I think, by those two pre-eminent sources we have been using to describe the moral vision of Jesus: the Beatitudes and the Mandates of the Kingdom. We may understand the first, the Beatitudes, as indicating attitudes that must be encouraged in any Christian. We may understand the second, the Mandates, as examples of specific acts in which these attitudes are expressed. Both go hand in hand, the attitude and the activity, though the attitude has priority of concern. Our care for each other cannot be effectively expressed, after all, if our attitude is fundamentally one of indifference or competition or aggression toward each other. The evil from which we must first ask deliverance is consequently the evil within us, the frame of mind, the motivations that find expression in our activity.

We noted in the last section that this frame of mind is largely the result of an acculturation process: The individual is shaped by his society to cherish or condemn certain patterns of behaviour. The most influential period in this process, of course, is the early formative years of childhood, though to a greater or lesser extent, depending on the individual, it continues throughout life. The experience of guilt emerges whenever this pattern of behaviour is broken—whenever the individual, through an autonomous decision, offends the expectations of his

culture as to appropriate and inappropriate ways of
thinking and acting. The presumption being made
is that the individual is committed to this pattern of
behaviour. Either he has actively committed himself to it through personal decision, or he is passively committed to it by the simple fact that he
continues to live within the particular society. In
either case, whenever he breaks this commitment he
is judged (and is expected to judge himself) guilty
of evil.

Sin, Culpability, and Punishment

Within the society of Christian believers we call
the above offenses "sins." A sin occurs whenever a
Christian breaks his commitment to the pattern of
behaviour demonstrated by Jesus as the will of the
Father. As such, however, and following our previous remarks, it is preceded by a specific attitude
(e.g., greed, envy, pride) of which the particular sin
is the expression. Whenever the Christian sins, in
other words, he sins both "in his heart" (to use the
phrase of Jesus) and in the deed itself.

Like any evil, of course, a sin can be of greater or
lesser seriousness; sinful deeds, like virtuous ones,
differ in the importance they possess for the individual's commitment to Christlikeness. In the early
church the most serious sins an individual could
commit were thought to be adultery, apostasy, and
murder. Of these, apostasy and murder would still

be sins of great seriousness for any Christian, though today the seriousness of adultery is in open debate—at least as compared to the other two. At any rate, the point is that the sin a Christian commits must be judged variously according to the extent to which it denies the example of Christ. Habitual deceit is obviously a more serious evil than the telling of a single lie. To murder someone out of spite or hatred is clearly more serious than to break his arm. To slap a child out of frustration is clearly less serious than to burn holes in him with a lit cigarette.

One of the more delicate issues the above remarks raise is that of the individual's culpability for his sin. On first glance this issue poses no difficulties. To be culpable means to be accountable for an evil committed, to deserve censure or blame for it. And to the extent that any Christian offends his commitment to Jesus he is culpable. His offense, after all, cannot be greeted with indifference, and certainly not with approval. Both make a mockery of his commitment from the very beginning, abusing its importance and sincerity. And if he experiences guilt over his offense, both reduce his guilt to insignificance.

Where the issue of culpability becomes delicate, however, is when we attach to it the question of punishment. Should the censure and blame imposed on the offending Christian be accompanied

by penalties—private or public penalties such as os-
tracism and physical discipline? We cannot deny
that the overwhelming answer to this question in
the tradition of Christian spirituality has been yes:
the sinner deserves to be punished. And insofar as
he lives within "Christendom"—that is, a particular cultural context whose center is the New Testament witness to Jesus—his punishment is decided
at the discretion of his fellow Christians, usually represented by some single individual or group.
The sin, after all, is an offense against the culture's professed norm of behaviour. Its punishment, therefore, is designed both to maintain the
moral integrity of the culture and to provide a
pedagogical tool toward preventing the sin's re-
occurrence in the individual himself or in others
tempted to do the same. It is an unfortunate but undeniable blot on the record of Christian history that
these punishments were often barbaric: prolonged
imprisonment, torture, even death. Some medieval
chronicles on this subject could have been authored
by the Marquis de Sade, or the experimenting phy-
sicians at Dachau or Buchenwald. And this judgment stands despite the outlook of some theologians that these punishments provided retribution
or "satisfaction" for the sin committed and
thereby re-instated the individual into the community's favor. The sin may indeed have been an
offense against God's will revealed in Jesus. But

the punishing response certainly left a lot to be desired, both in itself, its extreme forms, and in what it implied of the community's values.

The above remarks pertain to the punishment of sin that has been inflicted on Christians by other Christians. But what about the punishment of sin inflicted by God? Does God punish the sinner? Again, we cannot deny that the overwhelming answer to this question in the tradition of Christian spirituality has been yes, the sinner is punished by God. The answer, however, has a double context. The first context relates to our remarks in the previous paragraph. Here the punishment of the sinner by the Christian community is understood as satisfying the punishment judgment that God himself would mete out. The sinner can make retribution to God by accepting this punishment with equanimity, performing without complaint a penance proportionate in severity to the sin committed. The presumption being made is that this punishment or penance is somehow pleasing to God. It assures God, so to speak, of the individual's awareness of his sin, his sorrow for it, and his desire to reaffirm his commitment to God's will revealed in Jesus. The logic of this presumption, however, is a disturbing one. First, it isolates a particular quality of God that finds only remote recognition in the New Testament, namely, God's vengeful justice, his demand to be satisfied, paid back for offenses committed against his will. We cannot say, without distressing the message of Jesus, that this quality is characteristic of the Father he preaches. Secondly, it assumes that this satisfaction must take the form of suffering, as if there were something pleasing to God in suffering *per se*. But this again is a questionable viewpoint within the message of Jesus. The individual is being asked to demonstrate his renewed commitment to God's will by the pain he endures, whereas a more Christlike attitude would surely be to demonstrate it by the increased good he does (an idea we will take up at greater length in the following chapter).

The second context involves God's autonomous punishment of the sinner—that is, the punishment God metes out directly, without the mediation of the Christian community or the individual's personal choice. This punishment is generally thought to occur in either one of two ways. In the first, God personally intervenes in the sinner's earthly life to punish him. Concrete manifestations of this intervention are often described in exquisite detail: sickness, shattered hopes, the death of a beloved, barrenness, and so on. It is always presumed that the punishment is proportionate to the sinner's offense, since God's justice is unquestionable. In the second way, the punishment is not secured during earthly life but awaits the sinner after death. Again, however, a proportion is thought to reign: the punishment is either fierce but terminal (purgatory) or fierce and eternal (hell). Whichever punishment

greets the individual upon death is provided by the
direct judgment of God as the one most pertinent
to the evil committed during life.

Many Christian creeds have been comfortable
with the idea of purgatorial punishment. In fact, it
has been a general presumption in Christian spirituality that most individuals will need to spend
some "time" after death in offering satisfaction to
God by suffering for their sins. In some creeds it is
even thought that part of this suffering can be
shared by those on earth and applied vicariously to
those in purgatory. Comfort with this whole idea
derives from the belief that purgatory provides only
terminal punishment, after which the individual en-
ters into the joyful presence of God. On the other
hand, the concept of hell has been a cause for considerable distress among the creeds. This derives
from the belief that hell, unlike purgatory, involves
eternal punishment. The distress lies in trying to
conceive an individual so evil that God judges him
unforgiveable, someone completely beyond the
reach of God's mercy—someone who has either
eliminated the experience of guilt from his life (the
"hardened sinner") or experiences guilt but does
not allow the experience to affect his behaviour (the
"recalcitrant sinner"). And it finds its most telling
expression in the fact that while Christian tradition
has easily assigned individuals to heaven and purgatory, it has never determined that a single indi-

vidual inhabits hell. For the idea of eternal punishment has always aggravated the Christian understanding of the Father's love—God's willingness to forgive even when forgiveness is not sought.

Judging Sin

We may conclude from the above remarks that while we can readily affirm the culpability of a sinner in the sense that his sin deserves blame and censure, we cannot as unreservedly affirm that this censure should be accompanied by punishment. We are not thereby affirming that punishment is undeserved, but only that its determination must be carefully considered. When sin is understood as the evil an individual commits when he denies the Father's will revealed in Jesus, then the denial is fundamentally an issue between the individual and God. It is not, I think, any community's place to determine *as God's will* how a censure of this denial might be expressed in the punishment of the sinner. It is the community's right to voice *its own* censure, to oblige the sinner's awareness that he has broken the commitment that binds the community together, and to determine in a humane way how this commitment might be re-affirmed. But it is not the community's right to decide how the sinner might satisfy *God* for the offense. The community does not know God's will in this matter; whether God will require retribution at all, and if so, what this retribution might involve. All the community can do is encourage the individual to acknowledge in some fashion that he has sinned—to acknowledge his guilt—and to demonstrate in some way that he is still committed to the pursuit of Christlikeness. It is not within its authority to accompany this encouragement with savage punishment, nor to present this punishment as God's will. And it is certainly not within its authority to threaten the individual's punishment by God after death.

An additional point may be made here. Everyone knows of Jesus' scorn for certain religious authorities of his day: the scribes and Pharisees. What specifically seems to have elicited this scorn was their tendency to judge the behaviour of others, and then present this judgment as God's very own.

It might be helpful to rehearse his two-fold criticism of this tendency. First, he criticized the identification of human with divine judgment. While Jesus surely accepted the rightful function of religious authority to cherish and safeguard the revelation of God, he did not accept the unquestioning right of that authority to interpret this revelation. He saw flaws in many of these interpretations, as the gospels sufficiently record. Secondly, he criticized the attitude which could and frequently did result from this identification of human with divine judgment. Here he cut quickly to the core. Those who made judgments in God's name on the evil and guilt of others had an inclination first toward

pride—identifying their will with God's—and secondly toward ignoring or readily excusing the evil
they themselves committed and the guilt they
should have subsequently experienced. His language in this regard is harsh and uncompromising,
filled with metaphors. He calls such people "whitewashed tombs," a "brood of vipers," hypocrites
who strain gnats while they swallow camels. So re-
pelled was he by this inclination that at one point he
would not claim even for himself such goodness as
would allow him to judge in God's name: "Why do
you call me good? No one but God is good" (Mark
10:18). God speaks through men; but no man can
speak for God. If the function of a revealer is to be
a mediator of God's will, but not to decide what
God's will is, then this decision cannot be made by
those who are not even revealers but only followers
of a revelation. Christians cannot claim a goodness
or a wisdom or a hold on God's will that Jesus himself did not claim.

While we might appreciate, therefore, the literary merits of a great work like Dante's *Inferno,*
we would have to maintain a much different theological estimate of its worth. If the above remarks
are on target we would have to say that the work is
a conceit on Dante's part, because by his own discretion he has freely assigned to hell individuals he
deems deserving of it. Admittedly this conceit is
central to the structure of his poem—he needs to
fill hell with inhabitants in order to work his art.

But in doing so he is also claiming, or at least presuming, a knowledge of God's judgment that he clearly does not possess. For he is selective in his assignments to hell. Only those dwell there whom he thinks deserve it—and this is his conceit. He does what Jesus never did, in other words, and what the Christian community has never formally done. In this sense Dante is the medieval pharisee *par excellence,* not only in his *Inferno,* but throughout *The Divine Comedy,* deciding who has merited the eternal pain of hell, who the temporal pain of purgatory, and who the eternal blessedness of heaven. And the same judgment would hold true for anyone assuming a similar attitude.

Of course, we cannot ignore the fact that Jesus himself taught a doctrine wherein some individuals by their sin would be denied the presence of God after death. We can thnk of such passages as Matthew 10:28: "Do not fear those who can destroy the body but not the soul; rather fear him who can destroy both soul and body in hell" (cf. also Matthew 5:22; 8:9). Yet we have already noted that there has been a controversy since the time of the earliest church whether this denial is *eternal;* whether or not God will finally embrace in his presence even the most evil of men. There is no controversy, however, regarding the question of whether or not Jesus himself ever judged an individual worthy of this denial. He did not. He named no one, but only posed the denial as a possibility facing the sinner's

refusal of God's will. What Jesus did not do, then,
no one has a right to do. We may even say—grant-
ing our interpretation of Jesus' attitude toward the
scribes and pharisees—that offering such judgment
on others is itself evil, the assumption of a preroga-
tive that belongs only to God. It is, as we will suggest in the next chapter, the evil of self-righteousness, the denial of Jesus' own attitude, "I judge no
one" (John 8:15; however, see also 8:16), and his
saying, "Judge not lest you be judged" (Matthew
7:1).

The question the above reflections raise is not
whether we are capable of committing evil; we are.
It is not whether this evil deserves censure; it does.
It is not whether this censure should be accompanied by punishment; it might be. And it is certainly
not whether we should readily absolve or ignore the
guilt we experience from the evil we commit; we
should not. The question, rather, is whether or not
there is such a thing as irredeemable evil, evil that
God will not forgive. The answer to this question is
a blank, ignorance, our inability to answer it. The
reason is the ambiguity in the New Testament. On
the whole we are inclined to find that Jesus' preaching about his Father makes it difficult to think
there is any evil the Father would not forgive. We
may presume, for example, that the unqualified
forgiveness that Jesus teaches us to possess is also a
characteristic of the Father he preaches. On the
other hand, there are cryptic, difficult passages that

seem to imply that an individual is indeed capable of such unforgivable evil. I am thinking, for example, of Jesus' saying that "All sins will be forgiven you except the sin against the Holy Spirit" (Matthew 12:31)—a sin originally interpreted as apostasy, the denial of God as the author of his own acts, and later, by the Christian community, the denial of God's activity in the life and destiny of Jesus. The result of this ambiguity is ignorance. Or perhaps better put: the question of God's forgiveness of the evil we have done is only answered as we each come to judgment before God. As with the very question of life after death, so with the question of how our life is finally judged—the answer can only be secured for certain at death itself. Until then, despite all our faith, we live with the whispers of doubt and uncertainty. But this, of course, is precisely what we mean when we describe faith as a *commitment*.

Yet the judgment of God will not come unexpectedly upon us, like a surprise. It is not that we have no role in what this judgment will be. We do. And its determination is provided by the fidelity with which we have committed ourselves to the Father's will revealed in Jesus. The individual who has steadily and consciously refused the demands of this commitment, therefore, has already passed judgment on himself. His refusal is a preference for a pattern of behaviour other than that demonstrated in the words and deeds of Jesus. Is it likely that in death God will receive this individual in the same way as one who has steadily and consciously affirmed his commitment to the revelation in Jesus? If nothing else we cry out from our sense of fair play that it cannot be. But the truth is that we cannot answer the question definitely. For its answer is strapped in ignorance. No—the only thing we may say for certain, and only then within the context of our faith, is that if we strive to live out our commitment to the revelation in Jesus there lies before us in death the Father's blessing. This is the certain promise in the resurrection of Jesus. There are no certain promises that anyone will be damned forever.

Evil can be a monstrous thing. But it can also be quite ordinary. Commitment to Jesus may or may not demand spectacular or heroic actions on our part. But it definitely demands everyday actions. The evil that we do, therefore, just like the convictions we possess and the commitments we make, and so the guilt we experience, involves us above all in the ordinary and commonplace. It is there that we prove the type of person we really are—in the behaviour that characterizes our existence not just now and then, but from morning to night, each day as it is lived.

III

Forgiveness and Repentance

THE concern of this chapter relates directly to our remarks at the close of the last chapter. To the extent that we do not live by our commitment to the witness of Jesus revealed in the New Testament, we need forgiveness. To the degree that our fidelity to this witness is qualified by infidelity, we need absolution. For the presumption underlying any need of forgiveness is the awareness that we have offended a particular pattern of behaviour (or as we might say, a "moral vision"), that we are guilty. Seeking forgiveness reflects our consciousness of the offense—our feeling of guilt—as well as our desire to reaffirm our commitment to the moral vision. To ask forgiveness for some wrong is always double-edged in this sense.

1. *Forgiving and Being Forgiven*

In the first place, seeking forgiveness reflects our consciousness of an affront we have committed; it reflects our guilt. The meaning of this statement is clear. It is not possible to seek forgiveness if the individual is either unaware of his offense against a moral vision, or believes that his action does not in fact constitute an offense. In the first instance we are dealing with simple ignorance. Here the responsibility of those affirming the moral vision is one of *teaching*—to make the individual aware of why his action is an offense. In traditional catechetical terms the task is one of "pre-evangelization"—the attempt to educate and convince the individual that the moral vision is a worthy one for guiding activity. It is a responsibility and task, for example, that arises at some point in the training of every child. When a child lies "naturally"—to avoid punishment, to win favor, to damage an unliked peer— you educate him in the conviction that lying is neither a correct nor excusable manner of behaviour. You seek to eliminate the amoral ignorance with which he has approached his deceit. In the second instance, the approach must be one of *dialogue*. If the individual is aware of the moral vision and does not believe he has offended it, yet you think he has, then dialogue is required as a service to each of you. You may discover that his innocence is justified; he may discover that it is not; or both of you may still be left with your separate judgments. In any event, each of you must keep an attitude of openmindedness or the dialogue will soon deteriorate into a mere positing of separate opinions. In-

stead of one dialogue there will be two mono-
logues.

Secondly, seeking forgiveness reaffirms the individual's desire to live according to the moral vision.
Again, the meaning of this statement is clear. It
would make little sense to seek forgiveness for an
offense if one had no desire to continue living according to the offended moral vision. To ask forgiveness means that the individual has erred in his
desired pattern of behaviour, acknowledges his error, and seeks to re-establish himself within this
pattern. Or differently put: To ask forgiveness is to
confess sorrow for the wrong one has done and at
the same time to intend amendment of this wrong.
The businessman who habitually cheats his employ-
ees, for example, and has every intention of continuing to cheat them, will hardly ask forgiveness for
his behaviour. For he is clearly living according to a
moral vision that permits cheating. Either he does
not accept, or does not fully appreciate, the condemnation of cheating that is taught, say, within a
Christian moral vision. Only if he were sincere in
his commitment to such a vision would he feel a
need to seek forgiveness for his behaviour. Otherwise he would not judge that he has behaved
wrongly. Or he would judge that his behaviour has
not been *inexcusably* wrong.

This last statement raises an issue that we need
only touch on here—namely, the ease with which

we tend to justify our offenses against a moral vision. The premise of the statement is that the moral vision is adjustable to circumstances. We think that what is wrong in one context can be right in another. This is the premise underlying every naive understanding of situational ethics. While a man may cheat in his business office, therefore, he may not do so in his home; while he may lie to his competitors, he may not lie to his family. His moral vision, in other words, is double-faced. It loses its integrity, its wholeness, in the contradiction of asserting that what is wrong in one set of circumstances is justifiable in another.

Retribution and Resentment

A study of the dictionary definition of the word "forgive" is enlightening. The word comes from the old Anglo-Saxon root, *forgiefan* or *forgifan*. Webster's defines it as: "1. To give up claim to requital from (an offender); to pardon; as, to forgive one's enemies. 2. To give up resentment or claim to requital on account of (an offense); to remit the penalty of; as, to forgive a wrong." We may note from these definitions that the word is fundamentally a forensic term, that is, a legal term pertaining to the rights of an individual. The particular right in question is that of equal retribution for an offense committed against oneself by another. To forgive is to forego this right in favor of the offender. And to be forgiven simply puts the same act

in the passive voice: the individual is the forgiven
offender. By your forgiveness you give to another
the gift of not exacting satisfaction for an offense.
This is the point Jesus is making when he abrogates
the law of the talon (an eye for an eye, a tooth for a
tooth). He is saying that while you might have a
lawful right to see retribution equal to an offense
committed against you, the better response is to
suspend this right and forgive the offense.

The above definitions also imply the existence of
some common moral vision between the offender
and the one offended. Only as this moral vision is
mutually affirmed is it possible for the one offended to forego just retribution from the offender. Among Eskimos, for example, where wife-
sharing is a sign of hospitality from one man toward another, no offense is committed when the
guest takes the wife to bed with him. If there is any
offense given in the custom it would likely be on the
part of the guest who refuses his host's offer. The
guest might be thought rude and unmannered in his
refusal; or worse, insulting—to either the host's
generosity or the wife's desirability. In Peoria,
however, an entirely different moral vision regarding wife-sharing would prevail. The point is that
the commonness of a moral vision is a prerequisite
before the question of forgiveness can legitimately
arise. It would be ludicrous for someone in Peoria
to forgive the Eskimo his practice of hospitality.

The second definition above contains an element

that expands the meaning of the word beyond a merely forensic context. That element is contained in the phrase, "to give resentment." What we are now dealing with is not so much the legal right of an offended individual, his right of retribution, as with his attitude toward the offense. An offense, after all, is not *just* an objective deed committed against someone. It also elicits from the offended individual a subjective response. That response is what the definition attempts to capture in the word "resentment." We have not only been objectively offended through someone's deed; we also have certain feelings about the deed: anger, disappointment, frustration, depression, and so on. We do not stand apart from the deed as a cool and disinterested observer, as if the deed had been directed against someone else. No—we are right in the middle of it. It is this affective engagement that produces the attitude of resentment in us.

Webster's defines resentment as a "feeling of indignant displeasure because of something regarded as a wrong or insult." This is an adequate definition of the feeling. The *result* of the feeling, however, is the subjective response of repulsion, the desire to drive away the offending individual. The response goes hand in hand with its stimulus. We do not want to be in the offender's company; we find him repugnant or infuriating. The reason for this response, of course, is that we have not isolated the offending action but have allowed it to absorb our attitude toward the whole personality of the offender. It is no longer just the offense that elicits from us a "feeling of indignant displeasure." It is the offender himself.

Countless illustrations could be given of the phenomenon of resentment. We frequently find it in marriages, for example, when through some trifling offense the offended spouse reacts against the entire personality of his or her partner. The image springs to mind of the wife who lays her whole marriage on the line because her husband has forgotten their anniversary, or has insulted her mother, or has disagreed with her on some point in rearing the children. Her resentment over the offense is categorical; it now defines her view of her husband as a person. She is unable to see the offense for precisely what it is—a singular act (or several singular acts) that have intruded on her expectations of her husband's behaviour.

Nietzsche was right when he perceived the seriousness of resentment as a destructive power within human relationships. He saw it as a brooding, self-perpetuating power, destructive for both the one who resents and the one resented, eliminating whatever good will might exist between them. And he saw its seriousness because it involves not just passing thoughts, but an attitude. More exactly, it involves a conviction regarding what is justifiable behaviour from the one offended. For resentment always believes itself justified. It is one of the major defenses of the offended consciousness, an active defense that repels not just the offense but the source of the offense. And Nietzsche was again right, unfortunately, when he saw that some people are at their heroic best when they are most resentful. One has the impression that their resentment is engaged almost with delight; that the particular offense is no longer what is important to them but the motive it provides for a massive display of self-assertion, power, and control over the offender—especially by increasing as much as possible his sense of guilt.

When we are called upon by Jesus to give up resentment, to forgive another his offense without a feeling of indignant displeasure, we are being called upon to be Christlike. There is no question that Jesus took offense at what others said and did. There are passages in the New Testament where he demonstrates a quick and even harsh anger. The cleansing of the Temple and the rebuke of Peter come immediately to mind. But there is no indication that the offense of others resulted in an attitude of resentment. His anger does not brood or feed upon itself; his disapproval is not like a wound kept freshly open. If anything, Jesus habitually adopts just the contrary attitude, one that St. Paul was later to voice: "Be angry but do not sin; do not let the sun go down on your anger" (Ephesians 4:26). In fact, it was just this attitude—his teaching and demonstration of forgiveness—that seemed at times a folly to Jesus's disciples. For we can be certain that they were perplexed to hear of an abrogation of the law of the talon; of love even toward one's enemies; of a forgiveness that kept on forgiving, even seventy times seven times. Each of these statements and many more, the lessons of more than one parable, the attitude of Jesus himself before his tormentors: all these demonstrations of the spirit of forgiveness must have amazed, if not shocked, the disciples. For they were as foreign to common behaviour two thousand years ago as they are today. Whereas resentment would have been familiar enough to his disciples, Jesus taught them to dissolve their resentment in forgiveness. They could have easily understood the desire to "get even" with an offender (Peter still hadn't tamed this desire by the night of Jesus' trial, when he cut off a soldier's ear) and the harboring of a repugnance for him. But they had to strain to understand the lesson of Jesus to acknowledge in the offender his offense, yet greet it not with an attitude of retribution but of free requital.

To my mind this lesson reaches one of its most striking expressions in the metaphorical injunction: "Take the beam from your own eye before removing the speck from your brother's eye" (Matthew 7:5). What the statement means is that the resentment we direct toward the offense of others is often blind to the offense that we ourselves commit. While we freely indulge our resentment toward others, we remain conveniently unaware of the causes for resentment we have given; while we easily see reasons for their guilt, we readily ignore reasons for our own. This becomes particularly distressing, as the saying indicates, when the resentment we harbor for some small offense ignores the far greater offenses of which we ourselves are guilty. This is the ignorance of all hypocrisy. It is not ignorance in the sense of unawareness, but rather the refusal to admit that the wrong of which we accuse others finds a similar or greater expression in our own lives. It is the ignorance of the father who berates his son for stealing some trinket, while he himself is embezzling a fortune through fraudulent bookkeeping.

Self-Righteousness

The attitude described by Jesus' metaphor is less strikingly put in the word "self-righteousness." The self-righteous individual is one who takes quick offense at the deeds of others, and is just as quick to point them out to a listener. His response is that of moral superiority, an ease in judging the behaviour of his fellows. He knows for certain what is right and wrong, and believes himself gifted with inerrant insight into the motives underlying what others say, feel, or do. Yet aware of the wrong in others, he remains remarkably unaware of the wrong in himself. For his self-righteousness is premised on a view of himself as a paradigm of inoffensive—"correct," "upright," "faultless"—behaviour. But his premise is unconvincing. If anything, it indicates a disturbing lack of realistic self-evaluation, while at the same time giving us a clue to the meaning of the biblical concept, "the self-righteousness of the sinner."

The tradition of Christian spirituality is especially harsh in its condemnation of self-righteousness. Several outstanding examples could be drawn from the New Testament demonstrating this, but here I will limit myself to just two.

First, there is the statement of St. John: "If we say we have no sin we deceive ourselves, and the truth is not in us" (1 John 1:8). The statement is unequivocal; it is applied to everyone without qualification. Just as everyone has need to forgive those who offend him, so everyone has need to be forgiven his own offenses. Anyone who claims only the need to forgive, without the need of himself being forgiven, is a liar. St. John is subtle enough, of course, to realize that no sane man, even minimally self-aware, would actually *say* he has no sin. No one would risk the ridicule of others that would follow such a claim, the scorn or mocking laughter that greets any transparent deceit. No—the statement is referring not so much to a bald assertion of sinlessness as to the *posture* of sinlessness. St. John is directing his remark toward those who behave *as if* they had no sin, as if their past had suddenly disappeared and their lives are now described only by virtue. In doing so he is undoubtedly reflecting the same attitude of Jesus, in whose own life St. John's statement would have been applied pre-eminently to the scribes and Pharisees. Jesus' condemnations of their posture of sinlessness are eloquent and unreserved. He speaks of them as "whitewashed tombs." He describes their concern with the petty sins and offenses of others, while ignoring their own great sins, as "straining a gnat while swallowing a camel." In fact, if Jesus ever shows a quick contempt toward his fellows, it is toward those who assume in their behaviour an attitude of self-righteousness.

The second example is drawn from an incident and a saying in the life of Jesus. The incident is that of the woman caught in adultery whom the people are about to stone for her offense (John 8:1–12). The saying derives from what Jesus perceives as the self-righteousness of her would-be executioners: "Let him without sin among you cast the first stone" (John 8:7). Presumably Jesus meant a sin equally as serious before the law as adultery. Confronted with the hypocrisy of their self-righteousness, no one stirred and the woman's life was spared.

It is misguided to center the attention of the above incident on the issue of adultery. That is sim-

ply the given context for the lesson Jesus wishes to
teach. The incident does not demonstrate that Jesus
is approving the woman's wrongdoing. This is clear
in his final words to her, "Go and sin no more"
(John 8:11). It only demonstrates that his concern
is directed elsewhere. His thoughts are less on the
punishment she might deserve for her offense than
on the attitude of those who would willingly kill
her. And by preventing her punishment by his
adroit comment he seems to be presenting as the
greater offense not adultery but self-righteousness.

For Jesus, "God alone is good" (Matthew 19:17).
God alone is righteous; God alone may justifiably
judge the deeds of men. Only to the extent that he
has revealed his will do men know what is good and
evil before God. And only as their own judgment
reflects this revelation is their judgment free from
self-righteousness. What this means is that before
anyone passes judgment on another's guilt according to the revelations of God's will, he must first
become acutely aware of his own guilt before this
revelation. This will purify his judgment, making it
more closely expressive of God's will rather than
his own sense of self-righteousness. It is precisely
this purification of their motives that Jesus is seeking when he confronts the assailants of the adulter-
ess.

As we suggested in Chapter 1, a condemnation of
this inclination toward self-righteousness may be

traced all the way back to the initial book of the Old Testament and its record of the Fall. The sin of the man and woman, we said, is located not in their refusal of God's command regarding the tree of knowledge—God never expected perfect submission in the first place—as in their response once God confronts them with their refusal. For what do they do? Do they take responsibility for their parts in the offense? Do they admit their fault? No, they do not. Instead, each adopts an attitude of self-righteousness which finds expression in their excuses for their behaviour. The man excuses his offense by blaming the woman for it; the woman excuses her offense by blaming the serpent for it; and the serpent, a convenient scapegoat, is left alone as the culprit, there being no one else to blame. Neither the man nor the woman accepts responsibility for the fault committed. Each assumes an attitude of false innocence that all but says, "I am not at fault for what has happened; someone else is." It is this self-righteousness that fires God's anger. In fact, one midrash (commentary) goes so far as to suggest that had Adam and Eve responsibly admitted their offense before God, God would have spared them his just response and mankind would still be living in Paradise. But this suggestion, of course, goes too far, and we cannot accept it. For the plain truth is that every person who has ever lived, save Jesus, has more than amply committed the same sin as Adam and Eve. Each has made excuses for his offenses before God and taken an attitude of self-righteousness. We did not need two people, Adam and Eve, at the beginning of human existence to commit the original sin—as if the world would be a paradise had they not. Each of us commits it over and over again in his own life. Each of us is Adam, each is Eve.

The Fifth Request

The reason I have been stressing so far the activity of forgiving over the reception of forgiveness is due to the source from which I have drawn my reflections. That source is the fifth request in Jesus' great prayer to his Father—"forgive us our trespasses as we forgive those who trespass against us." We must note that the request possesses both a passive and active dimension: we are asking to be forgiven the offenses we commit, but only to the extent that we forgive those committed against us. The request, therefore, is in the nature of a contract or agreement between two parties: I ask that if I do this, you do that. Or differently put: We ourselves are imposing a qualification upon the forgiveness we seek, namely, our own willingness to forgive others. Yet we must also note that the structure of the request does not imply that forgiveness of our offenses is *automatically* secured upon our forgiveness of others. The latter is a pre-requisite for our being forgiven—but that is all. Our forgiveness of others does not force or compel God to forgive us in turn. Instead, it functions as a "demonstration," a necessary demonstration, of the sincerity of our request. Before the request can be granted we are required to indicate our worthiness.

This characteristic of the request sets it apart from all the others found in the Lord's Prayer. In the other requests we are asking something outrightly, something as a pure gift from God without any qualifiers attached: thy Kingdom come, thy will be done on earth as in heaven, give us this day our daily bread, lead us not into temptation, deliver us from evil. The present request, however, offers for the first and only time in the entire prayer a *direct* statement of personal responsibility. For this reason it is perhaps the most difficult to speak. It is much easier, after all, to voice a simple request and hope for its fulfillment, than to attach a promise of specific behaviour to the request before its fulfillment can be fairly expected. Yet that is exactly what is occurring in the present request. We do not say, "forgive us our trespasses," and let it end there. We go on to add the qualifying condition, "as we forgive those who trespass against us."

This qualification derives from Jesus' habitual concern with the character of human relationships. As noted in chapter 1, this concern reaches its highpoint in the double commandment he offers as a capsulized guide toward fulfilling God's will. The first commandment is to love God completely; the second, like the first, is to love your neighbor as yourself. This second commandment, we may note, has a remarkable structural similarity to the present request from the Lord's Prayer. You are to love your neighbor *as* yourself; you are forgiven your offenses *as* you forgive those who offend you. In each case there is a qualification in the statement centered on the individual's behavioural patterns. In the first case the individual's love of others is qualified by his love for himself. The presumption is that the individual loves himself fully, respects himself, cherishes his life, desires, goals. As he loves himself in this fashion so is he to bestow this same love on others, respecting them, cherishing their lives, desires, goals. In the second statement, as we have said, the forgiveness that the individual receives is qualified by the forgiveness he practices. In both statements the individual is understood as an agent whose activity (love, forgiveness) involves him in relationships with others. It is necessary, in other words, but not sufficient for the individual to love himself and God. He must also love his neighbor. Nor is it sufficient for him to seek forgiveness for his own offenses. He must also forgive the offenses of others. A proper understanding of Christian forgiveness, like that of Christian love, is other-oriented.

A further point must be made about the request; or better, the point must be made more explicitly.

The request being voiced is that *God* forgive our offenses, in the same manner and degree that we forgive those who have offended us. There is, I think, a clear and unmistakable implication here—namely, that forgiveness finally derives from God. If this is so, however, we must conclude that in forgiving an offender we can speak only for ourselves. We tell him that *we* have forgiven his offense, that *we* have blotted it from our minds and hearts. But our personal forgiveness cannot end his seeking of forgiveness. What it does is reestablish our own relationship with him so that the offense is no longer an effective influence. As we said earlier, it indicates that we harbor no resentment toward him. But the offender must still seek the forgiveness of God for his offense. We see this demand, of course, as a result of the faith that in offending another human being we are in fact offending God. The presumption of this faith is that God is not disinterested but involved in the deeds we commit toward others, the thoughts and attitudes we possess toward them. And again, the basis of this presumption finds perhaps its clearest statement in the double command of Jesus, and the connection he draws (the second command is *like* the first) between loving God and loving other persons. If this command expresses God's will for us, then God is clearly implicated in defining the character of our human relationships.

To the extent, therefore, that the words and deeds of Jesus provide the basis of our moral vi-

sion, and to the extent that we affirm these words
and deeds as the revelation of God—we must conclude that God is directly involved in the issue of
our behaviour. For it would be superficial to suggest that God reveals his will in Jesus for our benefit, and then becomes disinterested in our response
to this revelation. This understanding would make
a bad joke of the revelation from the very start. It
would imply that God did not seriously intend what
he revealed in the life of Jesus; or that he did seriously intend it, but only for a while. I am reminded
here of the story of Noah. The reader will recall
how God destroys men because of their depravity
and refusal to amend their ways after repeated
warnings. Their behaviour causes him to lose interest in their willingness to abide by his revealed will,
and so he condemns them to drown in the sea of his
now mute indifference. In the story only Noah and
his family, only a select few, are saved, because
God still perceives in them the spirit of obedience
he desires. Now I am reminded of this story for the
simple reason that it could never be the story of
God as revealed in Jesus. For there God never loses
interest in his creatures, or becomes indifferent to
them, or abandons his care for them. The rainbow
promise that appears to Noah in the sky—that God
would never again forsake the men he formed—
finds its final expression in the life and destiny of
Jesus Christ.

The revelation that occurs in Jesus, in other

words, occurs for a purpose. And the purpose is to provide us with the gift of God's will manifested in a human life. God does not reveal himself in Jesus for his own benefit, praise or glory. Nor does he reveal himself for the benefit of the single man Jesus, as if Jesus alone was to be gifted with the revelation. No—the New Testament and the tradition of Christian doctrine consistently point out that the revelation of God's will in Jesus occurs for *our* benefit, the benefit of all mankind. The gift is not given for the benefit of none, or the benefit of one, or the benefit of a few, but for the benefit of all. And when the gift is given, God does not dispossess himself of concern as to how it is received and used. God is not an indifferent giver, save in the sense that he gives to all without consideration of merit. The revelation in Jesus is indeed a gift, freely bestowed, but not one in which God loses interest once it is bestowed.

When we pray, therefore, "forgive us our trespasses as we forgive those who trespass against us," we are acknowledging that discernment concerning what constitutes our offenses derives from the revelation in Jesus. It bears repeating, however, that this acknowledgement can be offered only insofar as the possessive pronoun "our" refers to Christians. It is not to Socrates or Buddha, Marx or Mao that we look for the foundation of our patterns of behaviour, but to Jesus. These others may

be employed, of course, in the deepening understanding of this pattern. The teachings of Socrates
and Buddha, for example, can obviously assist us
in appreciating the role of ignorance in Christian
life, just as the teachings of Marx and Mao can help
us appreciate the meaning of devotion to the poor
and exploited. But they are used only secondarily
and in service to the primary source found in the
words and deeds of Jesus. This, I think, is what St.
Paul is also saying in his abbreviated proclamation
of what defines Christian commitment: "There is
one Lord, *one* faith, *one* baptism, *one* God and
Father of us all, who is above all and through all
and in all" (Ephesians 4:5). When we ask to be forgiven our offenses, then, when we seek the healing
of our guilt, we are asking forgiveness for our infidelities to the revelation of God's will in Jesus.
We are not asking forgiveness for having offended
the moral vision of Socrates or Buddha, Marx or
Mao. Save where any particular teaching from
these other moral visions is confirmed in the teachings of Jesus, the Christian could hardly speak of
his offense as an offense against God. For he does
not believe that in these others a revelation of
God's will has taken place. The revelation is in Jesus, and it is because he has offended *this* revelation, whether or not its content reoccurs in the
doctrine of others, that he seeks the forgiveness of
God. The Christian is not accountable to God for

the teachings of two or three or many men; he is accountable only for the teachings of Jesus.

The Judgment of God

This accountability before God is what we may otherwise call God's "judgment"—a topic not discussed much in today's spirituality. Even in this book we have given away little space to God's justice, preferring instead to emphasize such qualities as his providential care and mercy. Yet now we are obliged to give this quality its due, even if brief, recognition.

Popular images of the activity of God's judgment account for a large part of the above reticence. We have, for example, the image of the *stern* judge, the one for whom our behaviour is either black or white, good or evil. This is the judge who knows nothing of extenuating circumstances, whose judgment takes no account of contexts. You did this, or you didn't. And your deed, isolated and alone, taken in itself, is the sole basis of judgment. With this God there is no such thing as pleading or explaining. Unlike Jahweh before Abraham's pleading to spare Sodom and Gomorrah, this God never repents his decisions. The image is that of a just God, to be sure; but the justice is narrow-minded and severe. When this image is applied in Christic portraiture I am reminded of the fierce-eyed Judge portrayed behind the main altar of the National Shrine in Washington, D.C. There is no mercy, no pity, no forgiveness in those eyes. And no human being can possibly escape an unfavorable judgment before their gaze, since no human being is without sin. The question of salvation or damnation consequently becomes one of simple proportion: If your particular deeds of good "outweigh" your particular deeds of evil, there is the likelihood, or at least the chance, of God's favorable judgment. We have all heard someone say: "I've done my share of sinning, but *on the whole* I've led a good life." This is an acknowledgement (or a hope) that God's final judgment will be proportional.

There is very little to recommend the above image of God. But one of the merits it possesses is that God's judgment is *transparent*—the right and wrong deeds upon which it is based are clearly perceived as such by the individual. Everything is out in the open; there are no surprises. The individual knows where his virtue and vice have lain; he is as aware of his sin and sanctity as is God. However, a second image we might mention hasn't even this little to recommend it. God's justice is here understood as a *searching* justice, a prying, peering, probing justice. By this I mean that the basis of God's judgment is now provided not only by what the individual himself perceives to be the good and evil in his life, but by good and evil of which he might not even be aware. A classic expression of this image occurs in the book of Job. I refer especially to that part where the friends of Job argue that Job's suffering must surely derive from some sin he has committed. True to a general axiom of Old Testament spirituality, they cannot understand a guileless suffering, one whose source is not some offense committed against God. When Job protests that he can think of no such sin, his friends respond that still it must be there, that God knows it and that Job must strive to recall what it is. God only punishes evil, they say, but he punishes it whether or not the individual himself is aware of it. Job must have done *something* to win God's severe justice—and remembering it will at least give him the consolation of understanding the rightness of this justice. But Job can remember nothing that would make the loss of his land and flocks, wife and children, his own physical pain, understandable as an expression of God's right judgment of sin. And it is no consolation to presume that this sin is there if it is hidden from Job's conscience. For how can Job, or anyone, confess to a sin he cannot recollect? How can he regret or promise amendment for something he cannot recall? How can he feel a legitimate guilt in this situation? He cannot.

The response that the above image of God's justice elicits from the individual is *scrupulosity*. The individual now perceives God's judgment as dependent not just on the evil he remembers, but on the evil that has slipped his mind. Even worse, he be-

gins to question whether or not he has offended
God by an act which he had initially thought to be
without offense. He worries; he frets. He lets loose
his imagination upon his behaviour, thinking that
he may have done evil even when it was not his intention. Insecurity becomes a brand upon his mind
and heart. He is always uncertain of his ability to
make accurate judgments regarding good and evil.
He is forever suspicious that he has adequately
foreseen the consequences of his actions. And his
suspicion in turn breeds an unrelenting sense of
guilt.

Thus we have the situation, for example, of a
woman I know whom I will call Mary. Only in her
case scrupulosity has grown to include not only her
deeds but, in a peculiar though not uncommon
twist of conscience, her thoughts as well. For Mary
takes at face value Jesus' comment about "sinning
in your heart" (rather than the viewpoint on this
comment we offered in the last chapter) and is convinced that she is accountable not only for her "evil
doings" but also for her "evil thinking." Most of
her adult life has consequently been spent in a scrupulous self-examination of her behaviour that has
frequently led to a paralyzing guilt, self-vilifi-
cation, and finally despair. Most of it, I might add,
has also been spent in extensive psychiatric therapy.

Any scrupulous conscience (not just Mary's) is
demonic. It endlessly torments the individual. He is

never sure that he has sufficiently sought God's
forgiveness for his behaviour. He is always scour-
ing his memory, his motives, looking for some offense that he had previously overlooked. His belief
is that God will know this offense, and that forget-
fulness or lack of precision is not a legitimate excuse for failing to secure God's forgiveness. God
judges *all* our behaviour, not just the bits and
pieces of it we presently recollect. Even more, he
judges it with an objectivity that we must share in
seeking his forgiveness. As a result the scrupulous
individual is forever watchful regarding behaviour
that does not *appear* offensive, but which may be
in an objective view. If he is uncertain in any given
instance, he believes it best to presume the offen-
siveness of the behaviour and ask God's forgiveness. His guiding principle is that in cases of doubt
it is wiser to think he has sinned than to think he
has not. In this way when he comes before God's
judgment he will not be caught short on the forgiveness he has sought.

One key to overcoming both of the above images
of God can be found, I think, in the fifth request
from the Lord's prayer. The request is that God
forgive our offenses *as* we forgive those who have
offended us. We have already discussed the characteristics that should mark our forgiveness of others.
And it is clear that these characteristics do not describe those attributed to God in either of the above
two images. We are not encouraged in our forgive-

ness to become petty or picayune, to demand that
the offender admit to us every detail of the offense
he has committed. We are not encouraged to require that he ransack his unconscious and confess
all the reasons for guilt that we believe he possesses.
No—we are encouraged to forgive directly, to forgive the offense for which he is seeking forgiveness.
We are encouraged to allay all suspicions that there
is more to the offense—or that there are entirely
different offenses—that he is omitting. We are encouraged, in short, to forgive as we would want to
be forgiven, just as we are more generally encouraged by Jesus to do unto others as we would
have them do unto us.

Only a misguided conscience finds comfort or
consolation in a scrupulous search for the forgiveness of God. It is the same misguidance that demands of others a scrupulous conscience in their
search for our forgiveness. The error that occurs in
each case, therefore, is an error in consciousness itself. Instead of encouraging a consciousness that
relates to God as *abba,* Father—and allowing this
to determine his relationships with other people—
the scrupulous individual relates to God as if he
were an omniscient accountant. His seeking forgiveness for his sins is then reduced to a game of
statistics, a tabulation. And the sincerity of his contrition is judged proportionate to the excellence and
precision of his memory. It is basically a give-and-
take mentality that here prevails: God's forgiveness

is granted only to the extent that detailed reasons for it are presented.

The God who is *abba* allows us the freedom to determine our lives—the values by which we live, the desires we cultivate, the goals we seek. In this he is reflected in every good human father who does the same for his child. Yet in that act of generosity, that gift we call the revelation in Jesus, God also demonstrates that he is not disinterested in how this freedom is used. God is not an indifferent giver. As soon as we affirm in faith that his will is revealed in Jesus, we affirm God's involvement in our response to this faith. The result of this affirmation is that all judgment pertaining to our blessedness before God is made within the confines of our freedom. Either we accept the revelation in Jesus as the pattern describing our behaviour, or we reject it. But in either case—and quite obviously—we must first be aware of the revelation. For we cannot exercise our freedom of choice unconsciously or in ignorance.

Thus the individual who has never even heard the name of Jesus can scarcely be judged according to the revelation in Jesus, but only according to his own particular moral vision. Nor can an individual be fairly judged according to this revelation when his behaviour is determined by factors outside his control—what we once called "demons" but now call, with psychological science, by other names. In both cases the individual's freedom before the revelation in Jesus is reduced or absent, so that judgment on his behaviour must accordingly be altered.

The God who is *abba* does not demand that we experience guilt and seek forgiveness for offenses against a revelation we do not understand or cannot fully affirm. He does not expect the impossible from us. The expectation, rather, is a much more modest and humane one. We must acknowledge our guilt and seek forgiveness only when we have *freely* and *knowingly* acted against what we affirm is God's manifest will.

2. *Interlude: Guilt and the Good Deed*

Being forgiven is not just a passive experience; it also implies a certain responsiveness on the part of the person forgiven. The guilt we experience when we offend our convictions is not adequately healed simply by feeling sorrow for our offense. The healing of guilt also requires activity, the particular activity we have been calling *amendment*. Guilt indicates not only that we have done wrong in light of some commitment we have made, but also that in response to this wrong (to "make up" for it) we must do right according to our commitment. Remorse, in other words, is never a sufficient response to the experience of guilt. It must always be wedded to specific behaviour that reaffirms our commitment to a given moral vision.

The Old and New Testaments are especially sensitive in their insistence on the above point. And they argue this insistence in a particularly striking and persuasive way, I believe, in the spirituality of the *mitzvah* that appears like a refrain throughout their ethical teachings. Let's spend some time looking at this spirituality, especially its effects on the responsiveness called for in the experience of being forgiven. In the process we will see that this responsiveness—and the guilt that brings it forth—also involves a communal awareness that requires a view of guilt as something more than merely a private experience.

Mitzvah is the Hebrew word for "good deed," and the spirituality built upon it requires an organic model of human community, or what others may prefer to call a "synthetic" view of human living. What does this specifically mean for a given community (for us the Christian community), the patterns of behaviour its members profess, and the guilt they experience when these patterns are broken? It means several things.

First, it means that the members of the community have a clear perception of what constitutes good and evil. As we suggested in chapter 1, this will derive from the prayer and study, the obedience the members direct at the witness, the words and deeds of Jesus. Again, behaviour that reflects this witness in a given situation is judged good and issues in blessing; behaviour that does not is judged evil and issues in guilt. While this judgment may in some instances demand considerable discretion and subtlety, in most it does not. For one of the more striking benefits of the witness of Jesus, I think, is its remarkable lucidity. The practice of such "goods" as generosity and forgiveness, a selfless fidelity and hope, the worship of God, the care of children, and so on: all these are unquestionable criteria Jesus offers to determine judgment on our behaviour. There is an immediacy about the teachings of Jesus that suffers obscurity only with the demands of a reluctant or too suspicious mind.

Secondly, it means that our behaviour must have as its motive the health of the community. But health in an organism is described as balance, that is, the harmonious interaction of its various members for the benefit of all. Any event that disrupts this harmony, therefore, must eventually be recompensed by an event that restores it. What this means in our specific context is that for the sake of the community's health any evil an individual commits must be balanced out by a subsequent good deed (*mitzvah*) that is *appropriate* and *proportionate* to the evil committed. (This, by the way, is a viewpoint that is increasingly acknowledged but still largely unpracticed in our civil penal system.) If you damage or destroy someone's reputation, for example, the good deed required is to restore his reputation. It would be inappropriate, in other words, if you thought yourself acquitted of this re-

sponsibility by giving food to the hungry or shelter
to the homeless. For while good in themselves,
these activities are irrelevant to the evil you have
done; the reputation is still ruined. On the other
hand, we must also be very careful here. What we
are saying must not be mistakenly identified with
the famous law of the talon ("an eye for an eye, a
tooth for a tooth") that was generally approved in
the practice of Jewish jurisprudence—and which
Jesus, we know, abrogated in his own teaching
(Matthew 5:28-42). The law of the talon was concerned with the retributory rights of an offended
party (or what we might call today his right to "get
even"), and only in this context with the responsibility of the offender to compensate adequately for
his offense. In Jesus' teaching, however, it is just
the other way around. For unless we were mistaken
in our previous remarks, the offended individual
has but one task. And it is not to seek retribution
for but to forgive the offense committed against
him. It is the guilty individual, the offender, who
must seek to balance in good deeds the offense he
has committed.

Thirdly, and perhaps most difficult for us to understand, the spirituality of the *mitzvah* insists that
no behaviour, whether good or evil, is private in its
effects. This insistence is a direct result of the
organic model of human community the spirituality is presuming. To whatever degree, in whatever
fashion, the behaviour of any member of the com-

munity affects the existence of the community as a whole. "Evil (or good) always follows from evil (or good)" is the prevailing maxim here. But because the doer of evil or the doer of good cannot be understood apart from his place in the community, his deeds always produce an effect therein.

The commonplace parallel here is a wound sustained by some part of the body—let us say a burned hand. Everyone knows that it is not just the hand that suffers. The whole body suffers; the pain of the burned hand ripples throughout the entire organism. This is essentially the same point the Old Testament is making in such typical statements as the lament quoted by Ezechial, "The fathers have eaten sour grapes, the children shall grind their teeth" (Ezechial 18:2). Every individual deed, for good or ill, in some way and at some time will affect the life of the community as a whole. The guilt an individual experiences when he has been unfaithful in his commitment to a moral vision, just like the gratitude he experiences when he has not, clearly possesses a communal dimension. I might also add that in one sense the whole of my book, *Act of Contrition,* is nothing more than a sustained attempt to reinsert this third trait into what are frequently our overly self-concerned and "privatized" consciences.

Fourthly, the spirituality of the *mitzvah* means that whenever a member of the community commits evil and yet refuses to perform the appropriate good deed to recompense it, this responsibility falls to the other members of the community. For the evil *must* be redressed if the health of the community is to be maintained. If the evildoer refuses to do so himself, therefore, his refusal must be made up in the generosity of others. And if the evildoer's refusal is consistent, if he becomes what the Testaments describe as an unrepentent sinner—someone who continually neglects to redress the evil he does with an appropriate good deed, someone whose experiences of guilt are barren—then the community, because its health is at stake, should seriously consider the option of removing him from its membership. For no organic community, just as no organism, can be fairly asked to host a continual threat to its health. The first step should always be an attempt to heal the threat from within the organism. But if that fails, you remove the threat. Like all Christian activity, however, this removal, too, must clearly be motivated by the witness, the care and loving-kindness of Jesus. No matter how strong the temptation may be, it must never issue in the pain, the brutalization in any form of the offending member.

The foregoing remarks on the spirituality of the *mitzvah* have offered an outline of the sense of responsibility that guilt should engender within an individual. We have noted that part of this responsibility involves the awareness that guilt is not an end in itself but must function as a catalyst for further activity: The good deed that "balances" or "makes up for" the offense from which guilt is born. We have also noted that another part of this responsibility involves the awareness that guilt is not just private but also communal in its perspective: The guilty individual understands that his offense affects not only himself but the community in which he lives. What the spirituality presumes, as we said, is an organic model of human community—that is, a model which sees as an essential ingredient in defining the community the interlocking and mutually influential relationships that prevail among its members. That Jesus had just such a model in mind for the community of his followers is perhaps most clearly expressed in his celebrated metaphor of the vine and the branches. The very same model, of course, also underlies St. Paul's own exquisite metaphor defining the community as the Body of Christ.

What I would now like to do is examine more closely this communal dimension of guilt. Specifically I would like to set my discussion within the context of the relationship between guilt, hope, and repentance. For if the foregoing reflections have been accurate, then the three are clearly and closely related. Guilt, we may say, issues in a spirit of repentance whose foremost expression is the willingness to do the good deed that adequately atones for an evil committed. But this spirit of repentance can in turn survive only on the hope that the broken convictions from which our guilt derives are worthy of continued pursuit—not first for our own sake but for the sake of others.

3. *Hope and Repentance*

If we say that Christian spirituality of a generation ago, influenced by the luminous works of Bultmann, Barth, Ebeling, Althaus and others, had as its major concern the issue of faith and its relationship to past history—especially the history of Jesus—we could say that the spirituality of today, marked by the works of men like Moltmann and Pannenberg, has shifted this concern more to the issue of hope and the future. Today, perhaps for the first time in generations of Christian spirituality, hope is on center stage for appreciative study, and reflection on the future is enjoying pre-eminence to a degree it has scarcely achieved previously (an exception being the early apostolic church). This situation has been exciting and productive of some of the most fruitful theological insights achieved in this century.

My purpose in the following remarks can obviously not be to examine all the factors—philosophical, psychological, sociological—which have gone into this shift of theological emphasis. Instead it is the much more limited one of accepting both these issues (hope and the future) as inarguably central concerns of contemporary spirituality, and then relating them specifically to the experiences of Christian guilt and repentance. I have chosen this topic for the simple reason that this relationship between hope, guilt and repentance has, to my knowledge, nowhere been treated in quite the following way. For what I will be proposing are three basic models of hope and the future, only the third of which (especially given our concerns in the previous section) offers the most adequate framework for understanding the meaning of guilt and repentance in Christian life. Needless to say, in providing only an overview of each model (and out of sensitivity to the non-specialist reader) I will have to reduce to simplified terms an analysis that would otherwise be extraordinarily complex and intricate.

Pandora's Jar: The Wheel of Hopelessness

The first model I would like to examine is associated above all with the ancient Greeks—captured, for example, in that segment of Hesiod's great poem, *Works and Days,* which relates the famous myth of Pandora. Let's take a brief look at this myth, then, with the specific intent of discovering its possible application for our own everyday lives. Just this application, after all, is the purpose of every mythmaker (even those in the Bible, as we saw in chapter 1 when discussing the Genesis myth of the Fall and exile) if his myth is to succeed and not fade from human memory.

According to the myth, Zeus has taken a dislike toward men because of the favor shown them by Prometheus. He is specifically irritated by Prometheus' theft of fire for the use of men and by the deception that causes him to select a pile of dry bones as men's offering to him. Zeus' reaction to this double affront is to strike back at Prometheus through punishing the men whom he loves. And as usual his punishment is ingenious. In his rage he has created a woman of irresistible beauty, endowed inwardly "with treachery in her heart" and outwardly with a large sealed jar in which every god and goddess has placed a woe, a suffering for men. Both of these items, the woman and her jar, Zeus then presents to Prometheus' brother, Epimetheus. And against Prometheus' advice never to accept a gift from Zeus, Epimetheus (whose name, by the way, means "afterthought") gladly takes both the woman, "as a companion to fondle close to his heart," and the jar which she carries. The following events, of course, proceed exactly as Zeus had planned. In a secret moment Pandora's curiousity gets the best of her. She opens the jar and all its sufferings are released upon mankind. The myth ends by recapitulating in one sentence the moral which the whole story was meant to demonstrate, namely, "there is no way to escape the will of Zeus."

What principally interests us in this myth, however, is not so much these final words of Hesiod, and the spirit of fatalism they express, as it is the jar of the seductive Pandora. For we find in the course of the story that in this jar, which supposedly contains only woes for mankind, there is also contained hope (*elpis*). But when the jar is opened hope alone is prevented from escaping by an explicit command of Zeus. The question is why. And the answer is gained only when we understand both what hope (*elpis*) meant to the Greeks and how it was employed in this particular myth.

In nearly all of Greek literature *elpis* is presented as an illusionary, harmful attitude closely connected to the sin of *hubris* (god-like pride). This would explain its inclusion in the jar. But though in this sense it is looked at negatively and would thus be a cause of suffering (the gods always punish hubris), in another sense it has the positive function of "anticipation," or more specifically, "foreboding of ill." And in this sense it would provide a means for the avoidance of any suffering awaiting a person. Anticipating it, the individual would possibly be able to avoid it. Zeus' retention of it in the jar, therefore, also becomes readily understandable. It intensifies and exacerbates his punishment of men, since without *elpis* they cannot even foresee, let alone elude, the misery now set free upon the world.

The hopelessness in which Hesiod's myth leaves an individual is thus double-sided. It is positive in the sense that without *elpis* he is less likely to commit the capital sin of *hubris,* thinking himself like unto the gods. But it is negative in the sense that without *elpis* he cannot control his future, since he cannot anticipate the events that will shape it and so cannot constructively plan his existence. It should cause little surprise, then, to find that owing in part to the influence of this mythic substructure to their thinking, the Greeks were led to their famous cyclic view of history. For if human beings cannot anticipate and thus control the future awaiting them, in this uncontrollability the future must inevitably begin to appear like the past: every future event will seem like every past event insofar as in both cases no event can be anticipated and so possibly altered. Or differently put: the future is locked into its uncontrollable fatality just as the past is locked into its uncontrollable objectivity. Furthermore, since according to Hesiod's myth it is suffering which Pandora has released upon human beings, the past and future come to be viewed not as a cylce of just any uncontrollable events, but pre-eminently as a cycle of uncontrollable *misery,* from which, of course, like Zeus' will, there is no way to escape.

It is not difficult to locate commonplace examples of the way this hopelessness finds expression in ordinary life. We have one in the case of a businessman I know (you may know others just like him). His days are an indication that personal history can indeed by viewed as a spinning circle in which the same events (and their varying degrees of pain or tedium) are repeated over and over again. Even the variations that may occur here and there throughout the weeks or months or years only highlight all the more the overwhelming sameness of his life and the course of events it is following: the same chores, the same worries, the same sins, the same feelings of guilt, and so on. And so far as he can see there is no breaking out of this circle. Try as he might to embark on some newness in his life, he always seems to be dragged back into the same old cycle. His freedom seems chained, limited to only peripheral matters in the general course of his life: whether to buy this or that automobile; whether to wear this or that set of clothes; whether to go here or there on his vacation; whether to enroll the children in this or that sports program. Even here, however, in his freedom over these superficial concerns, he seems chained to a circle: for it is his *place* to exercise this freedom; it has *always* been his place to do so, and always will be.

In view of the above observations it is not hard to understand why there arose in Greek thought such distinct spiritualities as Stoicism, Epicureanism, and Platonism. For each in its own way was attempting to deal with the hopelessness of "natural" man and his condemnation to a seemingly endless cycle of earthly pain. The Stoics did this through counselling resignation (*apatheia*) toward

the events of life. The Epicureans did it again
through a counsel of resignation toward life, but
with the additional encouragement to seek actively
whatever pleasures life might hold. Finally, the Pla-
tonists, while also counselling resignation, did so in
the judgment that bodily life and its pain were unimportant anyway, since the proper joy of man was
only to be found in the soul's contemplation of the
"eternal forms." Taking these three cases, then, as
predominant representatives of Greek spirituality,
we may conclude that guilt and repentance within
this first model of hope (hopelessness) would foremostly involve: 1) the recognition that the individual is the prey of a future he cannot control (he will
repeatedly commit the same deeds that cause guilt
and call for repentance); 2) that any attempt to
change this future is therefore not only doomed
from the start, but a hopeless expression of pride
and rebellion against the will of the gods; and consequently, 3) that in place of hope one should cultivate in himself a spirit of resigned detachment to
the pain of his existence, since he can neither foresee nor alter it.

Memento Mori: Hope as Escape

Of the three schools of thought mentioned
above, the one having the most profound influence
on Christian spirituality has, of course, been Platonism. In fact, it is through a reflection on this influence that we come to our second model of hope,

for which I am suggesting the title, "hope as escape." What gives rise to this model, briefly put, is the localization of the "eternal forms" of Platonic contemplation (specifically the True, Good, and Beautiful) into a time ("after death") and a place ("up above") where they prevail as characteristics over all the pain and suffering of the cycle of earthly life. This time and place, as adopted by Christianity, has traditionally been called "heaven."

What we immediately notice as the major difference between these first two models of hope is that in the second model the future is no longer bound to the cycle of earthly existence but proceeds along a linear path and possesses a definite goal. Peace of mind and happiness, therefore, while still being in part the product of a resigned acceptance of the ills of existence, have also become the characteristics of a distinct spatio-temporal order toward which this linear future is heading. In this second model, in short, earthly existence is not all there is. Rather, it can lead to another type of existence in which all human woe is gathered back up and locked again into Pandora's jar. Or differently put: with the localization of the objects of Platonic contemplation comes the birth of hope understood as escape. Earthly time is now a path leading to a future goal, which, when achieved, halts the time of earthly misery altogether and begins the new time of heavenly bliss.

The steppingstone between these two times is death. It is the catapult which hurls the individual from the cycle of earthly ills into the eternal joys of heaven. But this movement clearly cannot be understood as fated or pre-ordained. For if heaven is indeed imaged as the locale of the True, Good, and Beautiful, then obviously only those whose lives have manifested these characteristics can find a home there. Those who live otherwise would be "foreigners" in this place; their dwelling here would be inappropriate. Instead, they must dwell elsewhere, and this "elsewhere" is what is traditionally called "hell." In other words, just as heaven is the locale of what is True, Good, and Beautiful in existence and so appropriate to those whose lives have matched these qualities, hell is the locale of the opposite qualities and correspondingly appropriate to those whose lives have matched these. In effect, then, we are saying that judgment has a role to play within this second model of hope, just as it does within the first model. But unlike the first model, wherein the judgment is passed (by the gods) before life even begins and is always negative, in the second model judgment is passed (by God) not at the beginning but at the end of life. It is then that the decision is finally made whether heaven or hell is the most appropriate result for the way one has lived. I would like to remind the reader, however, of the qualifying remarks on this decision we offered toward the end of the last chapter.

The role of guilt and repentance in this second model is by now transparent. It involves the recognition of what is not true, good, or beautiful in one's life—what is evil in one's life—and a commitment to the efforts to overcome these characteristics. Guilt reflects the individual's awareness of the evil he has done. Repentance is principally a disciplinary process (prayer, good works, ascetic practices, etc.) through which the possibility of repeating the evil is diminished and the good is increasingly brought forward as the primary characteristic of the way the individual behaves.

The above model probably represents the most common understanding of the relationship between hope, guilt, and repentance in Christians today. It perhaps reached its highpoint, though, during the tenth to fifteenth centuries. Throughout this period an unbroken *memento mori* was sung to remind Christians of their guilt before God's will (by definition true, good, and beautiful) and the need to repent their wickedness. For only then could they legitimately hope that when death catapults them from this existence into the next they will land in heaven rather than hell. Hope, in other words, is basically a divisive power in the individual, separating the negativity and unhappiness he experiences during earthly life from the bliss he believes he can merit in heaven. The individual lives for the sake of another life; his current life is something he has to endure.

As we noted in chapter 1, the negativity with which earthly life is approached within this model may be partly attributed to the prevalence of a view of original sin which sees its results as demanding a complete condemnation of life in this world. In this view earthly life is a "vale of tears," a terrain of sorrow and ceaseless labor, a maze of obstacles in which the individual must be ever alert on his path to God. Hope is the attitude which counterbalances the despair and pessimism which this situation can create in an individual and allows him to overcome it. But it does so through joining battle with the world, condemning it, and separating life in this world from life in the world to come. And the spirit of guilt and repentance which it creates in the individual is thus essentially selfish: the individual "uses" his guilt and willingness to repent in order to escape the pain of earthly life by passing through death into the joy of heavenly life. In this model one is dependent on his hope to overcome earth and gain heaven.

The Future Kingdom: Hope as Mission

To some extent as a reaction to the second model of hope outlined above we now offer our third. Instead of emphasizing the sin and fallenness of the world, it emphasizes the goodness of created being and human partnership with God in bringing the world to its proper fulfillment. In this model God's world is a world in the making, and we are called to the task of involving ourselves actively and positively in this making. Underlying this task and replacing the pessimism toward the world which marked hope in the second model, there is an optimism that together with God we are not only capable of this labor but have a duty and responsibility toward it. The results of the Fall recorded in Genesis, while seriously acknowledged, are given less emphasis than the mandate to exercise power over the earth, subduing it in obedience and devotion to the Creator.

In this third model, furthermore, we find that instead of using the term "heaven" to describe the goal of human existence there is a preference for the term "Kingdom of God." This becomes understandable, though, as soon as we recall that heavenly life as the object of hope in the second model is consistently opposed to earthly life—whereas in our third model the object of hope is not first a time and place separate from the earth but earthly life itself (though obviously transformed from what it now is). In our third model, in other words, hope is principally earth, not heaven, centered. And the fallenness of the world is not something the individual turns his back on and attempts to escape in another time and space dimension, but something within whose context he must labor to bring about God's presence and rule. Hope, therefore, is now understood as a creative and God-inspired attitude toward the world because of which the individual's desire to gain heaven becomes subsidiary to his responsibility to make God present on earth. In short, rather than being principally escapist, hope here is principally *missionary*.

Terming the object of such hope the "Kingdom of God" is thus highly appropriate. For "kingdom," of course, is a political term, which, if nothing else, means that it is a communal term. The Kingdom of God must consequently be defined as communal in its concerns—and so be immediately distinguished from the above, exclusively individualistic idea of heaven. Yet if we do define the Kingdom of God in this way as a community, and if we also say that in our third model this Kingdom is hope's goal, then we must accordingly say that within this view hope itself must be understood as communal. The goal of my hope, in short, is now not my own future and destiny alone, nor even principally, but the future and destiny of all.

It is only within this third model of hope that I would say the experiences of guilt and repentance, at least Christianly understood, are properly approached. This is so because like hope and its goal they are now approached within a communal context. The individual experiences guilt and desires to repent the evil he has done not because he selfishly fears its consequences for his own peace of mind or salvation, but because the evil he does affects others and so retards (to whatever degree) the actualization on earth of God's Kingdom. This, of course, was a fundamental point we were also making in the last section when discussing the ethics of the good deed (*mitzvah*).

The thief, for example, retards this process because through his thievery he has created suspicion and mistrust toward other human beings in the person he has robbed. In doing so he has thus offended the character of mutual trustfulness which must mark human relationships in God's Kingdom. His thievery is not only an objective wrong in itself; it is wrong because of the negative attitude it creates in others.

Within our third model, therefore, repentance would require the above thief to rectify the harm he has done not only by restoring the stolen object, but more importantly by attempting to recreate in the man he has robbed the trust he has offended. If he succeeds, then in a small way (if only in the community of two which he and the other compose) he has gone from retarding the growth of God's Kingdom to encouraging it. He feels guilt and repents the wrong he has done not out of a selfish fear that otherwise he might lose the bliss of heaven, but because he knows that the Kingdom of God is a communal reality which he and all others must help to actualize through their individual efforts. God's will, he believes, is that with God's grace we must ourselves, each and all of us together, secure a redeemed world and God's reign. There is in this model, then, no sudden or unexpected act of God, no catastrophic "break" which ends the history of this world and begins the "new time" of God's Kingdom. God's Kingdom, rather, is born from within this world; its parents are God's will and the hope-inspired efforts we all make to assist in bringing it to realization. Both these points (1. that the Kingdom is an *in-worldly* reality; 2. that bringing it about is a *communal task*) form key elements in our understanding of Christian hope, guilt, and repentance. Each, I might add, will again occupy us at some length in the following chapter.

We need only mention here that the specific vision of God's Kingdom which impels the Christian's hope, guilt and repentance is the one proclaimed in the gospels. Christian hope therein is the active trust that this vision *can* be realized. Christian guilt and repentance therein is the recognition that we repeatedly depart from this vision in our personal and communal lives, and that we continually need to set our steps aright. Unlike the second model, therefore, in this third model guilt and repentance are never the product of fear (of earthly or hellish punishments); instead they are the product of hope itself.

In the foregoing pages we have presented some brief reflections on three basic understandings of hope and discussed what possible role guilt and repentance might play in each. In the first model—hopelessness—we dealt with the question of hope's role within a cyclic view of personal history, and determined that here guilt and repentance involved basically a recognition of one's limits and a resignation to the repeating sameness of the future. In the second model—hope as escape—we dealt with the question of hope within a linear view of personal history, and determined that here guilt and repentance potentially (if not usually) involved a self-concerned interest in avoiding any behaviour that threatened access to heaven. In the third model —hope as mission—we again dealt with the question of hope within a linear view of history, only this time we saw that it was the *communal,* not the personal, dimension of hope which was here emphasized. In this third model we also determined that guilt and repentance were at heart catalysts for a constantly renewed commitment to assist in bringing about the community of the Kingdom of God through an ever-deepening appropriation of the gospel message of Christ. Finally, we suggested that it was precisely because of this communal dimension and positive awareness of the world's future as the coming history of God's Kingdom that this third model was the one most appropriate for understanding Christian hope, guilt and repentance. For of the three it alone replaced an understanding of guilt centered on a self-concerned repentance and hope for the future with one of repentent concern and hope for all.

In conclusion, then, let us say that if Jesus' preaching about the future coming of the Kingdom of God demands foremostly a communal dimension to hope—and if guilt and repentance involves foremostly an awareness and active rectification of wrongs obstructing the realization of this Kingdom —then all three (hope, guilt, and repentance) should indeed be understood as positive and creative powers within us. For only so can we constantly renew our commitment in hope to the universal Kingdom of God which Jesus preached, by willingly recognizing and righting the offenses retarding its coming which we have each and all together committed.

IV

Living in the World

THERE are some people who are satisfied with the world as it is. Their consciousness has a peculiar way of dwelling on the good they find in the world, while ignoring or reducing to unimportance the evil. If you tell them of starving, dying children in Calcutta, they will presume you are exaggerating. How can anyone, they think, let a child die of starvation? Or even worse, they might find a blessing in this starvation. Imagine the life of pain or deprivation awaiting these children; it is probably best that they die young. Whatever you tell such people of evil in the world—of racial hatred, torture, wars— they will disagree with you, either by questioning the truth of the evil's existence or by interpreting its meaning in some positive fashion. Or like Scarlet O'Hara in *Gone with the Wind,* they dismiss it completely from their minds. Scarlet's final words, "I'll think about it tomorrow," capture the attitude of anyone who refuses the truth that life is often ugly. Erich Fromm calls this attitude "optimism,'' and his judgment is that the optimist is psychologically maladjusted. Unable for whatever reason to see the evil clearly before his eyes—the causes for guilt in human behaviour—the optimist habitually blurs and distorts, ultimately dismisses, its reality.

1. *A Realistic View of the World*

Nothing can be gained from quibbling over Fromm's use of the words "optimism" and "optimist." While we may not care for it—we generally place a more positive value on these words—the psychological attitude and character-type he intends to describe is obvious enough. The optimist lives in a dream-world, where the good is always present, no matter how hidden or apparently unpracticed. He cannot accept the idea of irredeemable malevolence; that no good can be found in the indismissable fact of starving, dying children. He lives with a grand vision of prevailing benevolence, wherein the particular evils of the world are lost and "guilt" is a nasty word. He condones with a naive faith, and at face value, the saying of Liebnitz that this is the best of all possible worlds. It never dawns on him that this saying is no excuse for eliminating from his consciousness a serious and involved awareness of the worst the world has to offer. The optimist lives in a lucite block that evil and guilt never penetrate.

In some cases the above character-type is formed from influences during the early years of childhood. The common example here is that of the father who is over-protective of his daughter, his "little girl." The father is well aware of the malevolence and evil in the world. He knows the wickedness and want that prevail among us, our reasons for feeling a justifiable guilt. But under the influence of his paternal love he decides that he will spare his daughter the pain of this awareness. He isolates her, refusing to permit her to experience the sin and squalor of existence. He shapes her consciousness to think what is good, to value what is good, *and to expect* what is good—though in the process, of course, despite all his well-meaning intentions, he is in fact doing his daughter a great disservice. For he is locking her into a single pattern of thought, rendering her incapable of adequately perceiving or judging what is not good, what can never be good in the world of experiences that lies before her. Through no will of her own she is being manipulated toward reality. Her vision of life will be myopic, so that when evil finally does intrude upon her existence, as inevitably it must, she will be unable to understand or accept it. Forced to judge the guilt in much of human behaviour, she only becomes confused and frightened.

In other cases the source of this character-type is drawn directly from personal experiences. Here the individual's optimism is a reaction to events or situations that he cannot bear. He blocks off or suppresses their meaning as an effective influence on his thinking and behaviour. He cannot handle the sin, the reasons for guilt he has found in the world, so he refuses to acknowledge them, or at least to acknowledge their importance. His response is like that of a ball that bounces in the direction opposite from which it came. Experiencing evil too greatly has caused him to "bounce back" by henceforth ignoring evil. "I don't want to hear about it" is the frequent demand of this character-type.

When an individual cannot bounce back from his experiences of evil in the world, when he cannot ignore the causes for guilt he finds there, when he allows the sin and ugliness he sees to dominate his attitude toward existence, he becomes the antithesis of the optimist. He becomes a pessimist. Just as optimism is the steady refusal to acknowledge the evil and guilt in the world, pessimism is the steady refusal to acknowledge the good. Whereas the optimist sees only the light side of life, the pessimist sees only its dark side. Each represents an extreme character-type.

Some pessimists take a peculiar delight in their attitude. They are convinced that they are the true realists in the world. They understand their pessimism as the final product of a mature mind, just as they understand optimism as the product of a childish, immature mind. To the pessimist the world reeks of malevolence and guilt. Its true history is read only in tales of war, starvation, disease, torture—all the depravities that afflict human existence. The pessimist accuses the optimist of being blind to this history, refusing to take in the full scent of its evil.

But to this accusation the response comes easily that the pessimist too has been blind in his reading of history. He has ignored the tales of sanctity we find there, the art, the virtue, the beauty that the world has held. The pessimist is as myopic as the optimist in his view of reality; the difference between them lies in what each is unable to see. Neither character-type possesses that quality of thought we would call "open mindedness." Neither will allow his experiences *as a whole* to affect the way he thinks, the attitudes he forms. Instead, each prefers to be selective, allowing only certain experiences to affect his thoughts and attitudes—or perhaps better said, to re-enforce them.

Knowing Good and Evil

Somehow we must learn to steer a middle course between optimistic and pessimistic close-mindedness. We must learn to acknowledge not only the evil we find in the world but the good as well; not just the causes for guilt but the causes for blessing. Somehow we must learn to apply in our lives the words of Jesus, "Resist not evil" (Matthew 5:39), and add to them, "Resist not good." The world is neither black nor white, but grey. It is a mixture, a composite of conflicting facts and experiences. Side by side with the child dying of starvation, we see the well-nurtured child. Next to the sadist who delights in the slaughter of human beings, we find the saint who willingly sacrifices himself for others. Take your eyes off a Hitler and you see a Mother Teresa. The ancient sages were wise when they imagined the world as the battleground of good and evil, not as the exclusive dwelling of one or the other. We may not care to think of their too human terms—of good and wicked angels outwitting each other, of invisible struggles whose stake is the joy or misery of a human life—but the reality, the experience they intend to describe is a correct and familiar one to any realistic individual. For realism is not defined as being pessimistic; and it is certainly not defined as being optimistic. Realism is defined as open-mindedness, the willingness to take seriously the cause for both pessimism and optimism that we find in the world and in ourselves.

It is curious to note the interest, sometimes avid interest, that human beings take in the evil, the guilt-producing behaviour found in the world. This is demonstrated nowhere more clearly, I think, than in the fare "television societies" favor. Statistics repeatedly demonstrate, for example, that if there is a choice of programs between a story on war or rape and an opera by Wagner or Puccini, by far the majority of viewers will opt for the first program. Against a repeated criticism of programmed news stories—that they emphasize the violence, disaster, sickness in societies—broadcasters rightly respond that this is the "news" that people want to see. They would turn their televisions off in boredom if the emphasis was on philanthropy and works of charity, music, art, or science. From the publishing world we could add the statistics that the majority of the popular novels printed are those dealing with varying degrees of social and/or sexual violence.

We cannot analyze in detail why this interest in viewing the world's evil and guilt takes precedence over interest in the world's good. But one possible reason is that it serves as a counterpoint to the goodness with which most people try to live. Along this line I might suggest that the law of the attraction of opposites is not only a physical but a psychological phenomenon. There is an interest to share vicariously in deeds we ourselves would never commit. The motive may be sheer voyeurism, or the satisfaction of curiosity, or the procurement of a more exact understanding of the behaviour of human beings. Whatever the reason, however, the good man who himself would never think of spilling the blood of another human being is attracted to the individual who wouldn't hesitate a moment in doing it. The woman who would die of shame before she herself would practice sado-sexual techniques is attracted to the individual who cannot relate sexually in any other way.

In itself this attraction of opposites need not repel us. In fact, it may well be an indication of the passion with which we have invested our convictions regarding right behaviour. The faithful husband who is attracted to the thought of once, just once being unfaithful, might well be demonstrating by this attraction his committed devotion to marital fidelity. He could be showing that his commitment is the result not of a blind, unthinking habit, but of a conscientious resolve. Of course, should his thought be enacted our judgment would need to be altered. For then the attraction of the opposite has lost its psychological character as an attraction. It has become a fact. The husband is no longer *attracted* by infidelity; he *is* unfaithful.

The above remarks are only a suggestion toward explaining the interest we often take in guilt-producing behaviour, the wrong that infests our world and the wrong that attracts us personally. They conclude with the observation that if we concentrate on this wrong, if we isolate it as a formative factor in our consciousness, then pessimism—about the world, about ourselves—becomes a possible attitude describing our character-type.

The Coming of the Kingdom of God

I would like to take up again the suggestion made in the last chapter that a proper Christian understanding of guilt involves us in an appreciation of Jesus's doctrine of the Kingdom—specifically now in the request he makes of his Father, "thy Kingdom come" (Matthew 6:10). This request requires for its understanding a delicate balance between pessimism and optimism. The request is double-edged. On the one hand it recognizes that this Kingdom has not yet come; otherwise it would be cast in the present rather than future mode. On the other hand it recognizes that the coming of this Kingdom is a definite possibility; otherwise it would make no sense to voice the request. The first half of the request gives implicit recognition to the evil and malevolence that exist in the world, the causes for guilt; the second half presumes that this evil and malevolence, these causes for guilt are redeemable. Both halves together are intended to reflect a realistic view of existence in the world, an open-mindedness that takes into account the good and evil that earthly existence involves.

We may note again that the ancient sages were right when they mythologized the world as the battleground between good and evil. But they were misguided—or perhaps better said, too literal in understanding their myths—when they transformed the concepts of good and evil into personal forces battling for victory beyond the wills of men. In this vision human beings are only pawns, playthings, the populace of the battleground on which the good and evil gods fight their terrible war. The outcome will be determined by whichever of the respective gods finally possesses the greater power, the stronger will. Inevitably, of course, the myths favor the final victory of the good god. In fact, I know of no myth where this final victory is not stated or presumed. The evil god generally wins most of the battles, but always loses the war. We can well understand the psychological need that is here being met—namely, to dispel the tension or despair that would result if hope for the final victory of the good were doubtful or absent. For who could bear a world, an existence condemned to the sovereignty of evil?

The difficulty with this mythic structure, and the reason why we said it was misguided, lies in its anthropology, the role it assigns to human beings. Within the Christian understanding of the coming Kingdom of God (which we may understand is an analogue for the mythic triumph of the good over the evil god), the individual is not a passive but an active participant. In other words, the difference between the myth of the warring gods and the Christian concept of the coming Kingdom of God is reduced to the question of human responsibility. In the myth, human beings have no responsibility— and hence no motive for experiencing guilt. The outcome of the antagonism between good and evil is decided independently of their involvement. To repeat a metaphor: we are only pawns, playthings of the battling gods. We are fated to be used as the gods see fit, to serve their own purposes. The drama is played out in the world, but the scenarios are written in heaven and hell.

As we noted in the last chapter, there is a strain of Christian spirituality that retains remnants of this mythic structure. I am referring, of course, to the personification of good and evil in the figures of God and Satan. Here again the world is the battleground between two super-human beings, and the war is engaged in the midst of human existence. And here again there is an unquestioned bias that the good must ultimately prevail and win victory. Christianity, after all, is the faithful heir of the revelation to Israel. It has never considered Satan the equal of God; perhaps the greatest of God's first creatures, the angels, but never God's equal. For the old covenant of the patriarchs and prophets, and the new covenant of Christ, there is only one God, not two or three or many, just one. The result is that the importance of the conflict between God and Satan within Christianity is now reduced from a cosmic scale, where God *must* win, to that of the individual human being, where his victory is an open question. God will someday reign as the acknowledged Lord of creation, whose will is always obeyed. But until then the destiny of the individual who has transgressed God's will, already revealed in Jesus, is an open question.

Within the confines of each individual's existence, then, good and evil, God and Satan, may be understood as equal; the final victory of the one or the other is not pre-determined. Or differently put: it is the individual himself who is now the final arbiter of whether good or evil will prevail in his existence. He is an active not passive participant in the destiny that awaits him. The good lies ever before him as a possibility, but so does evil. The choice between them is his alone. Neither God nor Satan compels him to choose what he would not choose. A human being is the plaything of neither the divine nor the demonic. He exists as an autonomous being in his own right whose choices are not *forced* by other autonomous influences outside himself. He must recognize these influences, to be sure, no matter what he calls them—gods or demons, heredity, environment, neuroses, etc. But before them he always retains the singular ability, the authority and power which allows him to say yes or no. This, briefly put, is the basis for the doctrine of free will that underlies every Christian anthropology.

We can now see, I think, that the request Jesus makes of his Father (and each of us joins in making with him), "thy Kingdom come," requires some subtlety of interpretation. The request may initially seem to indicate that the coming of the Kingdom of God is completely an act of God, in which any of our acts are superfluous. God himself, alone and in his own time, will secure this Kingdom against the evil present in the world. The request would then be

simply a petition or recognition that God will so
act. This understanding, however, is too lopsided;
it doesn't go far enough. By itself, in fact, it represents a return to the essential structure of the myth
of the battling gods. The individual is again reduced to a cipher upon whom God in no way depends for his final victory. The psychological corre-
late is the neglect or denial of human responsibility
in overcoming the evil that is recognizable in the
world. And the result of this is the sterilization of
all experiences of guilt.

That the above understanding does not represent
an adequate reflection of Jesus' preaching regarding the coming Kingdom of God can be seen, I
think, in at least two important gospel passages.
We have referred to them more than once throughout this book. The first is Matthew's record of the
Sermon on the Mount in chapter five; the second is
his record of the Mandates of the Kingdom in chapter twenty-five. While both passages, especially the
second, are probably literary expansions of the actual teaching of Jesus, they are undoubtedly faithful to his intention, if not his precise words. In each
Jesus is clearly placing responsibility on his disciples to live in a way that is appropriate to the actualization of the Kingdom. The implicit judgment
is *not* that God will force or compel us to live this
way once he himself has instituted the Kingdom,
but that the Kingdom is instituted precisely to the
degree that we ourselves willingly live this way.

We may say that God's involvement in the above process is two-fold. First, it is God who gives us the *opportunities* and *strength* to enact our convictions regarding what Jesus taught. These opportunities and strength we may otherwise call "grace." Grace is the gift of situations and the power to be pure in heart and peace-making, to feed the hungry and shelter the homeless, and so on. It is what frees us from a hopeless condemnation to self-concern or indifference. It is what makes our guilt redeemable through behaviour reaffirming our commitment to the way of life Jesus lived. Secondly, it is God who will *confirm* the world once human existence is characterized by the qualities of the Beatitudes and Mandates. Upon this confirmation he will reveal himself as God, the one God, for the praise and obedience of all. This is the apocalypse of biblical imagery, when the world, now the place of Christlike activity, becomes the Kingdom of God. Jesus did not teach us only what God will do; he also taught us what we must do. He established a relationship between God's will and our will wherein each is respected as a factor in bringing about God's Kingdom.

There is a presupposition at work in the above remarks, and on the basis of what we said in the last chapter regarding hope and repentance it is easily detected. The presupposition is that the Kingdom of God is descriptive of an earthly reality, that is, a condition or situation that does not presume a spatio-temporal setting different from the one in which we live. The Kingdom of God is not a-worldly but in-worldly. What describes its essential difference from the world in which we now live is its future mode: the Kingdom is not yet, but will come. But when it does we cannot legitimately presume that it will alter the spatio-temporal setting in which we presently live. What its coming will do, rather, is confirm and complete in God's presence the characteristics whereby human beings relate to one another within this setting. This opinion admittedly differs from that of other (though not all!) theologians. But I think it is a good one—certainly a possible one—if we take the Beatitudes and Mandates as the foundation describing the essential traits of existence within the Kingdom. In this interpretation we would then draw an equation between the "blessedness" of which both the Beatitudes and Mandates speak and the manner of human existence within the Kingdom of God.

An obvious consequence of the above interpretation is that the concept of the Kingdom of God does not pertain to the issue of post-mortem existence. It is at odds with any notion of this Kingdom as being what awaits the individual after death. Rather, our word for this state of post-mortem life, following a steady Christian tradition, is "heaven." Whereas heaven, in other words, is a state of existence possible for all individuals, the Kingdom of God awaits only the future members of the race. You and I will not enjoy the earthly existence that will be the Kingdom of God, even though you and I may enjoy the blessedness of heavenly existence.

Yet we must each be concerned about the Kingdom. For it is only on the basis of our pattern of behaviour *now* that future generations will be able to approximate more closely the qualities of existence this Kingdom requires. It is only to the degree that we take our guilt seriously, and strive to rectify the failures in behaviour it indicates, that we can bequeath to our children a better, more Christlike world. The future is built on the shoulders of the past. To the extent that we presently seek fidelity to the Beatitudes and Mandates, the faith and hope that Jesus teaches, we contribute to a future where these Beatitudes and Mandates, this faith and hope will be more widely practiced. And when this everwidening practice extends to all men and women, the Kingdom of God will have become a close possibility for us—though its final actualization, as we said, will belong to the will of God. And this saying represents no pipedream, no wonderland that can never exist. It is not a saying born of fantasy, an easy saying that pops out of a utopian imagination. It is a hard saying, one that affirms unequivocally the ability of men and women, with God's grace, to live blessed lives. It is a saying, therefore, that clearly stands against the spirit of pessimism described a few pages ago. And just as clearly it cannot bed down with the spirit of optimism also described.

Our effort now toward bringing about the Kingdom of God is the greatest act of fidelity we can perform toward future generations. On the other hand, it is also the greatest act of fidelity we can perform toward those who have gone before us, who in their own times and places have contributed to this coming Kingdom. We are saying to each group, past and future generations, that their own efforts are worthy of our efforts now, in the present generation. In our willingness to engage the moral vision, the patterns of behaviour taught and demonstrated by Jesus, we are one with generations of Christians past and future. We are the current church, the community of Christ, upon whom the church past and future depends to carry on and expand the witness of Christ. This is no light and comfortable awareness, but the burdening acknowledgment of the responsibility we possess to contribute to the shaping and growth of this community—and the guilt that is ours when we do not. The Kingdom of God will not come of its own accord, automatically. Nor may it be identified with the church, the present community of Christians, at any point in time. What we say is that the Kingdom of God will come *from* the church; that it will be born from the community of Christians as each generation of this community succeeds another in an increasingly thorough witness to the revelation in Jesus. But again, the final moment of this birth, the final act that will transform the community into the Kingdom, belongs to God, not us. And what that final moment, that act, will involve, besides a confirmation of what has already taken place, we cannot say (see Matthew 25).

The Community of the Kingdom of God

We may now engage more appreciably another distinguishing trait of the Kingdom of God which we mentioned in the last chapter. It is implied in the word "Kingdom." For while we might dispute the relative merits of the political structure this word designates, we cannot dispute that it implies above all else a gathering or group of men and women with a common center. In a political context this center is the monarch, and the kingdom is described by the relationships that exists between this center and the other members of the kingdom. As noted in the last chapter, the same general description applies to the religious concept of the Kingdom, with the single but all-important difference that the center is now God.

What mediates the relationship between the members of the Kingdom of God and their center is the revelation that occurred in Jesus. Since the Kingdom is essentially a gathering or community, this revelation pertains to the manner in which the members relate first to God, and then to each other. In previous chapters we have outlined some general characteristics of both these relationships, though in chapter 1 we suggested that all are fulfilled (simplified) in the double command of Jesus: love God with all your mind and heart and soul, and love your neighbor as yourself (Matthew 22: 36–40). The reader will recall that Jesus places these two loves on an equal footing ("the second is like the first"). Each is essential as a defining characteristic of the community of the Kingdom of God. It is not enough, therefore, like the saint in Nietzsche's *Zarathustra,* to love God but hate man; nor is it enough, like Ivan in Dostoevsky's *Brothers Karamazov,* to love man but hate God. The Kingdom of God can exist only when two loves prevail among us: love of God and love of each other. And for the Christian, guilt must arise whenever either love is offended.

The responsibility for securing the Kingdom of God is thus arduous and pervasive. This again bears saying, I think, because there is an ever-present temptation to reduce it to an easily fulfilled "compartment" of life—for example, carrying out periodic prayers, rituals, charities. But if the responsibility is fundamentally one of love, then it can never be approached in this way; it can never be a sometime venture in life. For love does not respect times and places; it is not a variable but a constant in life, always with us, like the need to breathe. It is, as Gabriel Marcel liked to say, a *mystery,* something from which we cannot detach ourselves. There is no such thing as a timetable love or a now-and-then love or a fickle love: all these are contradictions in terms. Love is with us as a constitutive part of our being, or it does not exist.

To ask of the Father, "thy Kingdom come," is thus to ask for the time when the double love of Jesus will prevail in the world. It is also to ask for the grace—the opportunities and strength—that will enable each of us now to express this double love, and so contribute to that future time. It is to acknowledge that the Kingdom is *thy* Kingdom; that its characteristics are not determined by our own preferences but are revealed by the Father in the words and deeds of Jesus. The attempt to structure the future on the basis of our own predilections—what we conceive to be the proper destiny of our own existence or that of the race—is made errant by this request. A future that is not pursued along the lines of the witness of Jesus is not Christian; and for the Christian it is not worthy of pursuit.

The common designation of our present place in time as the "post-Christian era" is thus legitimate, but only to the degree that it indicates an understanding of the *structures* of Christian life different from that prevailing in previous eras. It is legitimate, in other words, to the degree that it is a *relative* judgment on contemporary forms of Christian living. It is illegitimate, however, whenever it goes beyond this and becomes an *absolute* judgment, indicating that the pursuit of Christlikeness in itself no longer makes sense. Worse than illegitimate, it is naive in the confusion whereby it has identified the pursuit of Christlikeness with acculturated beliefs from the past. Because medical science and technology, for example, have taught us to respect human authority over illness does not mean that the dependence of previous generations on God for this authority issues in the foolishness of *all* dependence on God.

What it means is that our dependence on God when ill (but not, therefore, our dependence on God as such) must now be balanced by a dependence on medical science. More broadly, the modern dissolution of many previous beliefs surrounding the pursuit of Christlikeness in the world does not dissolve the present responsibility of that pursuit. What it means is that the manner has changed, the contexts in which this pursuit must now be engaged, the forms that guilt may take when this pursuit is abandoned.

In one sense, of course, the pursuit of Christlikeness will always be foolish. The New Testament is filled with implicit and explicit references to this idea. By standards opposite to itself, by a moral vision that rests on different bases, the pursuit of Christlikeness will hardly make sense. Derision or stupefaction, for example, will greet any word of

Christ's generosity in a society that is premised on the value of the accumulation of wealth. Or any assertion of resurrection life will be dismissed as fantasy in a culture that presumes the rightness of the saying, "Dead men do not rise." But every judgment of the foolishness of Christian living is only an apparent one. By this I mean that it can only be made vis-à-vis some contrary set of convictions and responsibilities. In itself there is nothing foolish in Christian living, just as in itself there is nothing foolish in a Stoic or Marxist life-style.

It is only when we begin to compare different views of existence, therefore, and then determine one among them as the most appropriate for us, that the others begin to appear foolish. To the miser whose existence finds its purpose in the hoarding of money and its corresponding power, selfless generosity will always appear somewhat clownish, ridiculous, "unreal"; to feel guilt over selfishness will always seem to him naive. To the ancient Greek who could only suppose the immortality of a pure human soul, because he was disgusted by what he believed to be the baseness of the body, the idea of resurrection of a "spiritual body" surviving death, would be repugnant. But within a different context, a Christian context premised on other convictions and responsibilities, generosity and resurrection life are not all unreal or repugnant, but definite and desirable possibilities. Any commitment to the coming Kingdom of God will burden the Christian with a witness to such possibilities. And the burden is not light but heavy (see, however, Matthew 11:30). To the miser he must witness to the possibility of generous living; to the despisers of the body he must witness to the possibility of resurrection life.

From the foregoing remarks, therefore, we will conclude that the Kingdom of God refers to the future existence of the human community, just as the concept of heaven refers to the future existence of the individual. To this we will add that while heaven pertains to post-mortem existence, the Kingdom of God will be secured within the space and time of earthly existence. Each concept is concerned with a future mode of existence—this is their similarity. *What* that future mode of existence will be, and *who* will share in it, describes their dissimilarity. On the one hand, all can enjoy heaven without distinction; on the other, not all will enjoy the Kingdom, even though all can contribute to its birth. In both futures, however, guilt plays a critical role. It is the fundamental pedagogical tool, the experience that trains our fidelity to the behaviour we are convinced is needed to gain the future we cherish.

2. *Final Words: Guilt and Faith*

It is time to bring my reflections to a close. But before I do, let met offer a backward glance bringing together some of the more salient points I have tried to make throughout the foregoing pages. My intent from the beginning was to offer an understanding of guilt that views it as not only a negative but also a positive experience in life. From the start I have also deliberately set my reflections within a religious, specifically Christian context. This was not to deny that there are other contexts in which guilt can be understood. Indeed there are, as countless books on the subject amply demonstrate. My position, however, has been that even though the specific context of these reflections has been a religious one, my analysis of guilt itself could be just as legitimately applied in other contexts. Or to make the same point somewhat differently: my purpose has been to describe what the experience of guilt involves, and then insert this description within the specific context of a Christian way of life. Whether or not I have succeeded or been persuasive in this task is, of course, not mine to judge; it is yours.

I have not intended this book, therefore, to be a detached or dispassionate analysis of the experience of guilt, but only a thoughtful demonstration that the understanding of guilt I have presented, and its relationship to Christianity, is fundamentally a correct one. In the process I have sketched an outline of the path which I believe every Christian must tread to appreciate the role guilt plays in his faith, his conviction that God's will is described for us in the life of Jesus. For the convinced Christian, Jesus is the self-donation of God to humankind; he can be obeyed or disobeyed, but never ignored.

An Irremovable Guilt?

Christian faith is meaningless apart from a salvation-experience, as twenty centuries of Christian witness from the apostolic age on down has testified. From Jesus' affirmation that "your faith has saved you" through Luther's cry of *sola fides* and on into Vatican II, the theme has come through undisturbed: faith is salvation, and there can be no salvation-experience without faith. When it becomes clear to us that we are Christians only through faith—and the intrinsic connection between faith and salvation becomes evident—we will simultaneously understand why every individual must first experience the *need* for salvation, and then have it met through faith, if he is to claim the title Christian. And so the question arises: how does an individual come to perceive his need for salvation, and further, how is this need met through the faith, the conviction that is uniquely Christian?

Our response to this question centers on the ethical commitments, the patterns of behaviour that define an individual's life. These commitments indicate his awareness that the meaning of his life cannot be found in passing desires and delights but only in the obedient pursuit of ideals *he is con-*

vinced express the changeless will of God—ideals, in other words, and a pursuit, that can last his lifetime. As we argued in chapter 1, however, these ideals do not comprise "do this, don't do that" rules for each and every circumstance in which he may find himself, but rather are the "light" or moral vision which guides and specifies all his ethical decisions. The individual has removed his passing wants from the center of his life and is seeking to do God's will insofar as it is now the source of meaning and the provider of a destiny for his existence. And he pursues his search through submission to his ideals since this offers the most obvious answer to the question he is constantly asking himself, namely, "What must I do to gain salvation, the blessing and pleasure of my God?" And to be sure, this moral effort gains some success in the beginning. For he can always gloss over the lapses that inevitably occur by reflecting on his personal inadequacies and using them as excuses. But as his effort continues a new realization gradually introduces itself which causes his previous successes to be regarded in a new light: they are illusory. For it begins to dawn on him that in fact failure is unavoidable. Even under the most favourable circumstances and with the best of intentions, he finds that he cannot fulfill the ideals that guide his life. A grave disquiet grows each time he is confronted with the fact of his radical weakness and powerlessness before the inexorable demand of his ideals, his convictions regarding God's will for him. This disquiet gains another frantic note with each added failure, for he perceives that his destiny, what he wishes to make of himself before the eyes of God, is at stake and slowly slipping away from him as his incapacity becomes more and more apparent. Unable to fulfill his ideals he is unable to relate to God in the proper way and his destiny is thus placed in peril. And odd though it may seem, his weakness and powerlessness are felt as a personal, *permanent, and irremovable* guilt.

It is important to be clear about what I have just said in order to avoid any false impressions of what this powerlessness before a seemingly irremovable guilt might mean. For this type of guilt is unique. It is unlike that described in the last chapter—which is assuaged in the practice of the *mitzvah* (good deed) —and more like the unhealing guilt described in chapter 1. Let us examine it more closely.

As we saw in the last chapter, a permanent and irremovable guilt cannot arise from a single offense or even from a combination of single offenses because guilt of this nature is removable. It can be robbed of its sting by the forgiveness that the guilty individual can receive from the one he has offended. If, for example, a man steals some money, he can appear before the now deprived party, confess what he did, give the money back, and receive forgiveness. With this the matter is finished. In fact, he might even find that through the offense and the ensuing pardon, his relationship to the offended man is closer than it was before the theft. This is a phenomenon which often occurs in a marriage where a misunderstanding which is patiently and lovingly worked out may be the cause of a deeper and richer love. Even should the combination of offenses be as heinous, say, as Hitler's, it is still theoretically possible, though perhaps far from likely, to find all those survivors who were maimed by his insanity and induce them to grant him forgiveness. It is clear, in other words, that at this stage of awareness there is no need to seek the forgiveness of God and no need for the individual to despair over the offenses against his ideals caused by a single act or a mass of them. The question, then, still remains: What characterizes the irremovable guilt of which we spoke and its accompanying tension?

This guilt introduces itself precisely at the moment when the individual realizes the inevitability of his offenses continuing without end despite his best efforts to stop them. It lies in the hiatus between the absolute demand of his ideals (since their source is the will of God) and his radical incapacity to fulfill it. Initially responding to the demand as best he can, he eventually discovers vast parts of it which he did not even perceive—for upon reflection he soon realizes that an absolute demand is an unqualified or infinite one. He is, in other words, infinitely inadequate. In that moment the individual sees that he cannot relate himself to God in the way which God seems to require. It is here that the first note of desperation is introduced into the drama and the pessimism I described in the last section becomes a distinct possibility.

I have suggested in a number of places throughout this book that the powerlessness of the individual in the face of his guilt stems not only from any external circumstances but from his humanity itself. For even in the most altruistic frame of mind and with selfless love at an intellectual and emotional high, he still commits offenses against his ideals and his convictions again and again. In every instance failure is potentially present for the simple reason that the individual's humanity is always present. This is a fundamental point I was making when discussing the Genesis account of the Fall in chapter 1 and the experience of temptation in chapter 2. The infinite distance that yawns between affirming God's will and the human ability to do it cannot be bridged from the human side, since at no time can the individual step outside the context of his humanity. He is a human for better and, in many cases, for worse. Yet there still remains at this point a legitimate question which we cannot fairly side-step, namely, "How can this incapacity or powerlessness justifiably be called guilt?'' For no one's humanity is his own choice; it is not at root his own creation. And guilt is incorrectly understood or experienced if it is not personal and the result of a choice (despite the twisting and turning of some treatises on original sin).

To answer this question let every individual look back upon his own moral history. There he will see many times in which he has been unfaithful to the call of his convictions regarding God's will, even in those moments when he felt this call clearly and unambiguously. Not only has there been outright infidelity but also an astounding indifference to the claim of his convictions upon him. In other words, what is happening with each new failure, what happened in each failure in the past, and what will occur in the moment he fails again is that the individual has personally appropriated the infinite distance that lies between himself and God's will, accepted it for himself, and in this way made it his own responsibility. At this point every individual (if we were right in chapter 1) experiences guilt in the proper sense: he has willingly broken his convictions. And the desperation that results from this situation can achieve a perverse perfection when the individual also realizes that he can do nothing to get out of his state of alienation from God's will. No matter how little he likes it, he remains in his humanity and therefore as far from God as finite is from infinite. Even given the impossible situation in which he would never fall again, the infinite distance remains uncrossed because his memory rightly accuses him of having approved and chosen this desperate state for himself. This is despair at its height. For there is no way out of this situation which can be constructed from the individual's— that is, from humanity's—powers. This at last is the guilt which cries for salvation by God, for no human resources can heal the breach. This, too, as we noted in the last section, is the basic situation revealed in any serious discussion of grace.

How is the individual saved from this situation? St. Paul, at the height of the tension just described, cries out, "What a wretched man I am! Who can save me from this doomed body?" And he comes back immediately with the only answer, "Thank God! It is done through Jesus Christ our Lord" (Romans 7:24–25). The fact that distinguishes a Christian is not that he adheres blindly to magisterial dogma or certain rites of piety. He is not even unique in following the law of love: for many outside Christianity also follow it and follow it more faithfully. Rather, what makes a Christian (as Kierkegaard, among others, continually points out) is his embrace of the Paradox, the logical absurdity of the God in time. The Christian affirms that the eternal has become temporal and the infinite finite, for he is convinced that God has become man in Jesus. And because of this conviction, this faith he eventually perceives and understands that what was once felt as burden and guilt—his humanity—is now united to his relationship with God. What was before an obstacle is now the means; and should an individual continue to maintain his sense of irremovable guilt before God, it is an indication that he has not yet fully abandoned himself to the conviction that in Jesus the alienation between himself and God is overcome. For the humanity which had been his burden, the cause of his guilt and the source of his infinite distance from God, is precisely the thing which God has so united to himself in Jesus that "the two have become one." *In the eternal humanity of Christ, God himself takes on our limits and yet still offers us salvation.* It is through faith alone, however, that this salvation can be accepted; it is faith alone which can free us from a permanent guilt and bring us the possibility in its place of peace, of blessing. For in faith we affirm that our salvation is no longer found in *achieving* without failure the ideals set us by God—the convictions that guide our patterns of behaviour—but, like Jesus, in *striving* for them with all our heart and mind and soul. An irremovable guilt is experienced only when we think we have the power to achieve without failure our ideals, and then must admit our constant failure to do so. But when blessedness is found not in the achievement but in the striving for our ideals, there can be no such things as an irremovable guilt—but only the kind that trains us in a fuller, more developed and mature appreciation of what our striving means. In a sense this entire book has been nothing more than a sustained attempt to demonstrate the truth of this point as the one which most adequately reflects the witness of Jesus himself, and so of all Christian living.

If an individual takes seriously his own humanity and its limits, if he thoroughly appreciates his need to be saved, if he allows faith to evolve through the obedience we described in chapter 1, then he can truly begin to make sense out of what Christian scripture has to say about faith and its relationship to guilt. It will then become absorbing to reread St. Paul's letters to the Romans and Galatians in the light of this experience. One might also catch a glimpse of how apt is St. John's terminology for describing life before and after faith: darkness and light, death and life, a hunger and thirst that is fully satisfied. Such an experience will also reveal the uniqueness of the unqualified forgiveness God offers us. This uniqueness has always been pointed out and faithfully recommended by confessors and dimly felt by penitents, though it remains at root unfathomable as long as our minds are massaged by those spiritualities built solely upon human analogies of forgiveness. Such spiritualities can never adequately reveal the fulness of God's forgiving act. For while forgiveness may indeed be recognized in them, the offensive act is never entirely erased and its effect almost always perdures in some way. It thus serves to breed either an attitude of suspicion that some hurt or pain remains in the offended party (which he has agreed more to forget than to forgive) or that sad sense of inequality which frequently results when one person forgives another.

It has been my position throughout this book that any state of irremovable guilt we might experience is illegitimate because it has already been actually and permanently removed by God. But not by being glossed over or somehow ignored by him. Rather, in the moment of faith which affirms that God himself took on human flesh, what once was the source of guilt (our simple humanity) can be the source no longer. It is literally annihilated, made into nothing, and can no longer be operative in the total healing which our faith has secured. The infinite chasm between God and humanity is truly and completely bridged in the person of Jesus. And that sense of inequality which forgiveness can erect on the human level ceases to exist; for in the act of embracing our humanity God has made himself our equal in all ways. Kierkegaard expresses it best: "When the seed of the oak is planted in earthen vessels, they break asunder; when the new wine is poured into old leathern bottles, they burst; what must happen when the God implants himself in human weakness, unless man becomes a new vessel and a new creature! But this becoming, what labors will attend the change, how convulsed with birthpangs! And the understanding—how precarious, and how close each moment to misunderstanding, when the anguish of guilt seeks to disturb the peace of love! And how rapt in fear; for it is indeed less terrible to fall to the ground when the mountains tremble at the voice of God, than to sit at table with him as an equal. And yet it is God's concern precisely to have it so."

With these words this book, this "spiritual entertainment" as I call it in the Preface, is finished.

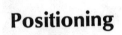

Positioning

Positioning
Belief in the Mid-Seventies

William J. Bausch

FIDES PUBLISHERS, INC.
NOTRE DAME, INDIANA

Permission to reprint from the following books is acknowledged:

Rumor of Angels, copyright © 1969 by Peter L. Berger; *Models of the Church,* copyright © 1974 by Avery Dulles; *This Man Jesus,* copyright © 1973 by Bruce Vawter; *The New Agenda,* copyright © 1973 by Andrew M. Greeley; *Believing,* copyright © 1973, 1974 by Eugene C. Kennedy; and *Faith and Morality in the Secular Age,* copyright © 1973 by Bernard Häring. Reprinted by permission of Doubleday & Company, Inc.

Faith for Today by Edmond Barbotin, copyright © 1974; *Our Idea of God* by Juan Luis Segundo, copyright © 1974; and *The Community Called Church* by Juan Luis Segundo, copyright © 1973. Reprinted by permission of Orbis Books.

The Meaning of the Sacraments by Monika Hellwig, copyright © 1972. Reprinted by permission of Pflaum Publishing.

Brown, Fitzmyer, and Murphy, *The Jerome Biblical Commentary* © 1968. By permission of Prentice-Hall, Inc., Englewood Cliffs, New Jersey.

The Reality of Redemption by B. Willems © 1970, Herder KG; *Theological Investigations,* Vol. X, by Karl Rahner © 1973, Darton, Longman & Todd, Ltd. *Does Jesus Make a Difference?* edited by Thomas McFadden, copyright © 1974. Used by permission of Seabury Press.

Jesus, God and Man by Raymond E. Brown, S.S., copyright © 1967 by Raymond E. Brown, S.S. *Mere Christianity* by C. S. Lewis, copyright © 1943, 1945, 1952. *George MacDonald: An Anthology* by C. S. Lewis, copyright © 1946 by Macmillan Publishing Co., Inc., renewed 1974 by Arthur Owen Barfield and Alfred Cecil Harwood. Used by permission of Macmillan Publishing Co., Inc.

The Theology of the New Testament by Werner G. Kummel © 1973, Abingdon Press.

Jesus, Lord and Christ by John F. O'Grady © 1972 and *Faith and Doctrine* by Gregory Baum © 1969. Used by permission of Paulist Press.

The Foundations of New Testament Christology by Reginald H. Fuller copyright © 1965, Charles Scribner's Sons.

Christ, the Sacrament of the Encounter with God by E. Schillebeeckx, copyright © 1963; *Faith: Can Man Still Believe?* by Louis Monden, copyright © 1948; *Sixty Saints for Boys* by Joan Windham, copyright © 1946; *Theology and Sanity* by F. J. Sheed copyright © 1946. Used by permission of Sheed & Ward, Inc.

ISBN: 0-8190-0606-8

Contents

To the memory
of my father,
positioned with God

Introduction

Change is the substance of our times. No one knows better than we Catholics not only how much has changed in the world but also how much has changed in our own Catholic tradition. There are all sorts of moderate and wild speculations about so many of our cherished beliefs. Startling statements in theology are being made daily and the average Catholic is not sure of his or her ground anymore. But we cannot just stand there and fret or throw up our hands. It is better that we try to understand what is being said and why. This book makes an attempt to answer both the what and the why.

There are ten chapters centering around eight major themes in current theological thinking. If we can come to terms with these themes then, I think, we will be in a better position to understand their many derivative ideas and practical applications. The eight themes deal with belief and unbelief, God, myths and symbols, dogma, Jesus who is Christ, redemption, the Church and the sacraments. There is a distinct thread that unites all these themes throughout, an overall impact that hopefully should give the reader an appreciation of, if not an agreement with, what is being said theologically these days.

As a parish priest, I have in mind several groups that might profit from the book. The first is adults who might either attend or give adult education classes. These ten chapters can not only provide the material for a course but also provide topics for much discussion. Secondly, I have in mind the educated parent who is somewhat taken aback with the newer religious ideas his or her offspring brings home almost daily from high school, college or CCD classes. It may help such a parent to cope if not to correct. Finally, I have in mind the high school and college students themselves, hoping that this moderate size book can form some kind of subject matter for their own classes or supplementary reading.

Because I am aiming at a general audience (although a somewhat educated and guided one) I have tried to tread the middle ground between popularization (with all of its dangers) and the presentation of direct scholarship in the use of readable quotations from those current theologians who are shaping our religious world to a large degree. Incidentally such quotations and their accompanying notes provide a generally very readable bibliography.

Finally, a word about the title. I have deliberately entitled the book *Positioning* because the one great truth that has come across to me is that there are as many positions on a particular religious subject as there are theologians, actual and aspiring. I have found the same wide varieties of interpretations in every other field from sociology to psychology. So I have used "positioning" as a title because the word carries with it the notion of a certain fluidity, a certain holding still of an idea that might, at the very next moment, suddenly shift. But nevertheless there *is* a momentary lull and the book's modest attempt is to take advantage of it. So, knowing that the last word has yet to be said, that new qualifications must be made before the reader turns the page, nevertheless I want to explore with the reader some of the fascinating and at times upsetting ideas that form the religious culture of our times. The alternative, as I have indicated, would be to stay quiet, to wonder and to fret. But the subject matter is simply too grand and too intriguing to be set aside so timidly. Better to brave the written word that might in some small measure help us all to see what the unfathomable riches of Christ might look like in the mid-seventies than to regress and by implication confine the Spirit to pre-Vatican II.

I wish to thank the people who have encouraged me to take up the task and especially members of my own adult education classes who have consistently inspired me. I also wish to thank Ann DeVizia who persistently and efficiently typed and retyped the manuscript.

1. Positioning Unbelief

— 1 —

It was St. Paul who remarked to the people of Athens that he noticed an altar dedicated to the "Unknown God." He appreciated that they threw that in among all the "name" gods to play it safe. They did not want unwittingly to offend a deity they never heard of. Nevertheless, Paul characteristically seized the opportunity to describe that unknown God as the One who revealed himself in Jesus. Were Paul living in the present day, however, he would come across, not an altar (we have gone beyond that) but a newspaper containing the "Humanist Manifesto II" which contains statements like this:

> We believe that traditional dogmatic or authoritarian religions that place revelation, God, ritual, creed above human needs and experience do a disservice to the human species. . . . We affirm that moral values derive their source from human experience. Ethics is autonomous and situational, needing no theological or ideological sanction. . . . We strive for the good life, here and now. Reason and intelligence are the most effective instruments that humankind possesses. . . . No deity will save us; we must save ourselves. . . .[1]

If this were not enough, a few months later Paul might pick up another paper and see the latest survey taken by Daniel Yankelovich, a respectable research firm, on a four year difference in college and non-college attitudes. Some of the information goes like this: In 1969 57% of the non-college youth thought premarital sex was morally wrong; by 1973 only 34% thought so. (The college goers began with 34% in 1969 and dropped to 22% in 1974.) In 1969 64% of the non-college youth thought an abortion was

1

morally wrong; by 1973 it had dropped to 48%. In 1969 77% of the non-college youth thought that "living a clean moral life is a very important value." In 1973 only 57% thought so. Among the college youth in 1969 45% thought affirmatively on this question and by 1973 34%. In 1969 64% of the non-college youth thought that "religion is a very important value," by 1973 this had dropped to 42%. Among the college youth in 1969 38% thought religion was a very important value and by 1973 only 28% did.[2] Even in his era of non-statistics, Paul might be impressed with the massive indifference to religion and its traditionally related moral questions. Putting down his paper he would sense that times have changed. No longer is there an altar to an unknown god. The altar seemed to be erected to the "Obsolete god" (small 'g') and underneath this main title is added the subtitle, "The Triumph of Secularism."

The extra irony here is that since Paul's own time and the rapid spread of the gospel Christianity had attained a large influence in every area of life. From the hierarchy of the Roman Catholic Church to the Consistory of Calvin's Geneva, society and religion were, for many centuries, intertwined. The churches had almost a monopoly over such public ventures as education, learning, the arts and sciences. Yet today all churches have lost their preeminence. Other rivals on the world scene have replaced them. Nationalism for one; the state, social agencies. The churches have been forced to retreat into their own spheres to compete for the private and voluntary allegiances of individuals. They have no direct impact on public policy any longer. They are almost entirely overshadowed by the large corporation structures, the mass media, big business, the government and the military. In a recent survey taken by *U.S. News & World Report* organized religion listed eighteenth among those large institutions which influence everyday life most profoundly. (For the record, television was first.)

How did it all happen? Are in fact people less religious today? Are there more atheists? Is God obsolete, useless, an unworkable answer for modern times, an embarrassment to the scientific age? Is there something more here than the traditional objections of brilliant men concerning the existence of God?

"Are you an agnostic or an atheist?" [asked writer Leo Rosen of famous philosopher, Bertrand Russell].

"Agnostic, of course. . . . Atheists are like Christians: that is, both dogmatically maintain that we can know whether or not there is a God. The Christian holds that God does exist; the atheist holds that God does not. But the agnostic knows that we simply do not possess sufficient grounds either to affirm or deny the existence of a supreme being. . . ."

I asked, "Let us suppose, sir, that after you have left this sorry vale, you actually found yourself in heaven, standing before the Throne. There, in all his glory, sat the Lord—not Lord Russell, sir: God." Russell winced. "What would you think?"

"I would think I was dreaming."

"But suppose you realized you were not? Suppose that there, before your very eyes, beyond a shadow of a doubt, *was* God. What would you say?"

The pixie wrinkled his nose. "I probably would ask, 'Sir, why did you not give me better evidence?' "3

This conversation at least thinks the question of God, of belief, is relevant. But is there something new today when only 42% of non-college youth and 28% of the college youth think that religion is a very important value? The Catholic Church seems to think so. So seriously has it taken atheism that Vatican II has bluntly stated "atheism must be accounted among the most serious problems of this age" and has gone so far as to create a permanent office of secretariat for dealing with atheism and studying everything that pertains to it.

So let us begin, in our attempt to position unbelief, by giving the reasons, in no particular order, for the decline of formal religion in our time.

— 2 —

1. Science and technological specialization have moved to center

stage at the cost of religion. Specialized fields of study have broken away from the churches and have their own internal logic, discipline and vocabulary. The scientific disciplines are considered on a par with, if not superior to, religion. Religion, once the unifying rationale for all things whatever, has been reduced to just one more department of human activity. In the popular weeklies such as *Time* or *Newsweek* religion is but one more department along with medicine, sports, education and entertainment.

This has happened because occurrences and events which formerly were explained by recourse to a divine power, as actions of the gods (or God), can now be explained by rational causes. We no longer think of thunder and lightning as the anger of the gods from which we must be protected by ritual and sacrifice. Now we go out and buy lightning rods. Thanks to the scientific revolution the world is simply no longer haunted by God's omnipresence, no longer perceived in the perspective of eternity. That is why Eric Hoffer, the longshoreman-philosopher, remarked that at some point in history God and the priests seemed to become superfluous while the world kept on going anyhow. All this is saying quite clearly that God no longer seems necessary in a scientifically explained and scientifically controlled world. Science, after all, has put a man on the moon and has taken the heart from one man and put it into another. The blind are healed today, not by miracles, but by medicine. The poor are saved, not by understanding, but by urban renewal. The imprisoned are freed, not by prayer, but by amnesty. No wonder the eighteenth century astronomer-mathematician Laplace, when asked about God replied, "I have no need of that hypothesis." No wonder twentieth century theologian Van Buren says, "Divine action is conceived as an intervention in this world by heavenly, transcendent powers. But men today can no longer give credence to such a way of thinking. The scientific revolution, with its resulting technological and industrial development, has given us another, empirical way of thinking and of seeing the world."[4]

What we are saying is that we have a scientific attitude now, an attitude which has hardened for many into positivism. This is the outlook which holds that the only reality is that which can be seen, measured and scientifically proven. "Unless I see the holes that the nails made in his hands and can put my finger into his side, I refuse to believe" (Jn 20:25). Thomas is the first positivist. So what do we need religion for? God? Belief? For us the sociologist has replaced the patriarch, the surgeon has replaced the witch doctor, the psychologist has replaced the confessor and the scientist has replaced the priest. Religion and its personnel have been subverted by science. Our attitude today is not one of believing easily in divine activity.

2. The rise of universal education. This is a variation of the above. Universal education has spread the gospel of positivism and inculcated the scientific spirit. The hold of the churches on the minds of men has been pried loose. Man now has more information about the world and, more importantly, the mandate to think for himself, to strike out for himself and to make himself the measurement of reality. He has grown quite conscious of his own personal worth, civil rights and self-determination—extreme luxuries in past days of collective turmoil in the effort to survive. Man is now free to make up his own interpretations of what is spiritually valuable to him and, thanks to the mass media, he has a large choice of life styles to choose from. He does not need nor much desire any official institutional guide as a church.

3. The rise of competing religions. Ever since the Protestant Reformation there has been in the West a variety of Christian religions to replace the old Catholic unity and the Catholic symbol interpretation of the world view. The result is that there is no longer any official model of religion anymore, no one official view of the sacred, no one officially and socially agreed on outlook of the world and the deity. The individual can shop for his own brand of religion suited to his tastes and liking. This novelty has obviously splintered the religious enterprise and weakened its impact on society. Furthermore, institutional religion was in principle weakened with Protestant insistence on a "spiritual" church:

Whatever the causal factors leading up to it [the Reformation], Luther and the other Reformers launched a fundamental attack on the Thomistic system. The crux of it of course concerned the status of the Church, especially through the sacramental system, as the machinery of salvation, and with it the status of the priesthood. The sacraments came to be by-passed by the direct relation of the individual believer to God through faith. The true church then became the invisible church of the faithful in communion with God, with no spiritual necessity for intermediary structures. The clergy then became spiritual guides and teachers but were deprived of the "power of the keys."[5]

The result of all this has been that no strong religions emerged with public impact. Such institutionalized religions as there are have had their strength siphoned off by other institutions which perform religious activities such as the courts, the VFW, the school and other organizations. They engage in what is called "civic religion." Add to this the impact of travel and the mass media which has introduced the Eastern religions and sects into the West, into the United States. This has enlarged the choice even more, especially for the young, and college campuses boast their share of Hindus, Hare Krishna and other exotic sects from the East. In brief, we have, in Robert Miller's phrase, moved from monotheism to polytheism. Once more the net result has been to reduce religion in general to a very private option and denominational religion in particular to one more competitor on the open religious market.

4. A change of life style. Here in the United States at least our life style, even with occasional setbacks such as gas shortages and a depressed economy, has become to some degree an almost endless round of busyness and entertainment. There is now the possibility of deflecting people permanently from any considerations or even the need to have considerations about the issues of religion. Religion is no longer seen as an interpretative thread lacing through everything; it is instead a leisure pursuit. No wonder our survey quoted at the beginning had only 42% of the non-college and 28% of the college youth thinking that religion is a very important value.

When life was unremitting toil for most men reward was conveniently located in a transmundane sphere. . . . As promises, rewards, reassurances and threats lost their purchase on men's minds, religious activity became a leisure activity: its intimate connection with work and the rhythms of life diminished as men's work activities came to have a less direct concern with nature and more with man's material and organizational products. . . . It is "after work" not "after life" which looms large in the thinking of industrial man—the arena in which reward is to be realized.[6]

Our life style emphasizes the immediate, the here and now. Direct experience is highly valued. Reality is now and it is here. People do not experience faith and God as vividly. Church life offers no comparable immediacy and, as we shall see, often no direct relationship with the world, with the secular, with what men are doing in their everyday lives. B. F. Skinner, the Harvard psychologist, bemoans the high emphasis put on the present, on the immediate, and praises the churches for helping people to defer immediate gratification for later goals. "The institutional churches have always been a great help in this regard because they arrange additional reinforcers that make people look toward the future while making sacrifices in the present. Religion has always helped people to do that, to be heroic in the present in view of a better future. . . . There is something very wrong with this . . . emphasis on now and getting everything right now. . . . There is a fantastic concern with the present in this country; all I'm really trying to do is to say that we have to look beyond this if we're going to be truly human."[7] The point is that he has pinpointed the fact of immediacy and in effect given one more reason for religion's decline. Religion which of its very nature speaks of the future can hardly be popular with the "Now" generation. Vatican II concurs: "Some never get to the point of raising questions about God, since they seem to experience no religious stirrings, nor do they see why they should trouble themselves about religion. . . . Modern civilization itself often complicates the approach to God, not for an essential reason, but because it is excessively engrossed in earthly affairs."[8]

5. The misplaced emphasis and at times the arrogance of institutional religion. Both Protestant and Catholic churches turned religion into a series of propositions and literal interpretations of the Bible. They frequently felt they had nothing to learn from others

much less from "the world." The churches became closed systems and soon lost rapport with science. As science advanced the churches clung desperately to the remaining gaps that they felt science could never fill. Then one day science was bold enough to claim to fill these also.

Had the enlightenment occurred first in a culture dominated by Zen Buddhism, for example, the outcome would have been very different, for Zen never set a date for the creation of the world, argued for the literal inspiration of any scripture, or based any claim on the alleged occurrence of miracles. But the Christian faith in the eighteenth and nineteenth centuries contained a weighty baggage of cognitive assertions about nature and history that could be either disproved or rendered improbable by a critical science. There were many, of course, who argued for the "reasonableness of Christianity," even as early as the eighteenth century. But they tended to place inordinate hope in the gaps in existing scientific knowledge which it was believed only religious truth could fill. When these gaps were closed by science itself it was a terrible blow. No blow was greater than Darwin's theory of natural selection which provided the first scientific theory of the origin of species. Before that no one knew how species originated, so a theory of special creation by God was at least a defensible position.[9]

No question but the theory of evolution was the biggest blow to the literal reading of scripture that most churches held to. Credibility, at least among the intellectuals, fell to a new low. As far as Catholics went, not only did they reel from the new science as did the others, but they too felt the stress of two world wars, the disruption of family life and the onslaught of industrialization—all of which forced them into contact with others. The Catholic ghetto started to break up and repressing novel notions became more and more difficult for those in authority. Vatican II came along and decisively thrust the Church back into the center of history once more. The Church was unprepared, caught off guard and has suffered the crisis of adjustment ever since. The result has been a deterioration of the religious images, exclusiveness and certitudes among Catholics.

We can go further. Most churches were not portraying God in the best light. He emerged from most official documents and catechisms as a most foreboding and forbidding deity, one rather indifferent to the stresses of the daily living of his creatures. He certainly did not emerge as the God who cared about the world, human science, dancing, waterfalls, kissing, pain, suffering. He did not appear as in any way involved in or concerned about the human enterprise. As such, this God was hostile to human progress and civilization. It was a feat for the churches to manage this caricature in view of the incarnation which they believed in. But they did, and sooner or later people rejected this God and, along with this notion, religion itself.

Finally, we might mention that with a renewed sense of social consciousness in the last several years plus the religious freedom given to non-Catholics and soon claimed by Catholics themselves, institutional religion came in for more criticism. "It may be," said Harvey Cox, "that the main reason for unbelief, whatever it is in our time, is not that people find the gospel incredible, but that they find the Church incredible. A church which calls itself the servant of the Prince of Peace but which is unable to take a decisive action against war; a church which proclaims the ideal of poverty but continues to accumulate property is not a church which is worthy of belief."[10]

6. The confusion of institutional renewal within the larger upheaval of constant and recurring change in society. People are caught up in "future shock" and have sought solace in the old certainties, particularly in an "unchanging" religion. But even this seems to be changing. People who are horrified with their churches that have gone liberal transfer to the conservative churches which project stability.[11] Some churches have gone so secular that they have adopted the jargon and terminology of the social worker and psychologist. The faithful looking for faith come back with therapy and this blurs the distinction between religion (as popularly conceived) and the social agency. There are those others, of course, who so welcome change that they feel that the churches, while doing a good job in the past, have now arrived at the point where they should be phased out. Among these there are those who have found secular organizations more concerned about social justice than their own churches. Even those remaining within the traditional churches

often ally themselves with secular and humanist causes that seem to be more relevant. Ecumenism officially offers the average man the encouragement to partake in a wider moral community of believers than his own particular brand of Christianity. All of these factors mentioned here have had the effect of weakening formalized religion among people.

7. Finally, there is a crisis of religious language. This is partly due to the theologians who have not kept pace with the world, who have lost touch with life. We are reminded that "theology lives and has its meaning only in relation to the wider religious matrix from which it arises. When it strays too far from its source or when it gets separated from other modes of expression in worship, ethics, it degenerates into empty and arid disputes; and of course, if it has become detached from its living background and then gets subjected in an artificial way to some formal analysis, we must not be surprised if it begins to appear senseless."[12] Indeed, much religious talk does not mean much to secular man today and while it is true that "secular experience without religious symbols is blind, unarticulated and terrifying; religious symbols without the content of secular experience are empty and meaningless."[13] In other words, if the language of religion has totally retreated to the monastery and the cloister the majority of people in the secular world can gather no meaning—and therefore no nourishment—from it.

But there is more to religious confusion besides modern theologians' opaque language. There is some general agreement among churchmen that the language of the ancient bible and of early Christianity is no longer meaningful to modern man either. The old language and concepts are outmoded today and make no sense to technological man. Words and concepts like "circuminsession," "hypostatic union," "transubstantiation" rest on discarded theories, world views and philosophies. So we are faced with the challenge of "how to *talk* about traditional Judaic-Christian beliefs in contemporary language. . . . Both the Old and New Testaments are human expressions of human theologies that express man's faith-convictions. But such human expressions are very old, having sprung from very ancient cultures that differ profoundly from that of twentieth century man. Neither Jew nor Christian can afford the luxury of resting his search for God in the primitive Testaments popularly known as the bible. . . . The challenge is to pass on to the younger generation an understanding of all that the bible means in language and with expressions that will have relevance to life as it must be lived today."[14]

Without relevant religious language, religion suffers and goes into decline. Else it's watered down as preachers try to be relevant and borrow from the social sciences. They might not use the terms "sin," "grace," "creation" or "the kingdom of God." They may resort to words such as growth, relationship, response, openness and so forth. But this re-translation tends to weaken religion as much as the language which tries to literalize those notions which by their very definition defy literal translations. In any case, as we shall see later on, there is a crisis of religious language and symbols and this crisis has added its pressure to the decline of institutional religion.

What we have given so far are seven formal reasons for the decline of institutional religion and belief. They have for the most part dealt with the historical basis for the religious-belief crisis. But there are other reasons, more sociological, more psychological and we shall examine a few of these.

— 3 —

There is an interesting theory by sociologist Peter Berger which maintains that people's worldview—we might say, their faith—derives not so much from intellectual deduction, but from the up-bringing, from the whole pattern of emotional overtones of the people that surround them from the beginning. We are social beings and most of what we know (or think we know) comes from the significant people in our lives. Furthermore, these people continuously and silently affirm in many subtle ways our inherited worldview. This view of life and our interpretation of reality will continue to flourish to the degree that they receive such social support. In some instances there is a rather elaborate system to keep the view intact. Berger mentions by way of example the Catholic

Church. It has its Catholic milieu, schools, priests, religious, sacraments, rituals, devotions, etc. All these persons and things conspire to keep intact the Catholic view of life. All conspire to make Catholicism plausible and almost "natural." The real threat comes, as we have indicated above, when the Catholic so "naturally" raised with a specific world faith-view moves into a pluralistic society, a society which not only does not believe as he does, but explicitly or implicitly mocks his beliefs.

It is relatively easy, sociologically speaking, to be a Catholic in a social situation where one can readily limit one's significant others to fellow Catholics, where indeed one had little choice in the matter and where all the major institutional forces are geared to support and confirm a Catholic world. The story is quite different in a situation where one is compelled to rub shoulders day by day with every conceivable variety of "those others," is bombarded with communications that deny or ignore one's Catholic ideals, and where one has a terrible time even finding some quiet Catholic corners to withdraw into. It is very, very difficult to be cognitively *entre nous* in modern society, especially in the area of religion. This simple sociological fact, and not some magical inexorability of a "scientific" world outlook, is at the basis of the religious plausibility crisis.[15]

His observation is borne out. Today Catholics, like other believers, are plunged heavily into a mass-mediaized world where their views are increasingly becoming only one of many. We have noted this already. But here we press the challenge this entails. The challenge is for individual Catholics as well as their Church to be assimilated into the American mainstream but not be absorbed by it. Church leaders and intellectuals try to enlarge the Catholic worldview so as to accommodate the Church to the contemporary scene and much progress has been made. What causes the strain on faith is when a certain line is drawn which the faithful cannot cross without diminishing or abandoning the faith. A prime symbolic case for modern American Catholics is the liberalization of the abortion laws and the virtual abortion on demand status of the law of the land. Attempts of Catholics both to have a hearing and to influence legislation have been generally futile as Catholics are more

openly treated as noncitizens whose interests are hostile to the
"people" at large. It may be that much of the Catholic belief system
will be viewed someday as hostile to America as the mass media and
secular liberals underpin situations, opinions and assumptions that
cannot be held by the religious Catholic.

In a society lacking any moral consensus, in which religion is officially
a private affair only, the civil law itself tends to determine moral
beliefs. An assumption develops that whatever is legal is also moral,
so that the Supreme Court's decision on abortion has probably had
the effect of convincing many people that there is no moral problem
involved. Groups which challenge, on moral grounds, practices that
the state has declared legal then run the risk of being read out of the
American consensus.

Groups which do not accept one or other major tenets of the
official American morality are increasingly driven to create special
conditions of living for themselves and special ways of handing on
their traditions to their children, a task for which American Catholics
seem at present very badly prepared.[16]

The point is that if faith flourishes best in a supportive community
then it fares ill where the community's consensus is anti-religious,
pragmatical and utilitarian. A crisis of believing may well be related
to the lack of emotional support, to the embarrassment of being different, to the tension of holding on to minority "antiquated religious
views" among majority peers whose world view is formed by the
mass media. Perhaps our statistics at the beginning of this chapter
bear this out.

Without commenting here on the moral issue let us look at
another symbolic issue: the question of masturbation. Karl Menninger in his book *Whatever Became of Sin?* mentions that for
centuries, even as far back as pre-Christian times, masturbation has
been condemned. But "the amazing circumstance is that sometime
soon after the turn of the present century, this ancient taboo, for the
violation of which millions have been punished, threatened, condemned, intimidated, and made hypocritical and cynical—a taboo
thousands of years old—vanished almost overnight! Masturbation,

the solitary vice, the SIN of youth, suddenly seemed not to be so sinful, perhaps not sinful at all; not so dangerous—in fact not dangerous at all—less a vice than a form of pleasurable experience, and a normal and healthy one!"[17] We are making no moral judgment here but rather using the example of how values can change so quickly and how therefore, as Menninger says, such reversals can call into question *all* formerly held cherished beliefs and attitudes. A certain lack of commitment, a certain holding back, a reserved kind of believing is inevitable. Faith and its commitments are positioned a little more cautiously today.

Next we may mention that religion goes into decline when devalued language and general irreverence assault it. Words usually associated with religion have been devalued to sell products. We have all kinds of miracle cleaners and fabrics, panty hose that "clings like sin," divine color schemes and heavenly decor and, as we shall note again, it is "Datsun saves and sets you free," not Jesus. Religious subjects and personages are now the subjects of mass media vulgarations. There are movies such as *The Divine Mr. J.* which *New York Times* critic Howard Thompson describes as "A dull, dirty-mouthed and utterly infantile 'religious satire' movie. . . . mocking the story of Jesus"; and another film called *Him* depicting Christ in a homosexual relationship. One issue of *Esquire* magazine showed President Lyndon Johnson crucified and an issue of the *New York* magazine showed President Richard Nixon in the famous pieta pose beneath the cross. The point is that religious language, religious personages and religious symbols are devalued in the way that George Washington is remembered on his birthday by stores having gigantic sales. The impact on the young especially can be eroding to the faith. Or at least it can blunt the readiness to use religious symbols tarnished by vulgarism.

Another point of confusion and uncertainty about formal religion arises from the religious writers themselves. It is no secret (as we shall see) that many religious phenomena, once thought of as completely or nearly miraculous, can be interpreted naturally. A Catholic student in high school or college may learn that what he believed were genuine miracles can turn out to be natural phenomena. The burning bush of Genesis from which God spoke to Moses is what is called St. Elmo's fire, a fire which emits static electricity. Manna is a natural phenomenon of the desert, as is the parting of the Red Sea. He learns that the infancy narratives of Jesus are theological inventions of the evangelists and that Mary's virginity is a high symbol of God's power to bring life from death (fruitfulness from sterility) and that Jesus himself did not say all of his words but that such words were put into his mouth by others; that those gospel people possessed by demons have striking similarities to modern day epileptics and that the resurrection narratives are riddled with questions and contradictions. These things can be perfectly legitimate and in reality open up whole new avenues of understanding and faith. But the point is that unless the teachers are careful and the classes sound, the student can come away with a rationalistic approach to religion. Personal skepticism rather than faith can be the result.

Finally, we go along with Andrew Greeley's phrase that the basic thrust in life for the infant is to learn that Reality is Gracious, Kind and Benevolent, that children will learn faith (in the sense of a transcendental interpretation of reality) from this primeval experience. The child learns forgiveness from forgiving parents. He learns joy and self-worth from them. John Shea says that the first hour that daddy comes home in the evening is the most profound religious experience that his child will have. It is at this time that the infant perceives the interrelationships of his father and mother and from this a faith-filled view of reality. Faith develops within other human values such as trust, obedience, knowledge, assent and commitment. Faith is nourished by the believers who raise the child. As psychologist Eugene Kennedy says, "Openness to God is mediated always by our human condition. . . . Faith grows in the context of relationship to adult believers."[18] All this means that as hostile and broken homes increase, that as divorce becomes more and more common, as family life is increasingly looked upon as the hotbed of all repressions, evils, frustrations for the child, then we can expect a greater crisis of faith as this child gets older. The difficulty of transferring, say, the notion of a kind, caring provident heavenly Father for one who has known only a harsh, demanding, deserting father becomes appreciated. The difficulty of a mature faith for the young man or woman who has not known self-worth and fidelity as a child can be acknowledged. We might note a parallel situation. Studies done on the outstanding radical students in the universities during the 60's by psychoanalysts show that these very students' radicalism and intense hostilities stem from their home life:

> Although most of the students interviewed did have parents with a left-wing or at least liberal background, their ideology proved to be less important than the fact that political discussions were the closest thing to personal exchanges that took place in the family — a circumstance that may have some bearing on the use of politics to express feelings that are personal. An atmosphere of polite estrangement seemed to prevail between these parents who got along well with each other on the surface but who were not deeply involved with each other. All the students felt their parents had not been physically affectionate toward them or each other. . . . Their feelings of abandonment and parental withdrawal have left them with a pervasive depression and a diminished self-confidence. . . . In the revolutionary culture many have found a "family" which understands their emotional needs better than their real families ever did. . . .[19]

Once more this seems to support Berger's theory, and others who maintain that none of us exists in a vacuum and that our outlook on and interpretation of life is highly colored and preconditioned by our families and the kind of supportive atmosphere we received. So with faith. Jesus' invitation to believe in him is "a statement that cannot possibly be grasped by anyone who does not know something about friendship and love. Faith language is human language, after all, and if friendship with God does not have a human face then it is beyond us completely. . . . We believe best, not when we escape our human condition, but when we are at ease and untroubled by it."[20]

There are other reasons why people do not believe. What we have tried to show are the more obvious ones. We have tried to position unbelief in the context of our modern day culture. But notice that most of the time we spoke of a lack of belief in relationship to institutional and denominational religion. That indeed, as far as external measurements can be applied, has declined. But belief itself? Has it declined? Is believing on the way out? Can man do without it? To these questions we must turn in the next chapter.

NOTES FOR CHAPTER 1

1. For a readable critique of the Manifesto see "The New Humanist Manifesto" by Louis Dupre, in *Commonweal,* October 19, 1973; also the December, 1973 issue.
2. *New York Times,* May 22, 1974, p. 37. The complete study will appear in a book to be published by McGraw-Hill.
3. *Saturday Review/World,* February 2, 1974, p. 25.
4. Juan Luis Segundo, *Our Idea of God* (Orbis Books, 1974) p. 47.
5. Talcott Parsons, "Belief, Unbelief and Disbelief" in *Culture of Unbelief,* edited by Rocco Caporale and Antonio Grumelli (University of California Press, 1971) p. 222.
6. Talcott Parsons, p. 265.
7. Eugene Kennedy, *Believing* (Doubleday, 1974) p. 140.
8. *Gadium et Spes,* article 19.
9. Robert Bellah, *Beyond Belief* (Harper and Row, 1970) p. 272.
10. *Culture of Unbelief,* cited above, p. 94.
11. See Dean Kelley's book, *Why the Conservative Churches Are Growing* (Harper and Row, 1972).
12. John Macquarrie, *God-Talk* (Harper and Row, 1967) p. 19.
13. Langdon Gilkey, in *Traces of God in a Secular Culture,* edited by George F. McLean (Alba House, 1973) p. 9.
14. William J. Duggan, *Myth and Christian Belief* (Fides Publishers, 1971) pp. 3 to 10.
15. Peter Berger, *Rumor of Angels* (Doubleday, 1969).
16. James Hitchcock, "Catholics and Liberals, Decline of Detente" in *America,* March 16, 1974; see also the editorial in *Commonweal* for May 3, 1974, p. 299.
17. Karl Menninger, *Whatever Became of Sin?* (Hawthorn Books, 1973) p. 36.
18. Eugene Kennedy, cited above, p. 40ff.
19. Herbert Hendin, *"A Psychoanalyst Looks at Student Revolutionaries"* in *New York Times Magazine,* January 17, 1971. Also, see the corroborative evidence in Merton P. Strommen's book, *Five Cries of Youth* (Harper and Row, 1974).
20. Eugene Kennedy, cited above, p. 40.

2. Positioning Belief

Religion, at least in its institutional form, has declined for the reasons we have seen in the last chapter. Religion in its personal form, however, is another matter. As we shall see there is no evidence that religion in its widest definition is on the way out altogether in spite of growing atheism. Men are still impressed to some degree by the various indications (some no longer hold them as strict proofs) of the existence of God. They are apt to have a favorable reaction to St. Paul's contention that "from the foundation of the world, men have caught sight of his invisible nature, his eternal power and his divineness, as they are known through his creatures" (Rom 1:20). Many will still be impressed with Frank Sheed's restatement of the classic argument for God's existence:

> If we consider the universe, we find that everything bears this mark, that it does exist but might very well not have existed. We ourselves exist, but we would not have existed if a man and a woman had not met and mated. The same mark can be found upon everything. A particular valley exists because a stream of water took that way down, perhaps because the ice melted up there. If the melting ice had not been there, there would have been no valley. And so with all the things of our experience. They exist, but they would not have existed if some other thing had not been what it was or done what it did.

> The effect of this is that none of these things is the explanation of its own existence, or the source of its own existence. Each thing . . . is essentially a receiver of existence. Now it is impossible to conceive of a universe consisting exclusively of contingent beings, that is of beings which are only receivers of existence not originators.

The reader who is taking his role as explorer seriously might very well stop reading at this point and let his mind make for itself the effort to conceive a condition in which nothing should exist save receivers of existence. . . .

If nothing exists save beings that receive their existence, how does anything exist at all? . . . Even an infinite number of beings, if no one of these is the source of its own existence, will not account for existence.

Thus we are driven to see that the beings of our experience, the contingent beings, could not exist at all unless there is also a being which differs from them by possessing existence in its own right. It does not have to receive existence; it simply has existence. It is not contingent: it simply is. This is the Being that we call God.[1]

Anglican writer C. S. Lewis gives a psychological variation:

Most people, if they have really learned to look into their own hearts, would know that they do want, and want acutely, something that cannot be had in this world. There are all sorts of things in this world that *offer* to give it to you, but they never quite keep their promise. . . . [Now] the Christian says, "Creatures are not born with desires unless satisfaction for those desires exists. A baby feels hunger: well, there is such a thing as food. A duckling wants to swim: well, there is such a thing as water. Men feel sexual desire: well, there is such a thing as sex. If I find in myself a desire which no experience in this world can satisfy, the most probable explanation is that I was made for another world. If none of my earthly pleasures satisfy it, that does not prove that the universe is a fraud. Probably earthly pleasures were never *meant* to satisfy it, but only to arouse it, to suggest the real thing. . . ."[2]

Modern writers add other dimensions in speaking about God's existence:

Look at the marvelous discoveries of science
and triumphs of technology;
the astounding energy locked up in matter,
the immense universe man is beginning to explore;
the wonders of the organic world and instinct . . .

This stupendous order presents itself like a problem
requiring a solution.

Chance? But, as Bergson said,
chance that follows law is
the opposite of chance! . . .

The need for strict accuracy and utmost precision
that the scholar accepts,
even if he is atheist,
comes from the same sense of dependence
on a supreme norm: truth.
The sceptic doubts, the atheist denies,
this or that idea of God
in the name of a truth they regard
as higher and purer.
Moral conscience, too, with its demands
for justice and retribution for rights denied,
likewise affirms an absolute moral value,
to which we must all justify ourselves.
In these ways, the Absolute, God himself,
ever bears witness to himself
at the heart of life.[3]

Another modern theologian says:

Schubert Ogden in *The Reality of God* builds his case on the deep,
underlying confidence that life is meaningful, a confidence he
finds also among those who consciously and explicitly deny the
existence of God. This confidence bears witness to a relatedness
to God, because it cannot be grounded in the merely phenomenal
or empirical flux of experience. What happens *really* matters only
if it matters everlastingly. What happens can matter everlastingly
only if it matters to him who is everlasting. Hence, seriousness about
life implicitly involves faith in God.

Whether or not this is to be regarded as in any sense an argument
for the existence of God, it does effectively and realistically point up
the alternative to Christian faith in God as being, not optimistic
secular humanism but genuine nihilism.[4]

There is one more way of discovering God that appeals to contemporary theologians which we must explore. They point out what we shall see in the next section, namely, that while science answers some riddles and gives us ever new inventions, it only makes more insistent the need to understand the *meaning* of it all. And not only is there concern over meaning, but also a concern over the ethical questions which science raises but cannot answer. We have nuclear weapons and the genetic manipulation of human beings. The ethical questions raised here must seek answers beyond science:

> Many geneticists and physicians feel the use of the new techniques should be limited to the detection, treatment and eradication of serious genetic defects and diseases. There is little medical or ethical debate about some of these flaws. But a number of prominent geneticists have much broader and, to us, more threatening notions of how the new technology might be used. . . . These eugenic predictions and proposals inevitably involve certain decisions about which "negative" human traits will be eliminated and which "positive" traits encouraged. But how does one make such decisions? What factors influence the designation of a particular trait as defective? . . . Who will make the decisions about the genetic worth of prospective human beings? . . . The real problem is the social and political context in which the new technology is developed and applied. The real question is, who will control its development and application? If left to the political and scientific experts, the results are bound to be increasing control by those of power and wealth over the weaker sectors of society.[5]

Some are beginning to realize that answers to the quantity and quality of human life, its very meaning, cannot be obtained from science alone and, in fact, there must be something higher than science that determines the answers. Again, all this points to the increasing interest, as science advances, in the meaning of human experience, human existence. That is to say, the more science advances, the more pressing becomes the human question.

Now using our motif of meaning, we can say that meaning as such is not a foreign desire for us. We have already indicated how believing is quite natural and integral to human nature. So, too, are those special moments when meaning becomes a moment of certainty and "reveals" a "Wholly Other" to us. What we mean is this: for most people in life there are certain precious moments that are best described as "catching us up out of ourselves." For example, we suddenly experience a lovely moment of intense friendship, we enjoy a stunning sunset such as we never have before, we come across a really selfless act of love, a sound, a child, whatever. In these and similar intense moments, an ecstasy of sorts comes along and we are pulled out of ourselves. Such experiences, such "signs of transcendence," have a wholeness about them, a definitive healing, an inner harmony which our basic instinctive intuition perceives as meaning. Everything for the moment has fallen into place. Suddenly life is not absurd. All of its diverse elements suddenly slide into place. We are faced with an experience, a calm, a peace. The harmony, the *meaning* (inexplicable but real) is absolutely compelling. We may go into a kind of trance, we may just feel the utter overpowering calm, we may break out in tears as a result of this experience.

Now it is this experience of well-being, of harmony, of absolute meaning that has intrigued some modern thinkers. They point out that this is exactly what happiness is: to perceive meaning and, conversely, to have conquered the absurdities and fears of living a meaningless life. If such meaning-experiences come across to most people at one time or another, it is argued, might not this indicate a larger Meaning—with a capital "M"? Might not that Meaning— God we would call it—be not really "out there" or "up there" but in the very heart of human history? In other words, might not the transcendent God also be immanent? Might not those moments of ecstasy we described be our discovery of a God who is already in human history and that therefore our faith in God begins with the study of man and his world?

If this is so, then our whole perspective changes. No need for miracles, angels and demons for the greatest miracle is with us all the time: God himself. No need for those old symbols that did great service for prescientific man in locating God up there somewhere: he is in the heart of this planet and those moments were moments of discovery of what was there (who was there) all the time. One of the interpretations of the transfiguration of Jesus in the New Testament says that his glory was present all the time. It is just that for the first time the disciples saw Jesus as he really was. All the other times he was commonplace to them but in their moment of ecstasy they saw him in his reality.

So, too, in this world. The world is God-filled; in those moments of ecstasy we see or perceive what is there all the time. He is the final Meaning of all meanings, the Answer to science's unanswerable questions, the final Ethic to pressing problems raised by science. Now these thoughts have several intertwined notions which we shall explore in the next chapter; for example, God's immanence, his discovery in human history rather than as a starry, detached extra, etc. But for the moment, all that we want to extricate from these paragraphs is the idea that God's existence and indeed his very presence is often verified (to the participants anyway) in those distilled moments of transcendence which cannot always be verbalized but which are genuine, real and indicative of a divine presence to those who have experienced them.[6]

Finally, whatever we think of these arguments for God's existence, theologian John Macquarrie reminds us that those who do believe are not dredging up outlandish positions that do violence to human nature or straining to put in man what is not there already. Rather, "it has been shown that the attitude of faith arises from the very structures of human existence itself. It is not a luxury but arises from our innate quest for selfhood and for a meaningful existence. No conclusive weight attaches to this point, but it is worth reminding ourselves that faith is not some strained perversion of our nature but an attitude that really does belong with the kind of existence that is ours."[7] Psychologist Kennedy adds his testimony:

Belief is at least as powerful as any medication known to man. . . . All we know, as psychiatrist Jerome B. Frank has told us in *Persuasion and Healing,* is that there is a dynamic associated with believing in other persons that transforms their chances. . . . Believing is not magic. It is profoundly human, a source of energy and self-integration, the like of which is not observed in any other human experience. In questions of growth, human relationships, and healthy achievement, the role of believing is crucial. It is faith, an active kind of believing, which makes men whole. . . . Faith involves struggle, an effort to sense the fullness of ourselves at the moment we commit ourselves in belief. And to believe is essential to the activation and coordination of all the processes through which we reach toward our own individuality and fullness. Believing is related to the complex human process we call growth; its character is keyed to the total development of ourselves.[8]

So to believe, to have faith, is not some alien strain imposed from without on unsuspecting man. To believe is as natural as to breathe. The quest for God, then, is not foreign to man. Whether he finds God or rejects him is not our concern here. Rather, what is our concern is the status of religion, not as an institution, but as a personal odyssey, a quest for cosmic interpretation that is open to a divine Being. So, defining religion broadly as a system of powerful symbols which seek to interpret reality, let us look at the record. What does it show?

— 2 —

The record shows that for all of the sophistication and scientific mind set which we saw in the last chapter, modern man is still very much after something to believe in. He may not be looking into the beliefs held out to him by the usual formal churchy institutions, but looking he is. Why? Because with all of his sophistication and science he has learned that he does not have all the answers or, as we may put it, the answer behind the answers. The reason is that:

Although man is reaching out towards the stars, he still feels anguish in his heart; although he has succeeded in transplanting vital organs such as the heart and kidney, he still trembles at the thought of death; although he has pleasure and comfort at his beck and call, he still has not succeeded in filling the bitter emptiness he feels within him; although he has crowded into huge cities, he still feels a piercing loneliness.[9]

And that about sums it up. In proportion as modern man has achieved technical control over his environment to that degree he now frets over control over himself, his life, his passions and his death. It is true that many natural wonders have been explained by science, but this only means that the mystery has just been pushed back one step further. This means that man has an ever new, always old mystery to contend with: the mystery of himself. And he wonders more and more about himself as his science produces nuclear bombs, dehumanizing slums and polluted air:

> . . . Allocation of massive sums of money has not bought off man's demons; proliferating governmental agencies have not brought them to heel. This is so, according to Daniel Moynihan, because the liberal establishment has failed to state adequately the questions facing men today. These questions, he maintains, are not those of poverty, or hunger, or population control, or war and peace, or race; the questions are those of human values—of morality and ethics, of behavior, in brief, according to norms that are not within man's power alone to construct. Moynihan does not hesitate to say that the questions are radically religious in nature, and that our failure to regard them as such is nothing other than a body blow to the culture itself, a blow from which the culture may not recover.[10]

This again is as good a description as any of where modern man finds himself. More than ever he is faced with the implications of his own science and its failure to come to terms with those human values which make life worth living. And each year the urgency grows stronger to find something beyond science to help man from becoming a cog in the great social machine. Each year it becomes more imperative to look beyond science to some kind of faith whose insights may have more healing power than machine made products. That is why Herbert Marcuse remarks that "where religion still preserves the uncompromised aspirations for peace and happiness, its 'illusions' still have a higher truth than science which works for their elimination."[11]

That is why one writer insists that

> . . . religion is not really a kind of pseudogeology or pseudohistory but an imaginative statement about the truth of the totality of human experience. So-called postreligious man, the cool, self-confident secular man that even some theologians have recently celebrated,

is trapped in a literal and circumscribed reality which is classically described in religious terms as the world of death and sin, the fallen world, the world of illusion. Postreligious man is trapped in hell. . . . In order to break through the literal univocal interpretation of reality that our pseudoscientific secular culture espouses, it is necessary for religion to communicate nonordinary reality that breaks into ordinary reality and exposes its pretensions. When ordinary reality turns into a nightmare, as it increasingly has in modern society, only some transcendental perspective offers any hope . . . religion, instead of becoming increasingly peripheral and vestigial, is again moving into the center of our cultural preoccupations.[12]

The search for meaning, understanding, interpretations goes on—and such a search is a seeking for a faith. Perhaps, as we have indicated, the old formulas and institutional religions do not give man satisfactory answers. Such answers may be lacking in vigor or conviction. Modern man, however, is still not lacking in his desire for answers to ultimate reality. What worries him is not so much the problems which his own intelligence and superior technology can solve, but rather those continuing mysteries "which reflect the transcendent content of his life: fate, meaninglessness, the unpredictable future, and death. Thus the fundamental traits of man's religious existence are as characteristic of modern secular life as they were of any life in the past . . ."[13]

As for the young, in spite of the survey earlier, they show signs of disillusionment with the limitations of science. In fact there has been detected a distinct turning towards the irrational, towards the mystical and to self-professed messiahs (saviors). Harvey Cox, the one-time high priest of the secular says:

All over the world today young people are looking for something which goes beyond the definition of reality as that which they receive through the mass communication media, or what they learn from their elders. Sometimes this search takes very bizarre forms, such as experimentation with astrological beliefs, or mixtures of Eastern beliefs, or it may take the form of experimentation with certain kinds of drugs, or exploration with the forms of sexual behavior which are not acceptable according to established Christian ethics. Nonetheless, behind this search there seems to be an authentic

reaching-out for something which is real, for something which calls
into question the more empirical reality around us. Although most
of these people are not willing to call their search or that for which
they are searching by the name of God, nonetheless, it is really a
search for the transcendent, for that which goes beyond the merely
empirical, and the natural, the socially and culturally defined. Are
we to think of these people as nonbelievers? I think not.[14]

Indeed we have witnessed something of a phenomenon in past years
with the popularity of the occult, satanism, witchcraft and astrology.
And it is precisely in the bastions of the secular, the universities, that
students are reading fantasy stories and dabbling in the occult—
which is another form of searching for faith. Consider:

- It is on the college campuses that Pentecostalism, with its high
  emotion, has begun and from which it has spread.
- Erich Fromm the psychoanalyst says in a newspaper interview
  that modern society's answer is to get back to religion.
- Karl Menninger, a founder of the famous Menninger Clinic,
  writes a book *Whatever Became of Sin?* that makes the best
  seller list.
- Eastern mysticism of all varieties enjoys a great vogue among
  the youth.
- The "God is Dead" movement dies and in fact one of the three
  principal theologians associated with it, Dr. Paul van Buren,
  has reversed his stand. In an interview he said, "Before I was
  asking, 'How can we make sense out of God?' " Now, he said,
  he has concluded: "The Christian gospel is not something that
  men have to make sense of. It is rather something that makes
  sense of men."[15]
- *The Exorcist* both as book and movie enjoys immense popularity. *Newsweek*'s religious editor Kenneth Woodward comments: "At a time of moral confusion among the sophisticated,
  the film harks back to starkly fundamental questions of good
  and evil. The phenomenon is undoubtedly faddist, but it
  speaks to a basic moral need, even if the coinage is somewhat
  debased."[16]

. . . When people are denied their heroes or the simple stories, such as the literal understanding of Adam and Eve, they encounter great difficulties in believing as they once did. They continue to believe, however, because they are impelled to search for something to make sense out of what they know in the world around them. In the interlude between the death of the old myths and the birth of new ones, man must believe in something. [Psychiatrist] Ehrenwald suggests that many persons turn to the negative image of traditional believing, to an embrace of superstition, devil worship, and other such activities. These do not constitute a sign of evil rampant as much as they provide evidences of the human need to believe and the urgent nature of the search for the believable.[17]

* A new magazine is launched in 1974 called *Man, Myth and Magic,* a commercial enterprise which eloquently bespeaks a well researched market.
* Gurus abound and people crowd auditoriums on transcendental meditations. Books on prayer have proliferated.
* Antiwar activist, Rennie Davis, is present among the 10,000 mostly middle-class whites in their 20's who welcome the fifteen-year-old, Rolls Royce-driving Maharaj Ji, sitting on a blue Plexiglas throne at the Astrodome in Houston, Texas. Said Mr. Davis, referring to the Maharaj Ji, "All I can say is, honestly, very soon now, every single human being will know the one who was waited for by every religion of all time has actually come."[18]
* Thirty-eight-year-old Swiss school dropout and ex-convict, Erich von Daniken writes best sellers for some 14 million readers who believe his gospel that man's religious history on earth is the product of beings from outer space. The newsman who wrote his story comments, "The millions of people all over the world (including China) who are obviously eager to accept his theories make up one of the amazing phenomena of a world that seems to be looking for new gods to worship."[19]

We could multiply the examples, but the fact is that all sorts of prayer groups, spiritual sessions, religious communes, splinter sects have sprung up, and sprung up among the mass-mediaized, sophisticated people of today. In fact, as Martin Marty points out, this is the puzzlement: it is precisely among the teachers, the sophisticates, the avant-garde of the secular universities and cultured suburbia who were confidently predicting the disappearance of the transcendent, the mysterious and the mystical who are now engaging in the mystical. "The middle-class, mobile, relatively affluent intellectuals who turn from the simply sensate-rational-secular style to the religious and even the mystical are interesting because they are the people most free to leave behind the concern for transcendent recognitions. . . . Yet precisely the people who could repress the vision that has led man to seek the gods are those who account for most of the renewed interest in the mystical."[20] Surely something is afoot when a worldly magazine such as *Saturday Review/World* in its science department can suggest that the feats of Skylab III might indicate that there is life elsewhere in the universe, intelligent life, and that in fact there have been serious attempts to try to contact it. After all, some scientists are dissatisfied with thinking that all living creatures on our planet came from the earth's own atmosphere. Could it not be possible that the earth is but an experiment from another planet, deliberately "seeded" by them? This would certainly explain why everything whatever on earth has the same genetic code. Are we in a "zoo" being observed by others? The science editor, Albert Rosenfeld writes, "I remember as a child, being puzzled by the readiness of people (and bibles) to attribute all-too-human motivations to God. I thought of that the other night when I was chatting about all this with a nonscientific friend, who finally commented: 'As an early reader of the Book of Genesis, I'm somehow not surprised at the idea that Someone Out There put us here. And if such a magical, mysterious, and powerful intelligence exists that is utterly beyond human imagining, can you give me a good reason why I shouldn't call it God?' I could give him no good reason why not."[21]

Modern man, it seems, is quite religious and the attempts of those to bury religion and claim that "God is Dead" have not been generally accepted. Instead the seeking is more urgent than ever and the basic human problems demand basically religious answers

and approaches. Despite the seeming triumph of secular consciousness man

> still possesses the capacity to experience within himself or within
> the world those powers, inclinations and depths which point be-
> yond a closed secular consciousness and perspective. . . .

No present religious thinker of any stature, however radical his posture, has been able to give up that faith. Leslie Dewart has been
able to let go of traditional Hellenic concepts of God, but he cannot let go of talk about the "presence" of God. Thomas J. J. Altizer
has been able to let go of a concept of the "sacred" understood as
radically separated from the "secular," but even he looks forward
to a rebirth of the "sacred" at some unspecified point. Michael
Novak has been able to let go of a transcendent God, but not of
the existence of an "unrestricted drive to know" which enables man
to transcend himself. Harvey Cox can suggest that we cease to use
the word "god," but not that we cease to believe that a new word
may be found which will better express what has always been meant
by the term as far as basic human experience is concerned. William
Hamilton finds in the person of Jesus a power and a mystery not
exhaustively encompassed by an experience of the secular. However strongly Karl Rahner has pleaded for a Christian acceptance
of profane secularity, his final faith is that the very progress of
secularization will lead to a reopening of the religious question in
the end.

Other examples could be supplied, but what is common to each
of the thinkers mentioned is their refusal to give up the last bastion
of religion. That bastion is precisely the belief that even in the most
secularized consciousness and society, man can find the presence of
experience and intimations which are potentially able to point to
something of ultimate meaning beyond man. We should not be
misled by the frequent assertions that a valid philosophy or theology
of God must today be cast in terms of a philosophical or theological
anthropology, that we must know man before we can know God.
Even this strategy, imposed in part by a secular consciousness which
seems to know only man, is meant eventually to find a way beyond
man.

. . . An outsider might, indeed, see radical theology as the choice of
that battle plan which gives up all such outer defense perimeters as

institutional religion, Hellenic concepts, feelings of dependence and finiteness, and political privilege in order better to defend the last stronghold. To extend the image, the real struggle between the conservative and the radical is whether religion can afford to raze the perimeter defenses; this is a question of tactics. On the central question of the ultimate validity of the religious quest there is no dispute at all, even though different ways of talking and acting may make it appear so. However shocking the language, the proposals, and the attacks of "radical" theology, they all rest on a very traditional premise: that the religious quest has a permanent human validity and will not be in vain.[22]

We have included this long quotation not only because it gives a valid observation about the seeming affirmation that both God and religion have expired, but it mentions names that the average reader will come across in the course of any discussion concerning religion in the modern world. Indeed, it may be pertinent to point out Brian Wicker's observation that there is no such animal as the truly modern secularized man but that he exists, rather, in the minds of such radical theologians themselves.[23]

In this section of many quotations—set forth to give the reader representative professional opinions about modern religion—we should end with one more by famed theologian Bernard Lonergan who is never easy reading, but his words bear thoughtful meditation:

It is a question that will be manifested differently in the different stages (this quest for a world view of reality or religion) of man's historical development and in the many varieties of his culture. But such differences of manifestation and expression are secondary. They may introduce alien elements that overlay, obscure, distort the pure question, the question that questions questioning itself. Nonetheless, the obscurity and the distortion *presuppose what they obscure and distort.* It follows that, however much religious or irreligious answers differ, however much . . . differ the questions they explicitly raise, still at their root there is the same transcendental tendency of the human spirit that questions, that questions without restriction, that questions the significance of its own questioning, and so comes to the question of God (italics added).[24]

So, in spite of the acknowledged vast amount of secularization, in spite of the surveys, modern man seems to be set on a religious quest even when he does not know it. Religion in the sense we have given it: a seeking for meaning, a set of symbols to interpret the world with a view to transcendence, this religion seems to be as much alive as ever. What gives the impression that religion is dying is the breakdown of the traditional forms of religion. We have implied more than once that the churchy institutions are in disarray. No one knows better than Catholics the breakdown in institutional religion for we have witnessed many changes and re-routings of traditional forms of piety and expressions. Even church-going, long a stronghold indicator of Catholic piety and strength, has eroded. A survey by the authors of the National Opinion Research Center on mass attendance, Greeley and McCready, lament the drastic and "catastrophic" drop in church attendance. They say: "It is well worth emphasizing at the beginning that the authors of this commentary are not pleased with what they have to report. On the contrary they present these findings with the greatest reluctance. . . . What is happening in the American Catholic population? Have the dramatic changes of the Vatican Council weakened the faith of the Catholic people? Have they simply decided that it is no longer a mortal sin to miss mass on Sunday? Have they been turned off by bad sermons? Do they find the new liturgy senseless? Are they angry at *Humanae Vitae?*"25 Whatever the causes, institutional religion is floundering. But not religion. And since the quest is real the churches at least have that in their favor. Now they are at the crossroads of crisis: whether to retreat into the past or to try to make the eternal truths more translatable to the modern secularized consciousness. Belief is positioned in the very heart of man, but to flourish it must have a credible and supportive community of believers; it must have a credible church preaching a credible God.

NOTES FOR CHAPTER 2

1. F. J. Sheed, *Theology and Sanity* (Sheed and Ward, 1946) pp. 33 and 34.
2. C. S. Lewis, *Christian Behavior* (Macmillan, 1943) pp. 56 and 57.
3. Edmond Barbotin, *Faith for Today* (Orbis Books, 1974) pp. 7 and 8.
4. John B. Cobb, Jr., "The World and God" in *Process Theology,* edited by Ewert H. Cousins (Newman Press, 1971) p. 168.
5. "The Politics of Genetic Engineering: Who Decides Who's Defective?" in *Psychology Today,* June, 1974.
6. Walter Kasper, "How Can We Experience God Today?" in *Theology Digest,* Summer, 1970.
7. John Macquarrie, *Principles of Christian Theology* (Charles Scribner's Sons, 1966) p. 72.
8. Eugene Kennedy, *Believing* (Doubleday, 1974) p. 37.
9. Juan Arias, *The God I Don't Believe In* (Abbey Press, 1973) p. 16.
10. Aidan Kavanagh, in *The Roots of Ritual,* edited by James D. Shaughnessy (Eerdmans, 1973) p. 146. See also the article, "Coming Apart at the Seams" in *Psychology Today,* February, 1975 in which economic historian Robert Heilbroner shares the same view. He comments: "After you've made some money and acquired some things, and after the initial excitement has passed, life goes on, just as bewildering as it always was, and the great problems of life and death once again come to the fore. We reemerge from our love affair with goods and know that consumption isn't the answer, and we ask ourselves what is. . . . In the end, our whole industrial way of life may have to give way to a new organization of society with less stress on technology, production consumption, and more on tradition, ritual, religion." See also Heilbroner's book, *An Inquiry Into The Human Prospect* (Norton, 1974).
11. Quoted by Juan Luis Segundo in *Our Idea of God* (Orbis Books, 1974) p. 127.
12. Robert Bellah, in *Culture of Unbelief,* edited by Rocco Caporale and Antonio Grumelli (University of California Press, 1971) pp. 79 and 281.
13. Langdon Gilkey, quoted in *Unsecular Man* by Andrew Greeley (Schocken Books, 1972) p. 79.
14. *Culture of Unbelief,* cited above, p. 92.
15. *New York Times,* April 15, 1974.

16. *Newsweek,* February 11, 1974.
17. Eugene Kennedy, cited above, p. 29. See also Peter Berger's article, "The Devil and the Pornography of Modern Consciousness" in *Worldview,* November, 1974 where he comments that the present day interest in satanism and the occult is in direct proportion to secular society's official suppression of the transcendent. "The current occult wave (including its devil component) is to be understood as resulting from the repression of transcendence in modern consciousness. This repression is socially and culturally institutionalized—in the schools, the communications media, even in the language of everyday life (in which, for example, curses have become domesticated as merely emotional expletives). In other words, it is institutionalized secularity that is playing the role of censor. If this is so, however, we can learn a useful lesson from Freud: Repressed contents have a way of coming back, often in rather bizarre forms."
18. *New York Times,* November 12, 1973.
19. *Newsweek,* October 8, 1973.
20. Martin Marty, "The Persistence of the Mystical" in *Concilium* 81 (Seabury Press, 1973) p. 38.
21. *Saturday Review/World,* November 20, 1973, p. 59.
22. Daniel Callahan, "God and Psychological Man" in *Religion and Contemporary Thought,* edited by George F. McLean (Alba House, 1973) pp. 124 and 125.
23. *Roots of Ritual,* cited above, p. 22.
24. Quoted in *The New Agenda,* Andrew Greeley (Doubleday, 1973) p. 59.
25. *National Catholic Reporter,* November 16, 1973.

3. Positioning God

A credible God. In the last chapter we saw that if modern man does not seek God in the old institutions or finds him irrelevant to his daily life, it is because he cannot relate God to his everyday experience. Deep down, modern man feels, God does not really care about him. And the reason for this? Because God is so remote; because he is traditionally understood as some static deity very far away up there somewhere. In turn this notion of a remote God is positioned in our inherited concepts of him as perfect. If he is perfect that means he is unchangeable, immutable, omnipotent, omnipresent, fulfilled, complete, immobile. This concept of God as a remote unchanging deity raised no major problems in past times when the world was conceived in like manner. The world was the world of Isaac Newton, which is to say, a world of fixed, immutable laws. Our planet was seen to be a vast complex machine, prewound and sliding into position, as it were, according to very fixed and discoverable laws of nature. An immobile God for a clockwork world was compatible enough.

There were unspoken problems about this view of God and world. As far as God goes, to call him perfect meant that no one or no thing could add any more to him or detract from him. Neither could anyone or anything make him any happier than he was once and for all. Our catechisms took note of this when it asked, if God were perfectly happy why did he create? The answer was that that is the way goodness is. It is diffusive of itself; it just naturally spills over. This answer was not really satisfying because it still left us with an image of a distant reservoir of goodness that overflowed slightly but which somehow left the main Source undisturbed. The

36

inference was that if perfection meant the full once-and-for-all plentitude of everything imaginable whatever, then the whole human enterprise is not really serious in reference to God. The human enterprise was a kind of playacting because in the last analysis, God could not and would not be affected by it all anyway. And his heaven? Was that like God too? Was it a place of total fulfillment, fullness and completion? With all of life's absurdities, maybe its adventures and passions were preferable to another, newer static existence in heaven where we were sure we would get bored after a few eons. We could make our own Hamlet's words:

> . . . who would fardels bear,
> To grunt and sweat under a weary life,
> But that the dread of something after death,
> The undiscover'd country from whose bourn
> No traveller returns, puzzles the will
> And make us rather bear those ills we have
> Than to fly to others that we know not of?[1]

That "dread of something after death" might not be hell, but heaven, if heaven is the place of passive perfection!

There is something of a caricature here, but there is much truth also. We had correctives to this image of God, of course, correctives in scripture itself. There he is spoken of as jealous and passionate and with moods; but, we were taught, this was human talk about God. He *really* was not like that. So philosophy once more overcame revelation. Then came the revolution. The revolution was the revolution of science and of all the things in science nothing so profoundly disturbed the current religious concepts of everything whatever as did evolution. Here was a world made up of evolving species. Further investigation in other fields unfolded also a world in constant flux. Beneath what looked like solid substance, everything was fluid movement. In fact when we finally came to the realization that there were moving atoms in everything, we also discovered that in turn there were subatomic particles and all were in a constant flux and in a constant network of relations. From gigantic galaxies to invisible protons and neutrons nothing is still.

We might even say that the old concept of substance is passe. Maybe the ultimate reality is not an objective substrata; maybe it is energy. In any case, we have today a whole new vision of the world. It is not Newton's prefabricated planet of fixed rules; it is a huge energy unfolding by virtue of its own evolutionary dynamic with a history before it and a history to come. It is in process in every part, great and small. So are we since we are a part of nature.

> We have set aside the Greek philosophers' notions of the universe. Copernicus and Galileo removed the earth from the center. Kepler discovered that the motion of the celestial bodies is elliptical and not perfectly circular. Newton's insights regarding gravity and the tendency of bodies in motion to stay in motion eliminated the need for Aristotle's First Mover who, as a Final Cause, effected the circular motion of the intelligent outermost sphere. Darwin's theory of evolution established the idea that the world is not static but enjoys a process of growth into greater perfection. After Einstein the ultimate foundation of physical reality is seen to involve relationships. Because the very worldviews which originally excluded any possible relationship with God have all but disappeared, some new options are possible in talking about God.[2]

And we moderns are seeking and finding new options because when we see the world running on its own inner dynamic we are apt to be less tolerant of the notion of a perfect deity up there somewhere. More than ever we want to know what such an immutable deity can have in common with such movement, such evolution, such action? He must view it much as we might watch the movements of an ant. But to be personally involved, to be concerned, to really *feel* for it—are such things possible? It is in the tension of this dilemma that new views of God are being taken. The predominant one today is to say that, as a matter of fact, we have to see God in a different way; we have to see him also in process; we have to challenge our view of perfection.

The notion of God as perfect, impassible, unmoved and unmovable is something we have inherited from the Greek philosophers by way of Greek influenced Christian writers. Plato and Aristotle held the concept of the Unmoved Mover. In fact, Aristotle in his work, *Magna Moralis,* takes his view of the unchanging deity to its logical conclusion. He says that God is so unchangeable that he cannot love us and we cannot in any way love him for that would involve movement. "God cannot even have any object of thought outside himself, for that would mean that he has an end outside himself. God, therefore, only knows himself."

The early Church Fathers accepted these notions part and parcel. Yet it is equally obvious that they were always struggling with the tensions, never satisfactorily resolved, between their philosophical, unchanging God and the biblical, passionate God. This is true from Justin Martyr of the second century to St. Anselm of the twelfth century who after a thousand years was still wondering aloud, "But how are you at once both merciful [which implies a change of heart, movement] and impassible?"[3] To them, the Greek philosophers and the early Church Fathers alike, God had to be perfect because their outlook taught them that any change is a sign of weakness. One only changed to remedy some prior defect. Obviously this cannot be so with God.

But, on reflection, there is nothing to indicate that change *as such* implies weakness. Perfection need not exclude change. Maybe one cannot be surpassed by another for this would imply lack; but how about surpassing oneself? What would seem to be more "perfect": an already complete and static being or one who can constantly grow and become? Perfection does not exclude movement. Our biggest problem is that we have all of that Greek philosophical baggage which makes us forget that "Many if not all the so-called metaphysical attributes of God—infinity, omnipotence, omniscience, omnipresence, and the like—are negative statements; they serve primarily as refusal to limit God to the specifically human or creaturely categories of finitude, of reduced capacity to act, or inadequacy in knowledge or wisdom and of confinement to specific temporal or spatial conditions. What they have to say positively is another matter."[4]

Now if God really can move and grow and change, then he is indeed more compatible with this world of ours; he has a definite affinity to it. For if this world has been found to be a world of change and dynamism, then it is not unlikely that its maker has these same characteristics, that he too is dynamic, living and related. "The concept of God is not the Greek unmoved Mover or changeless essence, but rather of a living, active, constantly creative, infinitely related, ceaselessly operative Reality; the universe at its core is movement, dynamism, activity, and not sheer and unrelated abstraction . . . the only reasonable explanation of the living cosmos is in fact 'the living God.' "[5] This whole concept of a changing, moving God is called process theology and the following quotation sums up its whole insight beautifully:

> Process thought is the name usually given to that view of the world which takes with utmost seriousness the dynamic, living, evolutionary quality of our existence and of the world in which we live. Ours is not a world of unchanging substances, of fixed entities, of permanently located "nows" and "thens"; it is a world in change, in which we have to do not so much with being as with becoming and in which we find ourselves caught up in processive movements rather than imprisoned in fixed habitations. From its lowest components—societal energies at the subatomic level—up to the highest grades known to us, we see this same energizing, dynamic quality. . . . The principle of explanation of such a world must in some genuine fashion be *like* that world. . . . God cannot, in such a world, be the exception to the metaphysical principles required to understand the world, but must be the chief exemplification of those principles. God is living, dynamic, energizing. He is also *related*. The perfection which can be claimed for him is not that proper to some unmoved or absolute essence; it is the perfection of his own identity as being himself, but that perfection subsists in his identity in and with relationships. He is the One who is sufficient to remain himself even while he constantly surpasses himself in his expression and activity. What happens in the world contributes to his satisfaction, enriches his possibilities in further self-expression, and provides ever new opportunities for his loving care.[6]

There are several conclusions we might draw at this point. First of all, when different theologians say that God is change and movement, this does not imply that he is all change. It means that such theologians make a distinction between God in his inner essence and in his relation to the world. There is a sense in which God does not change. He has an unchanging primordial nature (Whitehead), an absolute identity of character (Hartshore); he is the one alone who is sufficient to remain himself while he continually surpasses himself in his expression and activity (Pittinger). But beyond this primordial essence, God is change; in his relation to the world he is movement and energy. He changes in so far as he grasps or takes hold of this world. That is, in an incarnational way he is related to this world on its own terms (as later he would focalize this relationship in Jesus). But the world's terms are evolution, process, change, growth, movement. God is in the same state. He too is in process. He both participates in and reveals himself as movement and change. "God has an abstract, absolute aspect and a surpassing creativity."[7]

Secondly, this notion of God is far more in accord with the bible and does tend to free us from the old Greek philosophy categories. Consider, for example, Greek philosophy and the bible:[8]

Greek philosophy	Bible
No one and no thing can add anything to the Infinite Being	"Here I stand knocking at the door. If any hears my voice and opens the door, I will come in, and sit down to supper with him and he with me." (Rev 3:20)
The supreme will repose in its infinity	"My Father has never ceased his work and I am working too." (Jn 5:7)
Every created value remains extrinsic to God	"Father, I desire that these men who are thy gift to me, may be with me where I am." (Jn 17:24)

So God comes across differently in scripture. He is a God of movement, passion, adventure. He has entered this world on its own terms. We can, it seems, speak of him from our perspective as quite changeable, involved, caring. We can also say of him that he too moves with this world. Immanent to its history he can evolve with the world. He does not alter his transcendent Self, but he approaches us in the manner of this world's process:

> In his acceptance of man and his world God remains himself, the only basis and reason for the diversity from himself, differentiating himself from the non-divine other is his radical transcendence as its creator. Thus God's descent into the world does not compromise his transcendence; . . . the first effect of the incarnation is not a divinization of the world, but instead the clearest demarcation of the world in its secular otherness from the divine in its proper integrity. . . .[9]

This quotation mentions the incarnation. It is here, of course, most explicitly that God accepts process, growth, maturity, movement. "Philip, he who sees me has seen the Father" (Jn 14:9). And what people saw was a human being from birth to the grave, growing in wisdom, age and grace. Again, just as God became "moveably" incarnate in Jesus, so he grasps the world in the same mode: on its own evolutionary terms and to this extent he moves, grows and matures with it. We do not have a God therefore whose enduring and unchangeable identity has entered this world. Rather he is always related to it in terms of this world's movement, passion, growth and love, always in process and therefore always changing his appearance, as it were, to unfold with the world and to keep up with our own growing consciousness. In that sense God does change.

Thirdly, by accepting a "process" God we do not have to be embarrassed over prayer, for example. If God were really the immutable God of the Greeks, would our prayers mean anything? Can one move by prayer the Immovable? If God is so perfect then our prayers cannot pretend to inform him of what he obviously already knows. And, surely, our prayers could not dare to change the mind of the Unchangeable. Some have tried to get around this dilemma by pointing out that prayer is designed, not to change God, but to change ourselves:

> But if God is so good as you represent him, and if he knows all that we need, and better far than we do ourselves, why should it be necessary to ask him for anything? I answer, What if he knows prayer to be the thing we need first and most?[10]

There is some merit in this, but still this does not do justice to prayer itself and the many times we are urged to pray in scripture. On the other hand, if God is changeable, then he is really affected by what we do and we get a new sense of not only being heard by God but that what we do and what we are—and indeed, our whole lives— are really significant. Perhaps the holy minister who wrote the above quote was right when he wrote in another place more than a hundred years ago:

> What stupidity of perfection would that be which left no margin about God's work, no room for change of place upon change of fact —yea, even the mighty change that . . . now at length his child is praying! . . . I may move my arm as I please: shall God be unable so to move his?[11]

In passing, we might mention that the inability of the Greek philosophers and theologians to move God from the position of immutability caused them, quite logically, to stumble over the Trinity and the incarnation. These mysteries were compounded because these men felt that an immutable, impassible God could not move into another existence, much less really suffer and die. It was not without reason therefore that some held that Christ was not really God, but only an aspect of that immutable deity (modalism) or Christ was inferior to God (subordinationism) or one who was given a mandate too and made special by God (adoptionism). And all because God was forever himself which was interpreted as forever complete, perfect, and therefore incapable of change. Modern theologian Karl Rahner sees the problem but insists, "the acknowledgement of the unchanging and unchangeable God in his eternally perfect fullness is not merely a postulate of philosophy, it is also a dogma of faith. . . . Nonetheless, it remains true the Word *became* flesh."[12]

Finally it is worth pausing to note that our tendency to "freeze" God into some static, immovable mold has been transferred to Jesus. At one point Jesus' role came to be that of mediator between sinful man and the Father. This certainly was true, but the notion subtly grew that Jesus was the mediator between sinful man and a *wrath-*

ful Father. Jesus became "popular" precisely because he was a counterpoint to the stern deity who must be appeased. We could feel comfortable with Jesus. He was one of us and we were glad to have him to buffer the Father's anger. This of course was not only poor theology but bordered on blasphemy. From the beginning the Father is the Father of mercy and love and from the beginning Jesus *is* the visible love of the Father for his people. Jesus is the Father's "motion" of love; he is in Jesus loving us. In any case, people forgot that as Greek philosophy distanced the Father. But then a certain irony came in. As time went on Jesus' divinity became so emphasized that he too went the way of static perfection. He too became remote, powerful, fearsome, the *Pantocrator*. Having effectively removed Jesus from the human scene, having distanced him, what was left? Why, of course, the Blessed Mother. Remember all those cute stories about people being rejected at heaven's gate by Jesus only to sneak around to the back door to be let in by his more compassionate and kindly mother? We had reduced this Great Lover who became obedient unto death for our sakes to little more than a visible tyrant. We have reduced Mary to an appealing beggar unlocking the hard heart of Jesus. It is possible someday so to elevate Mary that we will need another saint to open her heart! The God of the bible was overcome by the static, remote deity of philosophy. If a "process" God can rescue us from that it will have performed valuable service to Christian revelation. It will remind us that "if anything is immutable in God it is the completeness of his love for us, which must include responses to our everchanging needs."[13]

— 2 —

If we see God as immanent in the world, as related intrinsically and dynamically to it, then we can take a second look at this world itself. We might recall that the medieval vision of the world was that it was parceled off into two spheres, the sacred and the profane, each impinging on the other. At times the sacred was quite evident in what were called sacred places, objects and persons. This was legitimate enough as long as such places, objects and persons were but indications of the sacred already existing in every part of the world. But a deviation set in. These sacred places, objects and persons slipped over into privilege and privilege slipped into idolatry and idolatry slipped into such self-justification that radical discrimination set in. That is, sharp division was made between the sacred and the profane as if God were not related to all the world, as if all the world did not manifest his glory. Soon the profane, the "worldly" became distanced and was the province of the many and the sacred was honored and became the province of the gnostic few. In other words, what happened was that a false distinction was made between the sacred and profane and this had far reaching consequences.

Actually, this did represent a deviation for both Old and New Testaments went to great pains to undo any false split between God and his world, between the sacred and the profane. Yes, the Hebrews did have sacred places but they were not to confuse them with the acquisition of automatic holiness. The only real holiness, said the prophets, is God's holiness and the only real profanation is not attesting to God's holiness. In the New Testament, Jesus made it clear that one is truly sacred not because he goes to a sacred place or is a sacred person but because he remains in love. This is the force of his parable of the Good Samaritan. The "sacred" priest and levite were in reality profane while the "profane" Samaritan was in reality sacred. Real sacredness cannot be separated from goodness, justice and truth. That is why Jesus told the woman at Jacob's well that all true believers will worship God neither there on Mt. Gerizim (an old sacred place, as many mountains were: they were "close" to heaven) nor even in the Temple in Jerusalem (a remarkable statement from a Jew!) but "in spirit and in truth." Later on, Saints Peter and Paul would insist that there is no longer a specific holy nation or people but rather all who are gathered in Christ's love and truth constitute "a chosen race, a royal priesthood, a dedicated nation. . . ."

Once more, this is not to mean that the early Christians did not have their sacred moments such as at the eucharist. The sacred was not an indifferent matter. It meant that the sacred was only such to the extent that it promoted the holiness that was in all the world; that it pointed up the presence of the transcendent God in all creation. The Christian concept of the sacred meant that especially since the incarnation all created matter was God-infested and therefore holy. The so-called sacred person, place and object that symbolized this reality were genuine and authentic. On the other hand, according to the Christian concept, any so-called sacred person, place or object that totally detached itself from the rest of the world and lost reference to it became an idol.

In spite of this biblical emphasis, this uniting of the sacred and profane, a division between them appeared in Christianity. It came in with the emperor Constantine in the fourth century. He, the liberator of the Church, brought his high titles of emperor and his trappings of office and his semidivinity status. Soon the newly liberated Church began to adopt such titles and concepts. Special offices, personal titles and grand churches began to appear. It was not too long after that the privileged clergy arose and the distinction between the clergy and laity was heightened by the introduction of distinctive dress, altar rails and holy roods. When the barbarians invaded Europe and the Church they brought in their world of demons. The later Middle Ages brought in specially distinct religious habits, indulgences and a host of sacred objects detached from the whole pattern of religion. Even though the Protestant Reformation of the sixteenth century essentially reacted against this complex sacralistic system it failed to go far enough and was itself saddled with a sacralistic atmosphere as is evident in its preoccupations with demonology, witchcraft and superstitious beliefs.

What we are saying is that even in Christianity, in spite of the Founder's distinct teaching and intent, the old split between the sacred and the profane came back and the static perfect God of distant Mt. Olympus was in vogue again. It was hard to escape the impression that the world was evil (as it was often preached by Catholics and Protestants alike) and that salvation lay only in certain sacred places (monasteries, convents: it is not without reason that most of the canonized saints are monks or nuns—or widows who have been liberated from fleshly marriage). The world as the place of the powers of evil rather than as incarnate by God himself became the theme. In this atmosphere the Church tended to pull back from the world, to disassociate itself from it, perhaps even to despise it. Holiness was confined to certain precise formularies and attached to certain precise places and persons. For the average citizen who lived, worked and recreated nine-tenths of his life "in the world," salvation prospects were dim indeed. As for the arts, sciences and politics, these were better left to the pagans to soil their hands with. However, a few of the disciplined faithful who periodically got away from the world in retreats and Sunday Masses might survive the wrath that was to come.

This of course is an exaggeration, but it serves to show the results of keeping a Greek God in his heaven and failing to see him as essentially immanent in the world itself. In the first chapter we spoke of the decline of formal religion. Now we can say that, in one sense, this has not been altogether disastrous. For such a decline has promoted secularization (along with, granted, the danger of secularism, the total divorce of religion from the world). Secularization detaches religion from public life and attempts to keep it confined in a small private corner. But religion, with its new concept of an immanent, process and incarnate God, can refuse now to be so compressed. Religion can break away from its "sacred" places and announce once more that the world is its domain. Religion can emerge from its self-imposed ghetto of sacred playthings. Secularization, by trying to push religion into a corner, can actually make religion free to reclaim the world. Religion can now have a new awareness that the truly worldly men of today "are not about to be misled into thinking that the true sanctification of the world can be realized by blessings and exorcisms; they are convinced that Christians will be saved by the testimony of justice and service to the needy. The true holiness of the world depends on the generous and disinterested commitment of believers for an authentic brotherhood among all men, a fraternal unity inspired by faith. . . . Today we have a pressing need to renew the expressions and forms of Christian worship in such a way that they are true testimonies of a living faith, one which tends to build up a brotherly world. . . . The encounter of religion and life can no longer be entrusted predominately to blessings and to propitiatory processions. . . . The conceptualizations of the *sacred* and *profane* inherited from antiquity and medieval times should be overcome in a loyal encounter of faith with the world of today in keeping with the spirit of *Gaudium et Spes*. . . ."[14]

So we are no longer (if we ever did) to look upon the world as evil or a place tolerated until we reach our real home. Rather we can discover that immanent God in the progress of this world, in our neighbor, in any activity that makes the world more true to itself. To bring the world to goodness and to draw it out is the Christian vocation. God is here, transcendent and immanent calling us ever onward. He is both our present and our future at the same time:

> From the beginning of the account of biblical revelation God has disclosed himself as the God of promise whose transcendence is not realized historically as the one who is timelessly above man, but as the one who is ahead of man, his absolute future. Thus, instead of being the alienating source of man's escape from his historical task, he liberates man for historical initiative. He calls man beyond himself and what are his possibilities at any historical moment into a future which can constitute for man the "Novum," the utterly new, that which is truly "not yet."[15]

Or, as St. Paul puts it, "for though everything belongs to you— Paul, Apollos, and Cephas, the world, life, and death, the present and the future, all of them belong to you—yet you belong to Christ, and Christ to God" (1 Cor 3:22ff).

So secularization has obliged believers to face the fact that religion is not to be confined to a little world of "sacred" objects and places; that religion can no longer be detached from a living faith that is coextensive with the world. Secularization can prevent us from evolving a ritual so esoteric that no one but a few initiates can know what it means; from erecting churches so portioned off from the world that only the "caste" priests may enter to pray; from a spirituality so monastic and apart that modern man can neither understand nor translate it into his daily life; from making God such a maneuverable object that we think we can capture him in a rite or formula or dogma; from making grace so quantitative that only sacramental manipulators can have access to it; from making the sacraments so defined that we prevent the Spirit from breathing where he will; and, finally, from holding to a religious rationalism so pervasive that he who recites the propositions of the creed by heart thinks he is a believer.

— 3 —

When we speak of God as not static but moving, entering and being a part of human history , we must go further and speak of him in terms of Trinity for the very notion of Trinity implies process and relation. But we must admit that the Trinity has always been something of a puzzle to us, that great mystery which we accept but can make no sense of, no place for it in our daily lives. The creed formulated at Nicaea in the fourth century says:

> This is the Catholic faith: to venerate one God in Trinity, and Trinity in Unity; not confusing the Persons, not dividing Essence. The Persons of the Father, Son and Holy Spirit are all distinct. But the Father, Son and Holy Spirit have all one and the same Godhead. . . .

A thousand years later the Council of Florence (1438) added its refinements:

> The Holy Spirit is eternally from the Father and the Son, and has his essence and subsistent being both from the Father and the Son and he proceeds from each of them eternally as from a single source and by a single act of breathing.

We give assent, but what does it all mean? Is it all a bad arithmetic problem or just a beautiful metaphor about God? What do we understand by person and nature and essence and being? It may help us not feel so guilty about our lack of good feeling about these terms if we realize that they are latecomers, the products of Greek thinking in the third and fourth centuries. The early church just did not speculate about the Trinity and in fact did not even use the term.[16] The scriptures, of course, are full of references to Father, Son and Spirit and the writers took them for granted. The first Christians knew that their Christian lives were related to the three, used their names in their baptismal formulas and dipped their converts three times into the water. So the Trinity was at the heart of their lives; they just did not speculate about it. They knew that God was involved in their history as Father, Son and Holy Spirit but did not define anything. This was left, as we indicated, to Greek philosophy. This was a necessity. After all, the gospel was being preached to the cultured Greeks and unless some precision came in about a Triune God, the gospel would be laughed off the scene, or at least grossly misunderstood. So men like Tertullian came up with precision terms such as person and nature and the formulas arrived at in Nicaea were genuine developments of revelation, logically derived from scripture.

Yet, as so often happens, the terms, clear and precise for one era, are difficult and obscure for another. As times have gone on we have lost the underpinnings for such terms. Outlook has changed, philosophical concepts have changed. So now the Trinity no longer means much to us except as a symbol of the most intricate of mysteries. Perhaps it is time to go back to scripture and the unspeculative feelings of the first Christians to position the Trinity aright.

The first thing to note is that our knowledge of the Trinity is a *revealed* one. It is obviously only in the context of Jesus that we can know about the Trinity. The knowledge comes to us at a distinct period of time. Without Jesus we know nothing of the Trinity. Secondly, what we do know from Jesus about the Trinity is that, whatever it is, it is constituted in *relationship*. That is to say, the revelation of the Trinity comes to us as an ongoing movement (process) of God with the Father (no inequality implied) eternally initiating his self-donation in the Son under the power of the Spirit. From Jesus we learn that it was the Father who sent the Son to seek and save what was lost and it was the Son who with the Father sends the Spirit so that we can cry out to the Father. This means that Jesus has revealed that the 'Trinity is a personal communication of a relationship which has entered into our history. Jesus himself is constituted by that relationship to the Father: "I always do the will of my Father in heaven." He is the revelation of the Father and together they send the Spirit. "No one knows the Father except the Son and him to whom the Son wished to reveal him." It is all of a piece, this Trinity: a concerted relationship, one loving source of revelation. That is why the first Christians never speculated on what distinguished the three persons (as the later Greeks did) but rather what united them. Yet, again, the three persons are distinct. Jesus had to struggle to bring his will in alignment with that of his Father in the Garden of Olives. And he did speak of sending *another* Advocate, the Holy Spirit. So there is distinction there, yet a unity of love.

In line with what we have written above, however, it shows us a deity who is community, a deity who is Father, Son and Spirit working in unison to reveal their nature of Love. "The unity or oneness of God is not the first thing, from which we go on to explore how three could spring there. The Christian message shows us *three, loving each other in such a way that they constitute *one. . . .*"[17] So the Trinity comes across as a community, a process, of love, as a mysterious unity and plurality with love on its mind. It is God who indeed is Father but one who is always approached through the Son under the inspiration of the Spirit.

The Father comes to us through his Son. This is a profound thought, full of meaning for us. It means that the Father is in Jesus and in Jesus we have seen his glory (Jn 1:14). But we must remember what we saw Jesus doing. He washed his disciples' feet, a great and distinct act of humble love. The Father is that. The Father is glory in precisely the way we see Jesus act and the way we see him surrender himself for us out of love. Jesus is the Father's "movement" of love towards us. When we see this we can abandon forever (as we have seen) any notion of a Jesus trying to ward off the anger of a wrathful deity, interceding for us to the Father in the sense that he will be only appeased by some blood sacrifice of his

Son. No, the Father loves us and it is precisely because of that love that he is in Jesus and that Jesus is his revelation of love. The Trinity represents a great movement of reaching out to us, a certain "flow" whereby the Father comes to us in Jesus under the impulse of the Spirit. This means that we approach the Father through Jesus. He is the Lover, the Object, the Goal and we reach him by way of Jesus because the Spirit leads us to do so. All spirituality is trinitarian. All approaches to God are trinitarian for the believer.

> For the Son is only Son by reference to the Father whom he manifests and whose name we can utter only because the Spirit has been sent into our hearts. After a while—it may be a long while if we are not brought up in a trinitarian devotion—we will automatically think of the Father when "God" is mentioned, and approach him through his beloved Son whose prayer is always heard for his reverence and in the power of the indwelling Spirit.[18]

Because of this movement to the Father through the Son the early liturgies show that Christian worship is not Jesus-worship, but the worship of the Father through the Son in the power of the Spirit.[19] So we modern Christians can do the same. We can approach God in a trinitarian way. We know that God has come to us in the process of a mediated relationship. And he comes out of love, not as a new love but the old love that beckoned every man who ever walked the planet, an old love now made new and concretized in Jesus Christ. We believers must therefore continue to follow the ancient practice of ending our official prayers "through Jesus Christ our Lord."

Moreover, in saying that God is in Jesus and that the Three Persons are in one divine nature is affirming the fact that Jesus' humanity is God's. This in turn means most profoundly that God has definitely entered into human history. This means, we repeat, that we are summoned not to some distant heaven hereafter and that we should just wait around and be pious until it comes. No, it means that here and now, in the human enterprise, in the human condition, in this human world, salvation is to be found. This history is our history, is his history. This planet is our planet, is his planet. The formulas that sound so quaint to us are desperately trying to preserve a vision of an incarnate world, not a world as a mere and barely tolerable antechamber to heaven. To have it otherwise is to put the static God back into his heaven (safely tucked away) occasionally to reach out by some miraculous intervention into the affairs of men. Worse, it sets up the possibility of a whole system of delegation whereby ecclesiastical or political figures speak for God. From there it is but a short step to identify their causes with his.

After we have pointed all this out we must confess that we can say no more. Whether we can work backwards from the notion of a triune relationship to conclude anything about the inner life of God himself in necessary terms of first, second and third Persons is problematical. We can only speculate and say that there must no doubt be some "structure" of a possibility which would correspond to Father, Son and Spirit which we have come to know from Jesus. Whether we can conclude that *therefore* this must be expressed in the terms of three persons in one divine nature seems to go beyond our logic, competence and understanding.

> There must be correspondence between God as we know him and God as he is, otherwise we would be hopelessly deluded, but to name this correspondence clearly and definitively is beyond the ability of man and his thought. . . . The Trinity is real to us not in terms of first, second and third person, but as Father, Son and Spirit present to us in the Christian experience. To try to delineate more precisely the inner nature of God by prescinding from his revelation as Father, Son and Spirit can only cause confusion.[20]

This makes sense. "Who can know the mind of God?" asks the prophet and we still make the observation. We must not push the Trinity too far and make the mystery less than it says. Even when we discuss the formulas of the councils we're still confronted by mystery. It might be well to remember that our belief in and dedication to the Trinity are precisely that of the Father, Son and Spirit of scripture and that whatever thoughts we have about it, whatever devotion to it, such thoughts and devotions must always be seen in terms of the Jesus who revealed the relationships.

To summarize: we approach God in a trinitarian way: through Jesus under the power of the Spirit. When we pray we pray to the Father, remembering that the Father is in Jesus and "He who sees me, sees the Father." We get into the "movement" of prayer and approach if we enter into Christ's life and style and imitate his prayer. Through and *with* him we pray at our liturgies because the Spirit has led us there. It is a matter of an attitude for us, of entering into the relationship when we pray and sing and live. It is a matter of not stopping at Christ, but going through him to the Father. After all, Jesus came to bring us not salvation but the revelation of the Father's love. The Father's will was his food and drink. The Father is all. But we can only come to him through the Son in the power of the Spirit. So again, it is a matter of attitude, of "rhythm" if you will. Once we get this attitude then we can let go of the embarrassing arithmetic problem of the Trinity and enter into it as did the early Christians.

Other people do not know this mediated relationship of the Godhead. God still reveals himself to them and summons them. But we have been given this revelation, not as a privilege but as a challenge. If God has been revealed to us as a mediated relationship it is only that we might know more forcefully than others that God is love.

NOTES FOR CHAPTER 3

1. Act III, Scene I.

2. Bernard P. Prusak, "Changing Concepts of God" in *Does Jesus Make a Difference?*, edited by Thomas M. McFadden (Seabury Press, 1974) p. 69.

3. Bernard P. Prusak, p. 67.

4. W. Norman Pittenger, "Process Thought: A Contemporary Trend in Theology" in *Process Theology*, edited by Ewert H. Cousins (Newman, 1971) p. 27.

5. W. Norman Pittenger, p. 26.

6. W. Norman Pittenger, "Meland, Process Thought and Significance of Christ" in *Process Theology*, cited above, pp. 205 and 206.

7. W. Norman Pittenger, cited above, p. 14.

8. Juan Luis Segundo, *Our Idea of God* (Orbis Books, 1974) p. 104.

9. Francis M. Tyrrell, *Man: Believer and Unbeliever* (Alba House, 1974) p. 36.

10. C. S. Lewis, *George MacDonald, An Anthology* (Doubleday, Dolphin Books, 1962) p. 65.

11. C. S. Lewis, p. 67.

12. Karl Rahner, *Theological Investigations*, Vol. IV (Helicon, 1966) p. 112.

13. Bernard P. Prusak, cited above, p. 74.

14. Bernard Häring, *Faith and Morality in the Secular Age* (Doubleday, 1973) chapter 3.

15. Francis M. Tyrrell, cited above, p. 315.

16. See *Christology of the Later Fathers*, edited by Edward R. Hardy (The Westminster Press, 1964). Remarks the author: "Clarity in general principles but uncertainty in details—such was the state of Christian thought on these important matters when the last great persecution suspended theological discussion" (p. 18);

"Though it may be held, I think, correctly, that the Nicene Creed presented the solid basis of the common faith, it introduced a sharpness of definition which was new, and in the process raised new and rather puzzling questions. If the Father and Son were clearly defined as of one substance, how were they distinct—and how, now that the point is raised, are we to think of the eternal Son as really 'made man' ? " (p. 21).

17. Juan Luis Segundo, cited above, p. 87.

18. Peter DeRosa, *Christ and Original Sin* (Bruce, 1967) p. 55.

19. Reginald Fuller, *The Foundations of New Testament Christology* (Charles Scribner's Sons, 1965) p. 158.

20. John F. O'Grady, *Jesus, Lord and Christ* (Paulist Press, 1972) p. 114.

4. Positioning Words

— 1 —

If we believe in God we instinctively believe that he has communicated with us; we believe that he has spoken. But of course if he has spoken and does speak to human beings, he must accommodate himself to our psychology, our understanding, our language if he is to be intelligible at all. It is with language, or better, with words in general and the sacred word of scripture in particular that this chapter is concerned. And its message is simple: there is more than one way to truth than logical speech. Truth is not tested by the intellect alone. Now to give a background to these assertions we must remind ourselves once more that we are the children of a scientific way of life; that the scientific mentality has dominated Western thinking for a long time. The result has been that we tend to see as truth only that which is literal, measurable, observable and objective. Our trouble comes when we apply this strictly to everyday life and especially to religion. If we make everything in religion—let us take the bible—objectively true and literal then we are bound to run into conflict. We all remember the Galileo case where the scientist said that the earth moves around the sun instead of vice versa. We also recall that the opposing churchmen said that this could not possibly be. To "prove" their point they opened to the bible where Joshua ordered the sun to stand still so that he could complete a battle. If Joshua ordered the sun to stand still, then it must have been moving. If it is moving, then it moves around a stationary earth.

Because these churchmen took the bible literally, and read as scientific words that were never meant to be so, the Galileo case became, in George Santayana's words, the first casualty of the scientific era. As other casualties mounted both sides became convinced of the stupidity and intransigence of the other. Church people tended to harden into fundamentalists and the opposing side tended to write off the bible as a collection of fairy tales, old legends and epics much like those to be found in any other nation's past. Belief eroded in proportion to the success of science in demolishing the (literal) bible and universal education spread the cleavage.

Since these nineteenth century battles, both sides (except for the diehards) have pulled back to admit a better perspective. For their part the bible proponents have finally accepted the undeniable demonstrations of science as to the age of the earth, the solar system's workings, and evolution. They have admitted to taking literally what was written in a style and manner that could only be called poetic. So the argument has been repositioned: the arguments, the discussions now revolve around words; they now revolve around the admitted premise that there is more than one way to truth besides a scientific proposition. Through modern studies it has dawned on many that there is more than one way to approach the real, more than one way of interpreting reality. As a matter of fact, it is not without irony that it was a scientist, not a clergyman, who brought this home. It was Freud who uncovered a whole powerful area of man's unconscious; that man is run by more than literal truths and that he expresses himself in many symbolic ways; that indeed literal words often hide subconscious meanings and interpretations. In brief, man is complex and so is his language. In this sense, man speaks science and he speaks poetry. His words have hidden meanings and layers of meaning. Truth is to be found in a careful understanding of what level people are speaking or writing. Truth is to be found in the intent and interpretation of the author. For example:

> A belief in witchcraft does not imply any abandonment of the rational process of thought. A person may accidentally be killed by a jaguar; he may succumb to a heart attack or tuberculosis. In a society in which witches are seen to be the causal agents of misfortune and death, people will acknowledge that the actual, efficient cause of death was the wounds dealt by the beast, or the stopping of a heart or the various organic traumas conditioned by

the disease. But why, they ask, did this particular man happen to encounter such a jaguar at that moment in time and space? Why did his heart stop now, rather than two years ago or ten seasons to come? The sufficient cause of death must be witchcraft. Our concept of "accident" or "luck" or "fate" is as irrational, in our sense, as a belief in witches; all such concepts explain the unforeseen, the random, or unpatterned by relating such incidents to a prior set of beliefs.[1]

Actually these concepts are not really foreign to us. We are quite at home with the interpretative language of secular literature, for example. We have always known the distinction between prose and poetry. Prose, we know, is the language of the journalist: it conveys objective, out-there facts without emotion or prejudice. Poetry, on the other hand, may convey the same truth, but colors it considerably; the poet himself makes no pretense to being objective for he in some way has been caught up in the reality. He describes it, but overtones it with much emotion, insight, and interpretation. Take, for example, Wordsworth's poem of his lady love:

> She was a Phantom of delight
> When first she gleamed upon my sight;
> A lovely Apparition, sent
> To be a moment's ornament;
> Her eyes as stars of Twilight fair;
> Like Twilight's, too, her dusky hair;
> But all things else about her drawn
> From May-time and the cheerful Dawn;
> A dancing Shape, and Image gay,
> To haunt, to startle, and waylay.

No one but the most literal-minded person is going to take the words as they stand. The poet is not merely describing a person: he is describing an experience (as Moses did in the burning bush? . . . the visions of Jeremiah and Isaiah?). The physical details such as height, weight, age, occupation (functional things the social scientist would ask) are not given because they are unimportant compared to the over all impression. They are insignificant compared to the total revelation of this fair lady (which is why there is no physical description of Jesus in the gospels?).

Or take Shakespeare when he writes of love:

> In faith, I do not love thee with mine eyes,
> For they in thee a thousand errors note;
> But 'tis my heart that loves what they despise,
> Who in despite of view is pleased to dote;

This is a variation of those little (sometimes maudlin) stories about the little boy who goes to the police station seeking his lost mother and the only description he can give is that she is the most beautiful lady in the whole wide world. It turns out that the mother is a worn, haggard, nondescript female. But, of course, there is truth in the boy's description. He is interpreting his total experience while the police report is looking for a sociological human being. So, as Shakespeare accurately says, love "sees" with a different set of eyes and writes with a different set of words and truth comes through in more ways than one.

Now the same experience applies to the bible. The bible is written, for the most part, in what we shall call the language of myth. We extend the word myth to mean any writing that is not literal prose. Myth here refers to both a different style from prose as well as the use of words to interpret events. So when we call the language of the bible myth we are saying that its language is not an informing one, but rather a *performing* one. It is the quite unliteral language that invites, demands, and unveils to us the ultimate meaning of life. The whole Galileo case amounted to this misunderstanding: trying to make literal what was myth, trying to make objective what was interpretative. On the contrary, "religion is not a matter of objective-cognitive assertion which might conflict with science, but a symbolic form within which one comes to terms with one's fate."[2] That is why the late modern theologian Paul Tillich was perfectly right in exclaiming, "There is no substitute for symbols and myths; they are *the* language of faith." So myth is a poetic, interpretative way of seeing reality. Myth rises above logical sequence and contradictions and can easily tolerate both (the resurrection accounts of Jesus, for example, have many logical questions). Myth takes for granted a world view of absolute power or powers, a higher form of life, an absolute Reality and seeks to make interpretations in this light:

> ...The myth-makers were far more interested in conveying an interpretative scheme about the nature of ultimate reality than they were in telling a story that would measure up to the strict scientific canons devised only centuries in the future . . . myth is a "different kind of truth." . . . It is precisely with the description of the *meaning of an experience* that the myth-makers in the historical religions are concerned.[3]

We, of course, have enormous difficulty with all of this. The reason is that we no longer think symbolically. We have seen in the first chapter that we are the children of the scientific era and we have been brought up on literal prose. So we must make an effort to put ourselves in the shoes of the ancients (anyone before the seventeenth century). They always saw two sides to an action as the example on witchcraft showed. One was the literal, objective side and the other the human meaning side. Now the ancients not only saw both sides but tended to favor the latter. Nothing was merely literal. Everything had to have some meaning for man. So they wrote and read on two levels: (1) they wrote literal happenings but intended the symbolic. So St. John, who frequently plays interpreter to make sure we do not miss the point, tells us that when Jesus said he would rebuild the Temple he was referring to his body. The literal statement referred to the building, but John clearly meant that to be a symbol of the resurrection. (2) they used and even invented literal actions *in order to* get at the symbolic meaning. Some of the gospel stories and miracles were invented in order to point up the meaning of Jesus. Now this strikes us moderns at the height of deceit: to invent a happening or miracle. We cry "untrue" but that is because we are so literal-minded. It would not occur to the ancients to even worry about literal truth. Their truth was always human truth. This is the sort of stuff legends are made up of. In her delightful book *Sixty Saints For Boys* Joan Windham says in the "Preface for Children":

... In this way we find out what kind of a person the Saint *was* as well as what kind of things he *did* by reading legends about him . . . I'll tell you something. . . . There is a legend about me. In my garden is a pond and once I dropped a trowel into it and I nearly fell in when I was fishing it out. A very little boy thought I *had* fallen in and every time he sees the pond he says, "Aunt Joan fell in there!" And other people hear him, and although it was some time ago now, a good many people describe exactly what they think happened and how wet I was and how there were water lilies round my neck and all kinds of other stories! But they all believe that I really did fall into the pond. I didn't; but it is just the sort of thing that I might have done![4]

Her point is well taken. The made up stories which we will call legends do in fact reveal something of her character and her ultimate meaning. Even a legend about her is symbolically true. So too we find the gospels telling us about Jesus multiplying the loaves of bread, healing the blind man and raising Lazarus from the dead. Such stories have no message if we take them in themselves for, after all, the people would get hungry again, the blind man would get old and his sight would deteriorate and Lazarus would die again. Period. On the surface, on the literal side, such stories have no meaning. But on the level of symbol they do carry meaning. Jesus is the real bread, he is the real light, he is the real life. "I am the way and the truth and the life." As food for the soul, light and life Jesus is active *now* and that is the point. Again, the literal events and stories are just not as important as the meaning. And that is why, we notice, there is positively no concern with the historical life of Jesus in the first Christian writings, the epistles. This is why the candidates for baptism received no instruction on the history of Jesus but rather on his meaning. As we read in Paul's epistles, the emphasis is on the Lordship of Christ, his redeeming death and Christian conduct. The gospels appeared in response to the desire to know more about Jesus and even then they were written not so much as to provide such historical details, as to provide interpretation.[5]

— 2 —

Let us press on. An example from the classic Japanese movie *Roshomon* will help. The picture shows a bandit discovering a man and his wife in the forest. There is a fight and the husband is killed and the wife raped. A woodcutter is also a part of the incident. The movie proceeds to tell the incident from each of the three persons' point of view. Interpretation and intent become obvious. Deeply shaken, each witness gives his own version. Which version is correct? What is really "objective" in the movie? Where does history reside? In one version, in none or somehow in all three? Because of questions like these the historian of today has long ceased to be satisfied with mere bare facts, causal indication and impartial description. Cause and effect do not make history.

The ancients had this sort of viewpoint. They wrote history as would one of the characters of *Roshomon*: openly interpretative and descriptive, conveying their truth. So with the writers of the bible. They made no pretense of not having a point of view. If God exists, if he is active in Israel's history then he cannot be ignored. He is the transcendent God who freely determines the course of history and takes part in it. It is he who gives promises, brings them to fulfillment and points to everything. The New Testament is not different. It openly "bears witness to the center of all history, not in the sense of a temporal sequence, but rather in the sense of a center which is decisive for the whole, to which everything is related and in which the ultimate goal of history is already anticipated and revealed in a unique way."[6] Therefore, the first and most important question to ask when we pick up the bible is not did this or that happen exactly as it is told. To know such facts may seem unquestionably crucial to our Western mentalities but such a question simply was not the primary concern of the authors and the first readers of the bible. So, following their lead, we should first ask, what is the *meaning* of this story and what exactly does it tell us about God and ourselves and the relationship between us? Why did the author choose to express himself like this?[7]

In the New Testament, then, we find no historical interest in our sense, no biographical interest as is shown by the absence of any statement about Jesus' appearance. What is there is history in the sense of conveying a person. As one writer says:

> In a positive sense, it means that the gospels in their form and character are anything but historical accounts, biographies and chronicles. Instead, they represent a unique combination, which has its only analogy, though a very instructive one, in the historical accounts of the Old Testament, namely, a combination of report and confession, of stories about Jesus and testimonies of the later community which believes in him. Both of these elements are so closely linked that we are even compelled to speak of a fusion: report *as* confession, and testimony of faith *as* a story about Jesus. The basis for this situation is certainly the fact that the authors saw Jesus not as a mere figure of the past who found his tragic end on the cross but as the living Lord, present through the power of the resurrection. Now they also saw and recounted Jesus' pre-resurrection history in a new and different light; on the whole they were unconcerned about the strict limits of history, which historical research would so relentlessly like to preserve.[8]

So, in the New Testament, the one large act of faith was the resurrection. As we shall see once the followers of Jesus became convinced of that then gospels flowed from it, the "good news." The evangelists, in other words, took the Easter faith and worked back from that. They too turned to myths (in our sense) to describe this unbelievable event and the man who was its center. Using myth is the original form of the evangelists' theology. That is why we cannot take every incident, every story, every saying of Jesus in the gospel literally. We made that mistake with the Old Testament and repeated it in the New. We are now trying to correct this mistake.

So, the major concern about the gospels is not necessarily getting the "facts" as we moderns would like; rather the crucial questions in a reading of the gospels are, "what is the *meaning* behind this story, this miracle, this parable, this saying, this action of Jesus? Why did the evangelists choose to express it this way? How does their own theology, their own intent color the events?" Scholars, in reading the gospels, not only detect accurately a definite theology for each of the evangelists but they can detect the various traditions behind their gospels; they can sense the oral reports and early liturgical hymns and practices. They can even sense the current apologetic in the minds of each evangelist; that is, what he was trying to convey and what he was trying to correct.

By this last statement we mean that scholarship in recent years has revealed that there was considerable diversity among the early Christians in their understanding of Jesus. Some of these opinions are clearly counteracted by the gospels. For example, there was a previous emphasis among some Christians on Jesus as miracle worker and wonder worker. The danger was to make Jesus too divine, too removed from the human condition. So Mark, in his gospel emphasized Jesus as one who must go through suffering and death. There were those who went in for special interior illuminations and spiritual experiences, so Mark gives no resurrection appearances in order not to add more visions to the agenda. There were those who thought that Jesus revealed some special secrets, so Mark goes out of his way to indicate that Jesus revealed and explained all things to his disciples. In short, Mark deliberately modifies previous and current misemphasis on the life and message of Jesus.

The same is true of Luke. He had in mind the gnostics who had a theory that light was the divine spark superior to matter, that matter was base and evil. Luke therefore puts a great deal of emphasis on Jesus being truly human: Jesus is circumcised, he suffered, he died on the cross; he ate and drank after the resurrection. The point is that both Mark and Luke "are dealing with the problem of earlier Christian diversity, and even images of Jesus that they are trying to normalize and correct. In the case of Mark it is the image of a powerful charismatic healer. In the case of Luke, if we read between the lines, it is the image of Jesus as a wisdom teacher who is enlightening men to find the divine within them here and now rather than waiting for a future moment of history. Jesus becomes a model of a man who has himself experienced this enlightenment."[9] In other words, what it all comes down to is that

We may not go on the assumption that because dependability of historical detail means much to us it had the same importance for the evangelists and their predecessors. They were greatly concerned that God had acted in history, and they told of his actions in terms of human, historical activity. In fact, however, they were reporting on what they were convinced was the outworking of a providential plan foreshadowed in the Scriptures, fulfilled in terms of the conflict of good and evil. They made their reports in a highly sophisticated way in the context of the theology of the times, but unsophisticated as regards the historiography of our day.[10]

Now that scholars understand that the bible is not literal history or a scientific textbook they are faced with two major problems. The first problem is understanding the myth and the second is how to reinterpret it for modern man. To attempt to answer both problems requires a great amount of scholarship and study and a knowledge of ancient cultures, mind sets and backgrounds. But the bible truths, to make sense and to nourish modern man, must be recast. We mentioned in the first chapter that intelligibility is one of the big problems today in religion. Biblical language and medieval theological language are neither appreciated nor understood today outside of scholarly circles. So we have the task of "re-mythologizing," that is, of unraveling and retranslating old myths into modern ones. At the same time we recognize that some myths are simply not translatable and we must therefore take them on their terms, not ours. Likewise we also have to resist the temptation, given our modern scientific attitude, of rationalizing the myths and in effect making literal what is poetic. (We shall see the result of this in the next chapter.) For the instant that we literalize the language or the myth itself we have lost them. For "in the modern age religious symbols cannot be believed in, they must be believed through. The goal of the symbol is not to bring man information but to lead him to experience. . . . Men and women passionately want their inherited religious symbols to speak to them of the sacred—to assure them, to critique them, to call them. . . ."[11]

We must note that all that has been written here so far does not mean to imply that there are no literal statements in the bible or that there are no truly historical books. It just means that in our over all approach to the bible and/or religion the strict objective, scientific canons do not apply; that there is a whole other dimension of truth and meaning that objective language simply fails to utter because, limited as is all human language, it cannot do so.

— 3 —

Let us give some examples of how scholars remythologize the old biblical myths. Now it must be stressed that much work remains to be done and that modern interpretations may have to be corrected in the light of later discoveries. But we include these samples from Old and New Testaments to show the trend of thought. Take the Old Testament. Scholars have learned that the first book of Genesis was written about the year 1000 B.C. This would put the author as a believer in King David's time, not Moses'. Therefore this writer, as a believer, already had preconceived notions and beliefs to draw on. So he expressed the story of creation in the commonly accepted science terms of the times. But of course his description was in no way an attempt to describe creation literally as it actually happened. (After all, who was there?) Rather his intent was mythological; that is, in our sense, it was a theological treatise with a point. It was an interpretative message and the message was this: Israel's God, Yaweh-Elohim, is the supreme creator and lord of the universe. Beyond this point there is no other. Certainly, the details in Genesis are not to be taken literally. There is no quarrel between science and religion here since each is talking on a entirely different plane. The creation myth is a sacred telling, if you will, a faith-proclamation of the greatness of the Lord.

Take the story of the Garden of Eden and the fall of man. Clearly these are myths. They are very creative, theological answers to the fundamental question, "Why is man so miserable?" As far as the bible goes in its opening chapters, "the Garden of Eden, the apple, the snake, the tree of knowledge of good and evil, form the mythological framework in which the Hebrew writer clothed his answer to the problem of evil."[12] "Adam" is not the name of a specific individual but a word meaning simply "earthling," which is an apt description of man's origin from the earth. In fact, the whole narrative of Adam and Eve is bent towards proclaiming that man came forth from the hand of God. There is really no attempt to say how and for this reason evolution is quite consistent with such a myth.

If we turn to the New Testament we find the same proclaiming and interpretative language, the language of faith. Take the infancy narratives of Luke and Matthew. Are they literal? Luke who wanted his gospel to be an eyewitness account certainly could not have been there at Christ's birth. It seems more likely that the infancy narratives were put there to counterpoint the real work of Jesus' redemption. They were not a part of the original apostolic preaching because that preaching concerned itself only with witnessed events and Jesus' redemptive ministry which began with his baptism by John the Baptist. The infancy narratives grew out of the desire to "flesh out" more information about Jesus as time went on and to be a symbolic form of his later saving actions. The infancy narratives "emerged out of the endeavor to impart an ever fuller understanding of the redemptive work and words of Jesus."[13] So we can sense the parallels: the swaddling clothes easily represent the winding cloths of Jesus' tomb. The lack of room at Bethlehem's inn is a retelling of John's phrase, "he came to his own but his own received him not." The shepherds were the outcasts of society. They were the prototypes of the publicans that Jesus consorted with in his efforts to save that which was lost. Mary herself is the embodiment of all those who say "yes" to God in Jesus. She in fact is a living parable for as her dead womb by God's power gave divine life, so the dead tomb on Easter issued forth the resurrected life by that same gracious power.[14]

Likewise Jesus' miracles can be taken more as mythical proclamations of the early community rather than as literal facts. The transfiguration is the community's way of saying that Jesus was the Lord. Feeding the crowds is Jesus' gospel nourishing mankind with truth. Lazarus is a picture story of the Dives and Lazarus parable. Jesus' walking on the water (always a scripture symbol of void, chaos and turmoil) is a symbol of his resurrection, treading the turbulent waters in triumph. Jesus, in other words, is victorious over evil.

Even the passion narratives have been treated to make the proclamation of Jesus. We can get at the basic facts *that,* not always at the *what.* That is, we can be content with fact *that* Jesus was arrested, tried, condemned and executed. However, the *what* is a problem: what happened, what were the charges, what was the trial really like, what did Pilate say? What, in brief, is interpretation and invention to bring home a point?[15]

These few samples of remythologizing from the Old and New Testaments will perhaps disturb the average Catholic. It might seem that all his old certainties are being explained away. True, there will be wrong guesses and exaggerations whenever scholars seek to reinterpret the old myths. The average Catholic should have confidence in the Spirit that truth will be served. He must see the necessity for reinterpretation for any living religion. After all, if he believes that Christianity is not a set of propositions but a way of life he sees the need for making it relevant for every age. He should also sense the truism that religion is therefore the least successful when it tries to legislate for all times, places and circumstances permanent rules and symbols; and most successful when it furnishes new symbols and rituals which give guidance and suggestions on how best to have the mind and heart of Christ.

The problem of much God-talk, as we said, is irrelevancy: trying to speak of God and all the symbols which interpret life in words that have lost their meaning. Some symbols must be changed altogether; others must be retained but reinterpreted in the modern idiom; for what is important theologically is not the reiteration of biblical phrases but faithfulness to the biblical witness. Our religious language, once more, is really not meant to explain everything and to "understand" God; rather it is meant as a verbalizing rationale to commit oneself to a Christian way of life. This might be hard if the language is a hold-over from the past which must be endlessly repeated. Language, symbols must change. Jesus himself remains our primary symbol that Reality (God) is gracious, kind and forgiving. He must therefore make sense to us so that we can "use" his life and death and resurrection as interpretations of our own: Faithfulness becomes a matter of giving his history priority over ours in the quest for meaningful symbols in life.

Existence is on-going, creative and always novel. We need symbols and language that will carry this load. So all that this chapter has meant to convey is to give us certain concepts that prepare us to look at developing dogma in a different light (Chapter 5) and, above all, to be better able to understand the Jesus who became the Christ (Chapter 6). It has sought to help us realize that logical truth is only a part of reality. There is room for the irrational, the illogical, the poetic, even the nebulous and the incoherent which test bits of reality that cannot be expressed by precise and correct language as any lover can testify. There is a need for taking one's era's language and recasting it for another era. Why not? It would be strange indeed if the Great Lover who is Father could be captured in prose alone or in one century's vocabulary. On the contrary, myth is religion's living language. Even more. It is, as we have indicated, the original form of theology.

— 4 —

There are two very critical points to review before we end. First, as we have said so often, myths are concerned with *meaning*. But when we talk about meaning we are bound to run into the same basic myths over and over again. The reason is that humanity is universal and its aspirations and motifs of interpretations will be common. That is why, in one form or another, certain basic myths called "archetypal" keep popping up. Some are the sharing of food (brought to fulfillment in our eucharist), denoting the sharing of the very substance that keeps one alive: hence the supreme hospitality, brotherhood, fellowship; the shedding of blood as a loss of vitality and drinking it as drinking the source of life. There are gods who died and rose again to explain the seasons. Miracles were used as proof of divine power. Virgin births were spoken of. The point is that these symbols are not unique to Christianity nor should they be. They are basic myths that express man's eternal hopes, his answers to the meaning of life, birth, death, tragedy and suffering. Therefore it would be expected that such long-standing, basic myths would and should be applied to Jesus. After all, he was the one who fulfilled all men's hopes. Those who believed in him would simply be forced to use ancient, deep-rooted, at-hand myths to get at the meaning of Jesus.

To get at the meaning of Jesus remains the point. So from the start comparison, language, cultural metaphors, expressions, myths were used to explain his uniqueness. The epistles and gospels reached back to the old myths to apply them to Christ. But how could it be otherwise? The deepest longings of mankind were at last fulfilled. Why should not the old myths be put to use? In other words, as we shall have occasion to mention again, no one should be scandalized to find out the ideas like the virgin birth and god-heroes and life after death existed long before Jesus. Since Jesus pertains to the deepest aspirations of mankind, mankind's deepest symbols must be appropriated to explain him.

Secondly, we must take note what the rest of this book seeks to do. It seeks to give contemporary insights into many of our cherished beliefs. However, it is crucial to remember that the ideas of the various theologians presented here are *not a mere translation*. Theologians are not taking former words and concepts and simply upgrading them. They are not taking patristic or medieval jargon and putting them into current language for our benefit. Rather what is going on is more profound than that. They are going beyond literalizing the symbols and myths of religion which have so long preoccupied them and led them down blind alleys. They have in fact come to the conclusion that they never simply translate the myths and symbols of religion. Rather they can only deepen them, for merely to repeat them in literal language is always to settle for far less than what they say. They are moving into a whole new appreciation of myths as we have explained it here and seeing exactly what that meaning of Jesus and the Church and the sacraments is. Too long we have all stopped at the observable, exterior and literal statements. We have endless catechisms and lives of Christ devoted to literalism and "objective" facts and history. We now know that such books are inadequate. Jesus is not only a fact, he is a meaning. The gospels are not biographies but theology. Too long we have objectified Jesus and the Church and the sacraments. Now the theologians are taking radical stances. They are returning to the original intent of the biblical authors. They are returning to the many leveled riches of myth.[16]

NOTES FOR CHAPTER 4

1. Christopher Crocker, "Ritual and the Development of Social Structures: Liminality and Inversion" in *Roots of Ritual,* edited by James D. Shaughnessy (Eerdmans, 1973) p. 64.

2. Robert Bellah in *Culture of Unbelief,* edited by Rocco Caporale and Antonio Grumelli (University of California Press, 1971) p. 46.

3. Andrew M. Greeley, *Unsecular Man* (Schocken Books, 1972) p. 248.

4. Joan Windham, *Sixty Saints for Boys* (Sheed and Ward). Introduction.

5. Tad W. Guzie, *Jesus and the Eucharist* (Paulist Press, 1974). See chapter 1.

6. Ferdinand Hahn, *What Can We Know About Jesus?* (Fortress Press, 1969) p. 13.

7. Peter DeRosa, *Jesus Who Became Christ* (Dimension Books, 1974) p. 102.

8. Gunther Borkhamm in *What Can We Know About Jesus?,* cited above, p. 75. Borkhamm goes so far as to say that Jesus himself, "his history and personality, imposed and forced this method of presentation upon the bearers of the first tradition and the gospel writers who later (in the last third of the first century a.d.) collected and molded this tradition" (p. 76).

9. Joseph A. Grassi, "The Challenge of Recent Research on the Gospels" in *Does Jesus Make a Difference?,* edited by Thomas M. McFadden (Seabury Press, 1974) p. 17. See also Robert L. Wilken's book, *The Myth of Christian Beginnings: History's Impact on Belief* (Doubleday, 1971).

10. Gerard S. Sloyan, *Jesus on Trial* (Fortress Press, 1973) p. 175.

11. John Shea, "The Second Naivete: Approach to a Pastoral Problem" in *The Persistence of Religion,* edited by Andrew Greeley and Gregory Baum, in Concilium 81 (Seabury Press, 1973) p. 109.

12. William J. Duggan, *Myth and Christian Belief* (Fides Publishers, 1971) p. 73.

13. Carroll Stuhlmueller, "The Gospel According to Luke" in the *Jerome Biblical Commentary* (Prentice Hall, 1968) p. 119.

14. See Peter DeRosa's book, *Jesus Who Became Christ,* cited above.

15. See Gerard S. Sloyan's book *Jesus on Trial,* cited above.

16. Tad W. Guzie, cited above, p. 116. See also Morton Kelsey's excellent book, *Myth, History and Faith* (Paulist Press, 1974).

5. Positioning Dogma

— 1 —

The discussion of words and myth leads us to consider the question of dogma. For Catholics especially dogma is a large part of their lives and even Protestants are willing to concede its value provided that the dogma always relates to Christ. In fact, they too have their sets of dogma although they are likely to use the word "confession" rather than dogma. We might describe dogma as the churches' concrete positioning of God's revelation. Dogma formulates the insight given by revelation; "it is the known and confessed truth of the Word of Holy Scripture heard and believed by the church." Or, as Protestant theologian Karl Barth puts it, "Dogma is the agreement of the church's proclamation with the revelation attested in scripture."[1] Catholics would not confine revelation only to scripture, but the thrust would be the same: dogma positions in concrete terms revelation. Now in order to understand dogma we will artificially break down the process that leads to it. We will list five categories or five steps to dogma.

1. *The Experience.* This is the primary, the core, fact. Someway, at some time, past or present, there was and is an experience of the sacred, the "otherness," the divinity. There is a decisive unfolding of the ultimate meaning to human life, an "ultimate concern" that is encountered. There is a revelation, a breakthrough of the divine. In all of these phrases we are trying to describe that there was an experience, whether it was a voice from a burning bush, an interior impulse or enlightenment, an unexplainable meeting with a Someone Other, a rising from the tomb, whatever. For us Christians, of course, the great revelation of God is in Israel's history and uniquely and definitively in Jesus. He *is* the revelation

of the Father. He is the experience, the Word eternally spoken, God's self-communication. However we put it, the main point to notice is that revelation initially takes place, not as a statement or a proposition but as an experience—which is why faith is never merely believing *that* but believing *in* someone.

We must add that although God's full self-revelation is uniquely in Jesus, his revelation is not confined to the Hebrew-Christian tradition. The Spirit breathes where he will. Vatican II's Declaration on Non-Christian Religions recognizes that not only Judaism and Islam but even faiths untouched by any biblical influence contain reflections of God's disclosure. Moreover the Constitution on Divine Revelation implies that God's self-communication comes to men independently of his special self-disclosure in the bible and that even atheists are open to God's influence. "Nor does divine providence deny the help necessary for salvation to those whom, without blame on their part, have not yet arrived at an explicit knowledge of God, but who strive to live a good life, thanks to his grace."[2] But for us Christians who know of God's presence in Christ, it remains the norm, the basis for whatever follows. Belief is rooted in the revelation, in the experience, the communication of the sacred.

2. *The Faith-Response.* Just as a sound needs an ear to hear it, so revelation needs a response, a reaction. When one responds to this revelation, whether directly or on the word of another, this is faith. Faith is always active. It is not an intellectual assent to a body of truth as we were taught in the past for then the most "faithful" person would be the one who knew the creed by heart. No, faith calls for a trust, a response, a reaction to God's summoning word. Faith is first and foremost a response to God's self-communication in grace. Only incidentally does it involve an assent to proposed truths. Essentially it is such a personal response that a man is pulled out of himself, so to speak, in surrender:

> Faith means stepping out of what is accessible, what is at hand—out of the atheism of my "totalizing world." It is the courage to "accept acceptance"; it is yielding to something which happens to

me from outside myself, to an event, to being forcibly grasped by an invitation—a yielding to a demand which snatches me away from myself.

Hence from the very beginning, faith has the character not of a word one speaks oneself but of response. It is a Yes, an Amen . . . to something, or someone who addresses me . . . authentic faith involves a risk, a leap—not outside one's own existence, but *with* and *of* one's whole existence—the overcoming of hesitation and doubt. . . .[3]

In his book *A Reason to Live, A Reason to Die!* Father Powell expresses it this way:

I heard a story recently—it was fiction I presume—of a man who had fallen off the edge of a high cliff. He manages to grab onto the root of a tree growing out of the side of the cliff, and was literally hanging on for dear life. He began to pray. Then he heard the voice of God asking him: "Do you really believe in me?" "I do!" protested the poor man whose life hung in the balance. "Do you trust me?" asked the voice of God. "Yes, Yes!" the man answered. Then the voice of God came back: "Then I will see to it that you are saved. Now, do what I tell you to do. Now . . . let go!"[4]

For Catholics brought up to think of faith as giving assent to a series of propositions or statements, this notion of faith may be uncomfortable. But the notion is accurate. In fact, the Church's saying that faith can be had even outside the Church and is to be found in men of good will everywhere underlines the essential difference between active faith and passive proposition:

In these and similar texts, Catholic theologians find an official recognition by the Church that an act of saving faith is possible without any explicit belief in the existence of God or any religious affiliation. This possibility is very significant for a correct understanding of the nature of faith. If it can exist under these conditions, faith evidently cannot consist essentially in the explicit acceptance of any particular doctrines. While the faith of the professed Christian implies the acceptance of certain revealed truths, such acceptance is not precisely identical with faith itself.[5]

3. *The Telling.* Not everyone has a direct encounter or experience with that "wholly other," though as we have seen many people at one time or another experience something that takes them out of themselves. But there are those who have had this experience. They are usually overpowered by it, give their faith-response and then, in the normal psychology of good news, they want to share it. When they share it, they speak it. When they speak it more often as not they turn to myth. We have already spoken of myth in the last chapter. Here we may recall that all deep experiences may often lie too deep for words. When words are used they tend to stretch and bend according to the desire to convey an impression. They are not used to inform, but rather to touch, to share, to reach over, under, around and within the person listening (or reading). "These are recorded so that you may believe that Jesus is the Christ, the Son of God, and that believing this you may have life through his name" (Jn 20:12). That is why, by the way, any language that pretends to "capture" God is suspect. Any language that objectifies him automatically reduces him. It forces the Hidden God into a proposition and thus makes him able to be manipulated. He becomes a department of the mind, not the jealous, unknowable, slightly mad Lover of the scriptures.

We remind ourselves that for Christians the normative "telling" is scripture but in turn we must remember that scripture itself is a product of tradition rising from it. Yet scripture, once formulated, becomes the definitive statement by which the original tradition is measured. But the larger point is the restatement that the gospels cannot be taken as exact, descriptive historical records about Jesus since they arose from the myth-traditions of the immediate past. We shall see more about this question in the next chapter but here we repeat that the gospels are proclamations and interpretations. They are the early church's faith-disclosures. They represent a collection of various traditions, but a collection that is geared to elicit a faith-response. The message, as we have mentioned before, must be retranslated for us moderns, but must still have a deep continuity with the Jesus who provoked it all if it is to be authentic and nourishing. ". . . All dogmatic statements about his universal meaning constantly require grounding in and confirmation by the historical particularity of the message, way, and figure of Jesus."[6] The message becomes revelation, we must remember, only when faith listens to it and interprets it. Hence "continuity and the retranslation of the message do not stand in opposition to each other . . . they are complementary aspects of the same fidelity of faith which call for each other. . . ."[7] This is why George Tyrrell in *Christianity at the Crossroads* says:

> As things are, the only test of revelation is the test of life—not merely of moral, but of spiritual fruitfulness in the deepest sense. It must at once satisfy and intensify man's mystical and moral need. It must bring the transcendent nearer to his thoughts, feelings and desires. It must deepen his consciousness of union with God . . . any other "sign," be it miracle or argument, will appeal only to the faithless and perverse. It may puzzle them, but it will never convince them; it may convert them to the Church, but it cannot convert them to God; it may change their theology—it cannot change their hearts.[8]

So the telling, verbal or written, is an important step in the spreading of the Good News. The only thing we must remember is to learn that we must always go "through" the language to the experience, to the Person.

4. *The Reflection.* Or we might call this, the theologizing. Sooner or later, when we read or hear about someone's experience of the sacred, listen to its telling in its various forms, certain people will begin to reflect on it all. They will compare this telling with others. They will even try to deduce other consequences implicit in the data. They will seek to form a unified pattern. They will look at how different peoples through the centuries, from different backgrounds have reacted and expressed their understanding of the myths. In short, they will reflect, draw conclusions and come up with a theology, "God-talk"; in other words theology results when we have "faith seeking understanding" (St. Anselm), faith seeking articulation.

We note that this reflection, this theologizing, is several steps removed from the experience both as to fact and to time. So theology can be wrong at times or incomplete. But theology is necessary and so are the theologians who explore the faith on behalf of the community. In fact theologians function best when they so serve the community and worst when they serve themselves. The religious experience is so rich and varied that it is the gifted who must take time to reflect, draw conclusions and enlarge the original communication for the community. Theology is further necessary because, to a certain extent, faith is a human acquisition as well as a divine gift and the theologians must also perfect the human element. The communication of God after all, comes to completion only in so far as it becomes also the understanding of man. Faith and reason are therefore not mutually exclusive. "Faith, as the supreme exercise of reason, arises when the spirit of man, borne by the divine Spirit, overleaps itself. Because human effort is involved, revelation does not come to man easily or all at once. . . . All truth, and perhaps explicated 'revealed' truth, is a laborious acquisition that takes the cooperation of many minds and the passage of many years. . . ."[9]

However, we must make three observations at this point. The first observation is that theology must always be self-corrective because it easily becomes rationalistic and out of touch with the original source, the Christ-event. In Catholic circles, for example, theology had become so heavily infected with rationalism and apologetics that it tried to "prove" the truths of faith. The impression was that one could think oneself into faith. If faith were at all supernatural it was frequently conceived as some kind of added value to the basic and indispensable platform of reason. The result was that religious mysteries became identified with the formulas in which they were expressed. But here is the danger. Once one formulates the mystery, he thinks he has possessed it. Once he possesses it, he reduces it. So theologians must be wary as they reflect on behalf of the community on the mysteries of faith. They must resist the temptation to declare that they have captured them completely, once and for all, in concepts, words or formulas.

The second observation is akin to the first: theology must not stray too far either from its source or other modes of worship and ethics. When it does this it degenerates into empty and dry disputes. Also, theology must not stray far from the magisterium of the Church (more on this below) or think that it replaces it. Both serve as a corrective to the other. The third observation is that since truth is so profound no one theology or school of theology will position it all. This is why it is healthy to have many schools of theology, many approaches, many traditions which refine the original experiences. When any one theology becomes so predominant that it suppresses the rest, then the danger is very real that only one theology will harden into fact and fact will harden into what appears to be dogma but which in reality is but one expression of a particular school. Karl Rahner's words are apropos here:

> It follows from the nature of human knowledge of truth and from the nature of divine truth itself, that any individual truth, above all one of God's truths, is beginning and emergence, not conclusion and end. In the last resort any individual human perception of truth only has meaning as beginning and promise of the knowledge of God.[10]

5. *The Dogma.* Last, both in time and importance is dogma. This is not to downgrade dogma for it is very important to religion and can serve it well. It is just to say that dogma is the most fragile of all the steps and needs the most care and the most reassessment. Dogma is the end statement of the first four steps. It is the formulation on the part of the believing community of some element of its faith which has come into full consciousness; or it can be the rejection of something definitively recognized as an error. Dogma is a quite necessary corrective to the necessarily personal limitations which would otherwise lead to an unbalanced sectarianism. "The universal witness of the Church safeguards the totality of God's revelation. The dogmas express what the whole Church is conscious of having seen by the light of faith."[11] We quoted before the statement that dogma is the "known and confessed truth of the Word of Holy Scripture heard and believed by the church." This is true and places dogma in its proper perspective.

— 2 —

It is interesting that in our day there are a few other things we can say about dogma that were not permitted a few years ago. One of these things is to admit that dogmas are provisional. By this we mean that dogmatic formulas are not and cannot be complete, positive, unchangeable, finished statements about God or his Christ. Since such dogmatic statements are necessarily human formulations they are subject to the laws of history. They are conditioned as all of our human utterances are. They are conditioned by the vocabulary, the adversaries, the politics, the thought patterns, the mind-sets of the times in which they were written. That is why so many dogmas seem so archaically expressed and even meaningless today. They are couched not only in language of another era but in the thought concepts that have long ago become obsolete except to a few scholars. Theologians can now make statements such as these:

In the search for what is available to us to be believed, we are aware of how far removed we are from the world of the mythology in which the gospel was first preached. This should make us reflect very deeply about the language we use today, in a world where we are torn between a refusal to merely repeat the language of a bygone culture and our inability to find a new language for ourselves . . . doctrinal and kerygmatic language should be seen as the product of a particular society . . . these must be evaluated within the context of the social environment for which they were intended . . .

Or:

We should also not make the historical expression of Jesus' words and actions in those concrete circumstances unhistorical and absolute by dissociating it from the historically conditioned linguistic categories of the period in which the event of Jesus was expressed. . . . To make the language of faith of a given period, even that of the New Testament, absolute, would be to deny that Jesus is the Lord of all history, including our own. . . .[12]

Or again:

> Nearly everybody recognizes today that the Christians of the first century thought in prescientific categories and that the biblical message needs to be radically transposed in order for its true meaning to come to modern man. To complicate the matter further, theologians are now saying that the thought patterns of Patristic and medieval man were likewise culturally conditioned, and that the whole dogmatic heritage of the Church needs to be critically reviewed before it can be authoritatively stated for modern man. This admission is highly disturbing to those whose concept of faith has been primarily that of an assent to dogmas.[13]

These views have so advanced that on July 25, 1973 a declaration (*Mysterium Fidei*) from the Congregation of Doctrine (formerly known as the Holy Office) states that, as a matter of fact, doctrinal statements are indeed conditioned in four ways: (1) by the human language they were expressed in at a given time and place; (2) dogmas are sometimes expressed in reference to a quite limited human context so that such a context may seem to be inadequate in the framework of a later one; (3) such dogmas are often directed to the solution of particular questions or the refutation of particular errors and that has to be kept in mind when reading them; and (4) dogmas are worded in terms that do as a matter of fact carry traces of changeable human conceptions. This last statement is a real turnabout from the days of Pius XII who rejected the notion that the concepts used in dogmas are time-conditioned. This last statement, however, follows faithfully the thought of Vatican II.[14]

The second thing we can say about dogma today is that most Catholics have erroneously thought of faith as something that has come down unchanged from apostolic times. Revelation, the saying went, was completed with the last Apostle. This could only mean that for two thousand years faith is repeating the same message. It also fails to observe that the Apostles would be obviously bewildered by such a complicated system of doctrine that the Catholic Church has. So equally obviously faith is not merely repeating the same message. Raymond Brown's observation is apt here: ". . . the explicit admission of Athanasius, the greatest of the Nicene Fathers, that in its formulation Nicaea was going beyond anything said explicitly in the New Testament."[15] So faith is a living thing and that is why Vatican II abandoned the static images of the Church in exchange for fluid images such as "People of God" or "Pilgrim Church" and spoke of Pope John's phrase that the Church must learn to "read the signs of the times"[16] through which God *continues* to address his people. This means that there is both a substratum (called the "deposit of faith") and an on-going unfolding. This substratum of the deposit of faith, namely, *the* revelation of God, his self-donation in Israel's history and definitively in Jesus, is unique and will always be the source and foundation for all believers for all times to come. The substratum, however, is not inert. It is there to be a jumping-off point of that God who continues to give of himself in this our day. This self-communication of God that took place in Jesus *continues* to take place in the Church in new and different ways. "God perpetually reiterates his Word spoken once and for all in Jesus Christ."[17] So we say that revelation is closed in the sense that it was made unconditionally and definitively in Jesus as witnessed by the apostolic Church; but it is open in the sense that God continues to speak the selfsame Word (Jesus) in the Church in this very age in which we live.

The third thing we can say about dogma is that since there is this primal substratum any continuity and development has definite limits. Development and present day communication cannot be an open-ended process. To the degree that it cannot it must always be continuous and homogenous. It must "remain always in unbroken and undistorted continuity with the eschatological meaning which the early Church discovered in this event" and "to retain authority all innovation must remain in full continuity with the tradition. All truth in revealed religion must be traditional."[18]

The fourth thing that can be said about dogmas is that they vary both in intensity and persuasiveness. No individual Catholic, for example, has to affirm every dogma with deep personal conviction. This applies especially to those dogmas which are so written and so technical that the average Catholic could not understand them anyway. Even the Decree on Ecumenism pointed out that "in Catholic teaching, there exists an order or 'hierarchy' of truths, since they differ in their relationship to the foundation of the Christian faith."

The fifth comment concerning dogma is to note that there used to be tags attached to them indicating how seriously they were to be held. Some dogmas were considered so essential to revelation that to deny them was to deny the truth. Others were said to be almost a part of revelation or closely allied to it. Others were considered to be of ecclesiastical opinion which it would be dangerous to ignore. These tags have pretty much lost their force today and as a matter of fact more is left to the individual to give proper and serious emphasis where it belongs. In other words, to be a member of the Church, not everyone has to repeat verbatim all the same dogmas, the same creeds and the same confessions.

The sixth thing about dogma is that, since it is a statement of a proposition, it should be let go of once it has done its job. (Scholars of course should keep it to examine and explicate.) The function of dogma, we recall, is to take bits of biblical poetry and myth and cast them into literal propositions so that we believers may be protected from error and excess. For this function dogma is of great service and a necessary one. We must be forever grateful to those Fathers and theologians who strove so mightily to bring precision to the great truths of life. But, again, after the dogma has been translated into literal words, then it should be given back immediately to the people so that it lives, so that it can be acknowledged that the experience of God is always larger than its definition, broader than its formula. Once dogmas have made their point they should be thawed and given back to the fluid, human depths from which they arose so that they, in a recycled mythological form, can nourish and challenge once more. We have already noted the mischief that occurs when distilled dogmas become their own justification and faith becomes equated with knowledge.

This is why there are reservations about the National Catholic Catechetical Directory which is being formulated at this writing. When it is finished it will probably be a splendid work, but one always with the inbred handicap of appealing only to the brain, of being a compendium of propositions to be believed in. It carries the danger that Christianity once more might be seen as a body of teaching rather than as an experience. Faith might be seen as the transmission of a body of knowledge rather than as living the life of Jesus in a community of believers. The Directory might deflect us from remembering that Christianity is less a content than a context; that it is mystery and experience. Robert Bellah reminds us:

> The intellectual formulas are like gutted, empty houses, offering no protection against the cold wind of contemporary reality, not because they are untrue, but because contemporary Americans cannot discern their meaning. . . . At the moment we need not so much an overall abstract explanation as to hear what the symbols—the bread and the wine, the fraction and the communion, the stone and the water—are saying. . . .[19]

We close this section with a lengthy quotation from theologian Gregory Baum:

> Doctrine is the Church's witness to God's self-revelation in Jesus Christ . . . Doctrine recalls and proclaims what God has done and is doing in Jesus Christ. Doctrine points beyond itself to the saving reality to which it testified. Even though doctrine refers to a reality that transcends it, it is strictly necessary. Without doctrine we could not talk about the redemption which is at work among us. Without doctrine we could not communicate with one another and form a fellowship of faith. Without doctrine we could not enter into conversation with other people telling them how the God, who revealed himself in Jesus Christ, is redemptively present in the whole of human life.
>
> . . . The role of doctrine in the Church is, therefore, ministerial. It serves the communication of the Word. It mediates divine salvation. Doctrine, moreover, is conditional. It subtracts nothing from the truth of doctrine to insist that it is conditioned by the culture in which it is formulated and by the problems of the Church to which it responds. Doctrine is the witness of the Church, at a particular period of her history, to the self-identical, on-going revelation of God in Christ. . . . There is an inevitable tension between doctrine and the transcent reality to which it gives witness. Doc-

trine can never exhaustively present the divine Word. . . . Though
doctrine is strictly necessary for men on this earth who wish to have
fellowship in the gospel doctrine is also a burden. It makes us im-
patient. Men become frustrated with the partial and historically
conditioned character of doctrine. . . . What is required is the
reformulation of doctrine. Vatican II has called the "accom-
modation of preaching" to the exigencies of the present "the law
of all evangelization" . . . the tension between doctrine and the
saving reality which it signifies has become so great that the reformulation of doctrine has become imperative.[20]

So, in summary, we have seen the five steps towards dogma: (1)
the experience or revelation; (2) the faith-response; (3) the telling;
(4) the reflection or theologizing, and (5) the dogma. It should be
obvious that only the first two really concern belief or faith. We
might however add the third, that is, "the telling." This implies the
larger question of community for there are those who rightly hold
that any real community among people presupposes a commonly
communicated faith and that faith in turn cannot achieve a healthy
growth except within the atmosphere of a believing community, a
church as we would call it. Ordinarily steps four and five are pro-
visionally necessary as long as we remember that theology is not
faith and dogma is not faith. In our terminology, both position
faith and must do so in order to be authentic, but such positioning
will alter from age to age as each era demands reinterpretation.

— 3 —

In our five steps we can see more readily where the pope and
the hierarchy fit in. They fit in, as it were, between steps four and
five. They, the hierarchy, do not make up the revelation, nor do
they invent its ways of telling. Rather they officially guide and
counterpoint the theological reflections and formulations of the
dogmas in service to the believing community. They are entrusted
on behalf of the community to preserve the truth as it goes through
cultural changes and expressions. They hold fast to the pristine
tradition. They teach, with an ear to the theologians, and correct
where need be. In their own collegiality they symbolize unity and

truth. Under the leadership of the pope they keep the original core traditions, the hand-me-down telling of revelation, intact.

When the pope and bishops—the hierarchy—wield the supreme doctrinal authority in the Church, the sum and consensus of what they teach is called the magisterium. To be considered a part of the magisterium, however, a dogma must not only be taught with moral unanimity by the whole college of bishops but it must be taught explicitly and definitively as something to be held by all the faithful. Otherwise the Church would be in trouble because, as a matter of record, some teaching which has generally been held by the college of bishops without notable contradiction over a long period of time has turned out to be problematic or outright erroneous.[21] That is why the magisterium is much more cautious today in proclaiming a teaching to be definitively held by the faithful even though a particular teaching may be common episcopal thinking.

To use a publicized example it is precisely this caution that has left the door open for the dissent over the birth control encyclical, *Humanae Vitae*. This encyclical is not an infallible statement, as the Holy Father readily acknowledges, but the teaching is considered part of the magisterium. Opponents say that here is an instance where the magisterium is wrong and point to the comments of some national hierarchies softening the encyclical's prohibitions. That is why Charles Curran can write, "On the other hand, the teaching authority of the Church on birth control is not infallible, not a matter of faith. The condemnation of contraception belongs to the ordinary, authentic magisterium of the Church to which we owe obedience. The very fact that the Church has not spoken infallibly indicates that the present teaching is open to development. To change the present teaching of the Church would be a case of development and not a direct contradiction."[22] That sentence was written before the encyclical was issued in 1968. However, even at the time of its proclamation Msgr. Lambruschini who was officially appointed to explain the encyclical to the press emphasized that it was not an infallible statement and that the possibility of a revised statement, if new data appeared, could not be excluded. Moral theologian Bernard Häring points out, "Noninfallible but very authoritative statements of popes were in the past officially corrected only after a relatively long delay." Häring goes on to recount how the burning of witches had been doctrinally justified by an encyclical of Innocent IV and that there was strong papal approval for castrating Vatican choirboys.[23] Papal appeal in *Humanae Vitae* to the "constant firmness by the teaching authority of the Church" is not quite accurate since that tradition is not all that firm, as the book *Contraception* by John Noonan has demonstrated. Again, all this tries to clarify that while papal and episcopal pronouncements must be taken with the utmost seriousness, nevertheless they are not so closed that revision and development cannot take place; that if there is revision, it must take place within the original spirit of the Revelation Who is Jesus and in the context of scripture and tradition which testify to him.

The pope's infallibility is always a question in the whole matter of the magisterium. We must always remember however that he is infallible when he officially teaches specifically and consciously in his role, not only as head of the Church, but as reflecting its own innate infallibility. As Vatican II expresses it, the Roman Pontiff acts not individually but as the "supreme teacher of the universal Church, as one in whom the charism of the infallibility of the Church itself is individually present, he is expounding or defending a doctrine of Catholic faith."[24] Since the Church's own infallibility has not been defined yet, papal infallibility leaves room for comment and discussion.

We have used phrases several times that the hierarchy serves the community. It is supposed to serve the faithful, making it more credible for them to be believers:

> It is the Church as a whole that is important. The magisterium is at its service and those who hold authority, the hierarchy, come later as it were: they preserve the community in faith and unity and to that extent serve it. It is not the other way around: the Church does not exist for the sake of the hierarchy. The Church is that fellowship which authority serves. As Jesus said, "You know that those who are supposed to rule over the Gentiles lord it over them. . . . But it shall not be so among you; but whoever would

be great among you must be our servant and whoever would be first among you must be the slave of all." Thus, following this, Vatican II says, "The people itself and the salvation of the people belong to the order of ends in God's purpose. The hierarchy is ordained to that end, as a means. The people must first be envisaged as a whole. . . . "25

When the hierarchy's concerns are shallow, self-serving or irrelevant they lose credibility.26 Such lapses notwithstanding, the hierarchy is in a unique position and their guidance has been invaluable. They are our leaders bearing the apostolic tradition and their official duty is to hand on that tradition intact—not as one hands down a closed volume from one generation to another, but as one hands down a living, vital, moving, alive, multi-faceted experience. The hierarchy should permit that experience to get dressed up in all kinds of cultural forms and expression, letting it be turned around like a diamond so that the light of one time may reflect on one aspect as the light of another time reflects on another, yet always preserving the initial impact of God's revelation in Jesus and never mistaking information about the person for the person himself.

In summary, if we were to put what we have written into propositional form, it would look like this:

	The Interpreters, Protectors & Teachers
The Reality	
1. The Experience or the Revelation	1. The Pope and other bishops with the Living Community of the Faithful
2. The Faith-Response	2. Ordinary Teaching: The Magisterium
3. The Telling (Scripture, Tradition)	3. Extraordinary Teaching: Infallible Pronouncements, Church Councils
4. The Reflection (theologizing)	
5. The Dogma or Conditioned Formula	

We the people are more a part of this whole scheme than we think. We may not have had the experience of the primal revelation of Jesus or have had a part in the early normative faith-response. But we do respond on the words of another; we have access to scripture; we have a magisterium dedicated to our service and we, as the Church, partake in infallibility. And, of course, we must make our own personal response else all is in vain. Our yes is essential if religion is ever to be more than a system of thought or a sociological fact. Our yes must make it live; our yes must make us think of the Lord Jesus as did the early Church: not as someone who died and was raised but as someone who had died but is *now* living. Our proclamation must always be for what is and what shall be as well as for what has been.

NOTES FOR CHAPTER 5

1. Wolfhart Pannenberg, *Basic Questions in Theology,* Vol. 1 (Fortress Press, 1970) p. 182.
2. Dogmatic Constitution on the Church.
3. Louis Monden, *Faith: Can Man Still Believe?* (Sheed and Ward, 1970) pp. 34 and 37.
4. John Powell, *A Reason to Live, A Reason to Die!* (Argus Communciations, 1972) p. 97.
5. Avery Dulles, "The Modern Dilemma of Faith" in *Doctrines Do Grow,* edited by John T. McGinn (Paulist Press, 1972) p. 19.
6. Wolfhart Pannenberg, cited above, p. 199.
7. Louis Monden, cited above, pp. 168 to 170.
8. George Tyrrell, *Christianity at the Crossroads* (Hillary House, 1963) p. 87.
9. Avery Dulles, cited above, p. 17.
10. Karl Rahner, *Theological Investigations,* Vol. 1 (Helicon, 1961) p. 149.
11. Avery Dulles, cited above, p. 23.
12. "The Crisis of Religious Language" in *Concilium* 85 (1973) pp. 20 and 33.
13. Avery Dulles, cited above, p. 26.
14. *America,* August 4, 1973, p. 57.
15. Raymond E. Brown, *Jesus, God and Man* (Macmillan, 1967) p. xii.
16. See chapter 9 on "Positioning the Church."
17. Gregory Baum, *Faith and Doctrine* (Paulist Press, 1969) p. 45.
18. Louis Dupre, "The Religious Meaning of Secularity" in *Religion in Contemporary Thought,* edited by George F. McLean (Alba House, 1973) p. 320. We must recall that scripture and tradition are two inseparable interacting modes of revelation. Scripture alone is simply self-defeating since it itself is based, as we have seen, on tradition. Tradition alone is self-defeating without the normative declarations of scripture. Tradition interprets God's revelatory action and scripture does the same. But still scriptural interpretation is a limited interpretation of what God has done; limited by all of the historical conditions during which it was written. There must obviously be an on-going interpretation since God revealed himself in Jesus for all time and for all men. So "the subsequent role of the Spirit in the history of the Church and in the history of men, the writings of the Fathers and theologians, the pronouncements of the Church—all of these enter into

what we call tradition, which is the post-scriptural interpretation of the salvific action of God described in scripture. . . . The importance of scripture is that it contains both the narrative of that action and the fundamental interpretation of that action, but there can be subsequent *normative* interpretation of God's action that is not found in scripture." Raymond Brown, cited above, footnote on page 58. See also Reginald Fuller's book, *The Foundations of New Testament Christology,* page 249; also a question about tradition in Jaroslav Pelikan's book, *Development of Christian Doctrine* (Yale University Press, 1969) p. 40ff.

19. Robert Bellah, the 1971 speech to the Federation of Diocesan Liturgical Commissions.
20. Gregory Baum, cited above, pp. 31 to 37.
21. *Sacramentum Mundi,* Vol. 3, p. 356.
22. Charles Curran, *Christian Morality Today* (Fides Publishers, 1966) p. 75.
23. Bernard Häring, "The Debate on Birth Control" in the *Twentieth Century Encyclopedia,* Vol. 7, p. 43.
24. Decree on the Church, article 25.
25. Boniface A. Willems, *The Reality of Redemption* (Herder and Herder, 1970) p. 89.
26. For example note the criticism in this editorial from *Commonweal,* Vol. XCIX, 10, December 7, 1973, p. 253. "The Roman Catholic bishops of the United States suffer from one real drawback: a significant number of people, Catholic and non-Catholic, regard their activities as irrelevant and meaningless. We do not include ourselves in this number, for we do not see how anyone still concerned with the well-being of the institutional church can take such a position. However, we encounter enough people with such views to know that they constitute one of the facts of religious life in this country, and this fact militates against any recognition of merit in what the bishops do."

6. Positioning Jesus

— 1 —

As one walks into the Capitol building of the United States in Washington, he looks up to the great classic dome. There, high above his head, is a painting of George Washington looking for all the world like some Greek god on the clouds of Mt. Olympus. In fact, the painting is called the "Apotheosis of George Washington." The dictionary defines apotheosis as the elevation of a person to the rank of a god or the idealization of a human being. That is what happened to George Washington in the painting: he is no longer a mere fallible man who happened to be the first president of the United States. Rather he is there as founding father, more than human, idealized, with overtones of divinity, to perfection. If we can pretend for a moment that we had no factual history about the man but this one and only painting we can begin to appreciate the problem of what is known as the "Jesus of history versus the Christ of faith"; and because no discussion in contemporary theology can bypass this question we must take time to position Jesus as we understand him today.

The problem arose when scholars studied the written accounts we have about Jesus, the New Testament. Even a cursory reading reveals (as we have noted in chapter 4) not a mere man, not only a journeying rabbi from Nazareth, but a super-human, elevated, exalted Lord and Master. Just as we know (let us pretend) George Washington only from that Capitol painting, so we only know Christ from the "painting over" of the New Testament writers. The question then became: can we find a real, genuine, historical Jesus of Nazareth underneath it all? Some have gone so far as to ask if there *is* a Jesus of Nazareth. Others have maintained that even if there is a Jesus of Nazareth, it really does not matter for we are saved, not by this Jesus, but by the Christ of faith, the idealized Christ who comes through the gospels which represent the reflections and faith-experiences of the first Christian communities. Even the very word we use, "gospel," is an "apotheosis" word; it means "good news." This clearly implies that "what is involved is not only some kind of historical account, but the 'glad tidings' of salvation."[1] In other words, the word "gospel" clearly indicates a colored account. More. Even the very combination we use, "Jesus Christ" poses the question. "Jesus" refers to that man from Nazareth who lived there two thousand years ago, was a child of his time, preached, ministered and was killed along with other rebels. "Christ" however is not a mere earthly last name; it is a title, and a title of sovereignty.[2] So this is the problem. Do we know only the Christ that the faith of the early Church has left us in the gospels and can we really know anything at all about the Jesus of history, that man from Nazareth? Can we work through the medieval church, the early Gentile mission churches, the Greek church to get at the Palestinian Jesus? Do we have solely the "apotheosis" of Jesus? Beneath the paint, as it were, is there a real historical personage? In search of an answer, we must go back to the initial and pivotal act that raised the whole question to begin with: the resurrection.

— 2 —

We of a later time cannot possibly imagine what the resurrection meant to Jesus' first followers. It was an event they did not expect (perhaps, as we shall see, not even Jesus expected it); their hopes had been dashed, their whole lives suddenly shattered. When therefore the Risen Jesus became apparent to them this was such a stunning, fantastic reality that the impact of it all motivated all their actions thereafter. And not only their actions but their thoughts and preaching. The resurrection became the entire basis for the new religion of Christianity and the interpretation of Jesus. Not that there were no teaching and preaching while Jesus was alive, but it was the resurrection that unified and sparked what went before. And why not? Whatever the resurrection was, it was something powerful. The one whom they had seen crucified like a common criminal was alive! And, as the scriptures remind us frequently, Jesus was alive not as a corpse come back to life, but as being alive in an entirely new way and dimension; so much so that he was unrecognizable. There was life all right but such a different life, such a new life in God who raised him up! In fact, we might speak more of a *transformation* of this Jesus. In any case, the problem is that there are simply no critical tools to measure such a thing as this risen, transformed state. Perhaps that is why, although the evangelists attempt to describe both the ascension and Pentecost, none of them tries to describe this resurrection itself. In this sense we might say that the resurrection, because of its unique position, is something really outside of history and not reducible to it (although Jesus' risen appearances certainly affected history).

> Something happened in which the disciples in these appearances were confronted with a reality which also in our language cannot be expressed in any other way than by the symbolic and metaphorical expression of hope beyond death, the resurrection from the dead. Please understand me correctly: Only the name we give to this event is symbolic, metaphorical, but not the reality of the event itself. The latter is so absolutely unique that we have no other name for this than the metaphorical expression of the apocalyptic expectation. In this sense, the resurrection of Jesus is a historical event, an event that really happened at that time.[3]

Picking up this theme another theologian expresses it this way:

> . . . Something happened between Jesus' death and the faith of the early disciples. That something is noncategorizable, unique, without analogy to anything previously experienced. It could, and can continue to be expressed only in a mythic mode, in terms of appearances and empty tomb. . . . Something has decisively formed [the consciousness of the early believers] either after or coincident with Jesus' death, to convince the early communities of belief that, no matter what the contrary appearances may seem to be, Jesus lives, and lives in a new and radically unaccountable way. . . . For the disillusioned, disheartened disciples to have come to the confidence

of his being "alive," *something* had to have happened. . . . What happened was the "resurrection." The resurrection is the thematization of an experience within the community of belief that the very dead Jesus lives. How he lives remains unknown. . . . The how of Jesus' being alive . . . comes to be expressed in terms of resurrection from the dead and of appearances to chosen witnesses. . . . Did the disciples not, then *see* Jesus? . . . They saw Jesus in the sense that they came to know, as an inescapable fact of faith-consciousness, that Jesus lives. . . .[4]

So Jesus was raised up, not physically like Lazarus or Jarius' daughter as resuscitated corpses. There was something different here. There was "something," an "aliveness" so profound and mysterious that Paul could only stammer in a general way:

What is sown is perishable; what is raised is imperishable. It is sown in dishonor; it is raised in glory. It is sown in weakness; it is raised in power. It is sown a physical body; it is raised a spiritual body.

That was the best he could do:

Jesus' risen body was no longer a body as we know bodies, bound by the dimensions of space and time. It is best to follow Paul's description of risen bodies as spiritual, not natural or physical; he can even imply that these bodies are no longer flesh and blood. Small wonder that he speaks of mystery![5]

The mystery of the resurrection, whatever it was, seems not therefore to be a mystery of a returned corpse, but the mystery of some decisive and dramatic change in Jesus and the impact of that change on the first believers. Moreover, the resurrection bears not only dramatically on the community's faith, but on Jesus himself, and his change of status. Recall that the affirmation is not simply, "we have seen Jesus" but rather "we have seen the *Lord*." In other words, the witnesses have enjoyed not only the sight of Jesus (in whatever sense this is meant) but, most of all, *insight*. Jesus has been transferred to the realm of Lordship by the resurrection (cf. Acts 2:32). So the resurrection was not only an encounter with a transformed Jesus, but also with an exalted Christ.[6] This is the key, and this is why the resurrection is *the* experience that would measure all past and future events. When Paul said that "if Christ had not been raised, then our preaching is in vain and your faith is in vain" (1 Cor 15:14) he was placing the resurrection squarely at the center of Christianity. It would be seen as God's approval and vindication of all that Jesus stood for while on earth and the definitive act which ushered in the final age of the world,[7] "the beginning of a new existence in which the life of the Messiah becomes the enduring life of that group which continues his mission."[8]

— 3 —

Now that we have positioned the resurrection as the keystone event let us follow the steps before and after it that led to the transformation of Jesus of Nazareth to the Christ of faith. The following diagram (on page 98) will be our guide for this and the next chapter (dates are approximate).

In studying the diagram, let us start backwards with step 4, the writing of the gospels. We must recall that it was the careful reading of the gospels that raised the question. For many centuries, except for some scholars, people who read the New Testament took it as it was: a telling of the life, times, and message of Jesus Christ, the founder of Christianity. People were not overcritical and besides for most of Western civilization the critical tools needed to study any work of art, music, sculpture or literature were unavailable. Manuscripts and critical texts were lacking and not much was known or not much importance was given to the culture and times of the first centuries. But then in the eighteenth century all this changed. It was the time of the Enlightenment. Everything came under scrutiny of man's reason and there was no hesitation or fear in treating the bible just like any other secular work. Soon rationalism and positivism moved in with its message that what was real was only what could be proven.

It was this spirit that took a look at the scriptures. Even before this time, however, certain critical essays were being written. Cer-

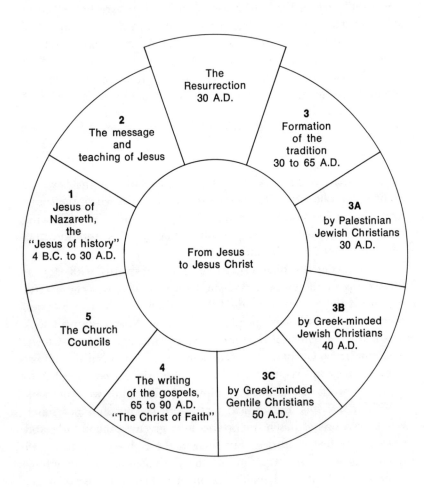

The
Resurrection
30 A.D.

2
The message
and
teaching of Jesus

3
Formation
of the
tradition
30 to 65 A.D.

1
Jesus of
Nazareth,
the
"Jesus of history"
4 B.C. to 30 A.D.

3A
by Palestinian
Jewish Christians
30 A.D.

From Jesus
to Jesus Christ

5
The Church
Councils

3B
by Greek-minded
Jewish Christians
40 A.D.

4
The writing
of the gospels,
65 to 90 A.D.
"The Christ of Faith"

3C
by Greek-minded
Gentile Christians
50 A.D.

tain discrepancies were noted in scripture and the view was emerging that the New Testament was not as simple as it appeared to be. In later years interest in psychology grew. Scholars wanted to know more about Jesus himself: his life, times, thoughts, consciousness and so on. The big discovery, if we may put it that way, was that a straightforward, clear biography was so hard to come by as to be impossible.[9] What led to this conclusion?

The answer was that the gospels emerged upon scrutiny, not as biographies of Jesus of Nazareth who lived in first century Palestine, but as highly idealized, highly colored propaganda pieces written from the very definite point of view of the resurrection experience. Propaganda is used here in its widest sense of trying to persuade and coax with all of the implications of treating the material to fit the purpose of the writers. In some respects Jesus is seen as walking metaphorically a few feet above the ground. He multiplies bread, has a dove descend on him, hears a voice from heaven, walks upon the water, battles with Satan, speaks majestic and lengthy prose at the Last Supper, etc.

To go back to our old example, it is as if the scholars discovered the apotheosis of George Washington but could get no factual, biographical details about him. So the scholars concluded that what we have in the gospels is not Jesus of Nazareth, whoever he was— and if he was—but the Risen Christ of faith. By this they mean that the gospels do not give a biography of Jesus—there is not even a physical description of him!—but are expressions of faith in the Risen *Lord*. The evangelists in other words have read back into the gospels later thoughts and developments about Jesus. In our diagram, it would be as if steps 1 and 2 were obliterated in the interests of steps 3 and 4 in virtue of the resurrection.

Books started to appear such as Albert Schweitzer's book with the provocative English title, *The Quest for the Historical Jesus*. That title told it all: could the real Jesus of Nazareth be found in the gospels? Was there some discernible residue of a real personage under the obvious risen Christ of faith? In answer to this, towards the end of the nineteenth century a famous lecture was given by a man named Martin Kahler. He said the whole quest for the historical Jesus of Nazareth was a waste of time. After all, he argued, people are saved not by this Jesus of history but by the Christ of faith, by what God had exalted him to through the resurrection. It is therefore neither desirable nor necessary to seek such a historical personage. Otherwise, he said, people's faith would forever depend on the discoveries of historians. What is more, what about all those millions of people who lived and died believing in Christ? Certainly it was the Christ of faith they believed in, not a constantly revised man of history. How could Jesus of Nazareth, screened through a rigorous historical process like Caesar or Napoleon, be an object of faith? The resurrection is the main event that changed it all and made Jesus the Christ of faith. Contrary to the slogan, *Christ saves* not Jesus.

Criticisms like this, however shrewd, left many others determined to search further. They decided that since the gospels were written faith experiences, perhaps some clues could be obtained from the traditions that gave rise to the gospels in the first place. After all, if Jesus died in 30 A.D. and the gospels were written sometime between then and 65 then there are some thirty-five years unaccounted for. In other words, if the gospels portray an idealized Christ of faith, where did they get their material? We can recognize the validity of this question—nor is the answer something surprising for us. The answer is from theology. Theologizing took place right after the resurrection and its forms—sayings, proclamations, creedal statements, liturgies,[10] stories, parables, doxologies—all formed the matrix out of which the gospels were formed. The gospels, then, are the product of previous theologizing as well as the theologizing of the evangelists. They tried to make Palestinian Jesus relevant to the Greek Gentiles and it was to be expected that the Jewish Jesus would be overlaid with the Greek Christness. Besides, we must remember that the New Testament which gives us the only picture of Jesus we have is the product of this half-century tradition of varied Christian theologizing, and all of it formed in an uncritical age.

In all of this new investigation it was but natural that, with renewed interest in the traditions that produced the gospels, new approaches were used. One, coming into being after World War I, is called form criticism. This was a method of trying to deal with the tradition itself: its "climate," its culture, its general literature, folklore, etc. If one can find out what a particular epoch's "life situation" is, then the content and broad suppositions of its literature can be discovered. These critics wanted to know what was in the minds of the first Christians when they formed the tradition, what led them to begin this or that tradition, why they shaped as they did the ultimate writing of the gospels and what did they freely invent (according to the proper "mythologizing" and literary license of the day) in order to express their faith.

Since understandably the first Christians wanted to know all about Jesus, stories about him (the critics deduce) were gradually reshaped in three ways: (a) by the adaption of these stories to practical needs (for example, having the Risen Jesus eat to counter those saying he was a mere phantom); (b) by the community's postresurrection experience and viewpoint, and (c) by the community's desire and need to sense that they still had the Risen Christ among them. They were not interested, these early Christians, in history for its own sake, but for the sake of the faith. Therefore they easily transmuted historical data into their own projections. No incident of Jesus that appears in the gospels but has some coloring by the community's faith. What the critics seek to do is to peel away the layers of the community's additions and projections to get at the core. They cannot always do this with certitude. The reason is, once again, that the Christ of faith has so overshadowed the Jesus of history that the gospels remain first and foremost written witnesses to the faith of the early Church. Only in a secondary way are they commentaries on the events in the ministry of Jesus.[11]

So this is where we are: the gospels are the product of tradition. This is evident. The traditions themselves are resurrection-prompted reflections of the early Christian communities, reflections which appear in their liturgies, creeds and doxologies. But one more observation remains to be made. If this whole process is as described then the implication was that the evangelists who patched all these traditions together were nothing more than compilers. It was not long before a reaction to this notion set in. More research showed that the evangelists were more than scissors-and-glue men. They were actually creative with their materials. They shaped them and molded them in line with their own theologies.[12] Scholars who worked on this tack claim to find distinct contributions and emphases. Matthew, for example, sees everything from the Church's viewpoint, the community. Mark (whose gospel was the first written and which possibly drew from prior traditions known as "Q") centers on the mystery of the person of Christ and the inability of his listeners to understand his message. Luke emphasizes the proclamation of Jesus' teaching and kingdom to both Jew and Gentile. These special emphases and perspectives are responsible for a change of detail in many of the gospel stories. So the challenge is to extract the traditions from the evangelist's own shaping in order "to differentiate between the theology of the writers themselves and the tradition which they incorporate into their writing."[13]

All of this has been a long approach to the problem but at least we have positioned it better. Now we move on to steps 1 and 2 in our diagram. To come back to our original question: beneath all this tradition, idealization, creative writing, can we still detach Jesus of Nazareth, itinerant rabbi and executed prisoner?

— 4 —

In spite of the obvious reading back into Jesus as a biographer might understandably do should he refer to "President" Lincoln as a youth (though in his youth he was not of course president) we can detect the teachings and life of Jesus of history. We can connect the earthly Jesus with the Risen Christ. This is in contrast to some scholars who have too easily written off the gospels as entirely creations of the Easter-struck community. They have given up too easily any hope of discovering the historical Jesus. And they have gone too far when they jump from the observation that a cultural form in the gospel narrative is that of the early community to concluding that therefore the core event or saying did not really happen. This is something that cannot be assumed but has to be rigorously proved in each and every instance.

On the contrary there seems to be evidence that the evangelists themselves tried precisely to avoid the split between the Jesus of history and the Christ of faith. They are constantly reading back and retranslating the gospel stories precisely *in order to make the connection.* And why? Why should the evangelists even bother with a prosaic narrative gospel form after the high flown enthusiasms of the early liturgical hymns and doxologies? Why should they bother with gospels at all since many of the letter forms (epistles) were already around? Why, if not their desire precisely to soften the over-enthusiasm which was taking the historical Jesus too far afield? Why go back and tell the story of the preaching rabbi of Nazareth and the suffering man of Calvary if not to counter the danger of making Jesus unreal and glorified to the point of losing his earthly identity and continuity? "The reversion to the form of the gospel narrative, to the story of the Palestinian preacher, to the 'once upon a time' as against the 'once-for-all,' to a historicizing presentation within the framework of the kerygma [proclamation] and, last but not least, to Jesus as he wandered through Palestine; all this occurred as a reaction—theologically relevant and therefore initiated and maintained by the Church—directed towards restoring the autonomy of the Christ, of the Spirit and of faith itself."[14]   In other words, the gospel narratives are latecomers. Hymns, liturgies, doxologies, epistles, were already around. But they tended to emphasize the Christ of faith. The gospels were written to ground this Christ in the figure of Jesus of Nazareth.

We can go further. In Luke's gospel, for example, he has the two disciples on the way to Emmaus discover the real meaning of Jesus in the light of his resurrection. What is this but a linking of the two? The Risen Christ *is* that same Jesus of Nazareth who they hoped would redeem Israel. When John has Jesus tell his audience that if they destroy the Temple in three days it will be raised up again he felt compelled to remark that Jesus was speaking of his resurrection so that his readers would know that the Risen Savior and the Jesus who spoke were one and the same. It was the Church that put such a great emphasis on the incarnation of the Son of God and confessed that Christ *Jesus* is the Christ of God, which is to say that Christ is rooted in the Jesus of history.[15]

Gunther Bornkamm goes so far as to say that the movement from the Jesus of history to the Christ of faith had to be made by the community if it were to be faithful to Jesus himself. He was the way, the truth and the life, God's ultimate act for the world, the turning point. The community therefore had to take up these statements and make the proclamation of them the best they knew how lest Jesus be forever reduced to a mere Master honored and revered only by his immediate disciples.

John Ashton is right when he says:

> The gap opened up by form criticism between the Jesus of history and the Christ of faith was precisely the gap the gospel writers were concerned to close. . . . The evangelists were interested neither in what we call the Jesus of history nor . . . the Christ of faith. . . . The fundamental affirmations of the Christian belief were, as we have seen, "Jesus is the Christ" and "Jesus is Lord." And the evangelists' concern was precisely to hold together Jesus of Nazareth and the risen Christ in this single affirmation, . . . an act of faith. They were neither historians nor theologians, but combined the functions of both in declaring their own faith and eliciting the faith of their readers. It would not be too far from the truth to say that the main trouble with nineteenth-century biblical scholarship was that it searched the gospels for history, whereas the main trouble of post-Bultmannian exegesis is that it has searched the gospels for theology. Nothing could have been further from the intention of the evangelists than . . . to record what actually happened; they are certainly more like theologians than historians; but to speak of them as primarily theologians is a dangerous half-truth.[16]

We might also note that with all of the post-resurrection titles that the early Church conferred upon Jesus, it still refused to let him get buried underneath them. Jesus' personality is not reduced to a function. The people of the early Church had a real consciousness of membership in Christ, the living experience of him and dedication to a personal Christ. Neither they nor the apostles clung to a function. They embraced a person. That is why they felt it necessary to write the gospels to go along with the early creeds and epistles. It was one thing to know what Christ did and profess faith in these things. It was another to seek to know him, who he was. In brief, their faith was in the Christ of the resurrection, but this faith was in the Christ who nevertheless was Jesus. No wonder St. Peter exclaimed, "Let all the house of Israel therefore know assuredly that God has made him both Lord and Christ, *this Jesus whom you crucified*" (Acts 2:36).

Perhaps we can show the connection best in several quotations from modern scholars:

John O'Grady:

> Scholarship seems to have made a complete circle: from the acceptance of the gospels as completely historical to a denial of historicity as a result of the failure to develop a biography or psychological portrait of Christ, to a further denial of the historical aspects of the life of Jesus by Bultmann, now a return to the gospels as historical. This returning circle, however, should not be judged useless. In the process we have learned a great deal about the gospels and the Christ of our faith. Today we readily accept that the gospels are not biographies but are expressions of the faith acceptance of the early community based upon a historical appreciation of Jesus Christ, an important gain for Christian understanding.[17]

Reginald Fuller:

> An examination of Jesus' words—his proclamation of the Reign of God, and his call for decision, his enunciation of God's demand, and his teaching about the nearness of God—and of his conduct—his calling men to follow him and his healings, his eating with publicans and sinners—forces upon us the conclusion that underlying his word and work is an implicit Christology. In Jesus as he understood himself, there is an immediate confrontation with "God's presence and his very self," offering judgment and salvation.[18]

Hans Kung:

> The background to the gospels and in particular the first three synoptic gospels, is not legend and speculation, but living experi-

ences and impressions, reports handed down about the living Jesus
of Nazareth. If not directly, at least through the evangelists' testimonies of faith we can hear Jesus himself speaking.[19]

Norman Perrin:

> Knowledge of the historical Jesus is, then, important in that it can
> contribute positively to the formation of the faith-image, i.e. it can
> help provide faith with its necessary *content,* and in that it can act
> negatively as a check on false or inappropriate faith-images, or
> aspects of a faith-image. Can we go beyond this? Yes, we believe
> we can, and we reach, therefore, the third aspect of our position:
> the fact that historical knowledge of Jesus can be directly relevant
> to faith, . . . We reach this by calling attention to the nature of
> the narratives in the synoptic gospels; like the sayings, they reflect
> the equation earthly Jesus = risen Lord. . .[20]

Hans Conzelmann:

> To what extent, then, can continuity between Jesus and the com-
> munity of believers be shown? In its own understanding, the church
> takes for granted that the Risen One is the Crucified One; the Risen
> One is firmly held to be none other than the man Jesus of Naz-
> areth. . . . Thus, according to the church's understanding, Jesus
> himself remains the presupposition of faith.[21]

Gunther Bornkamm:

> Yet our four canonical gospels contain no shorthand notes of Jesus'
> sermons, no official records about his deeds and fate, no biography
> in either the ancient or the modern sense of the term. And yet it
> would be senseless and quite unjustified to leave a blank space at
> this critical juncture or to insert a mysterious X. For the gospel
> tradition has unmistakably preserved—though to what extent may
> be disputed—the word of the historical Jesus himself, and generally
> in such a way that each fragment reflects the whole.[22]

Ferdinand Hahn:

> There are more than a few things here which can undoubtedly

stand up to a critical test. To mention only a few: Jesus' baptism by John and his initial adherence to the movement of the Baptist's disciples, Jesus' withdrawal from it shortly thereafter, and the gathering of a new circle of disciples in the setting of his first activity in his native land of Galilee, his conflict with scribes and Pharisees, his journey to Jerusalem and Judea, the conflict with the Jews and the Roman hierarchy and finally his trial and end on the cross. Indeed these facts are not few. . . .

The church can no more live from the mere fact of the history of Jesus (as attested and confirmed to us even through non-Christian sources), than it can ignore the concrete life and ministry of Jesus while holding fast only to the significance of his appearance and revelation. . . .

Attention should be directed, however, to John's unbending insistence upon the historicity of Jesus. The assertion that the Word became flesh in John 1:14 is not only a general theme but is also actually upheld in the entire account . . . everything is set within the framework of the earthly ministry of Jesus. . . .

When I speak of the historical Jesus I go behind all the statements of the community, limit myself to the facts of his earthly life, his ministry and proclamation, and attempt to gain a picture which is free from all post-resurrection conceptions in order to grasp the history of Jesus in its own terms. Such a retrogressive quest of the historical Jesus is quite possible. . . In spite of the knowledge that all tradition is already stamped by faith, this tradition still points so clearly back to the history of Jesus that a clear over-all picture arises of this special character of his life and ministry, even when we are not able to produce from it a complete account or a continuous biography.[23]

All of these quotations affirm one point: Jesus of Nazareth is the Christ of faith. There are and will continue to be scores of questions about Jesus—his knowledge, his self-awareness, his sense of messiahship—but no one can remain in the genuine Christian tradition and deny the unity between Jesus and Christ. This is what ultimately sets the Christian faith apart from all other faiths, from all other perspectives.

There is more to be explored in the next chapter. For the moment we might do well to return to our diagram. We see that the central reality, the keystone, is the resurrection. Moving *forward* from that we see it as sparking the formation of traditions about Jesus and the eventual writing of the gospels from these traditions. These gospels necessarily therefore reflect the theologizing that went on in the Easter-minded community. The gospels, as Vatican II said, were written "with that clear understanding which the authors enjoyed after they had been instructed by the events of Christ's risen life and taught by the Spirit of truth. . . ." Moving *backwards* from the resurrection event we see that Jesus himself and his teaching have been interpreted in the light of the resurrection and with post-resurrection theologizing; however, this theologizing is not so total that he is obscured as a historical person or that his words and teachings do not have a significant bearing on the gospels. So we summarize:

1. There is a historical Jesus whose deeds and words and person can be detected, known, appreciated and loved. Jesus of Nazareth still remains normative.

2. His teachings, though clothed in later terms, come through to us as genuine, as carrying his authority.

3. There was a formation period under the impact of the resurrection around 30 to 65 A.D. when the eager, early Christians, reflected, sang, ritualized and put into creeds their theologizing about Jesus. The Spirit unfolded many implications and made known what was hidden. The community thus learned to give the titles of Lord, Messiah and Savior to Jesus of Nazareth.

4. There was the writing of the gospels, a writing which reflected the formation of the Christian tradition which used freely the newly unfolded, newly impacted titles of Jesus; which had a point of view in mind; which reflected both history and theology and therefore which had no intention of presenting a strict biography of Jesus of Nazareth any more than to present solely a strict theology of the Christ of faith.

There is one more related question that should be explored. If all this process took place how can we be sure that, in the last analysis, Jesus' revelation has not been distorted and that in fact we are getting someone else's interpretation rather than his own teaching? The answer lies once more in the gospels themselves as credible narrations. First of all, for all the variants in the gospels there is unanimous convergence of vision about Jesus. There is a very obvious unity among all four gospels and other New Testament writings that form one piece, one message that indicates that the traditions were indeed kept free from contamination and rumor. Secondly, the faith about Jesus in not only unanimous but unhesitant. "The authors never write like philosophers groping for the final answer, nor does the language of doubt ever appear in their religious testimony." The writers knew what they had been taught, they believed in it, lived it, died for it and proclaimed it with conviction. Thirdly, there is the utter novelty of the New Testament. We must note that there is nothing in the Jewish tradition to predispose the first disciples—all Jews—to accept what they did. Their traditions would never have prompted them to accept what they were proclaiming. If they had set out to construct a messiah they never would have come up with a back-country carpenter as their candidate. Fourthly, the Apostles themselves were profoundly changed and they in turn changed the world. The message had to be authentic to take a motley crew of fishermen and make them the mission band for the world. In a word, the claims of Jesus and his Apostles are too ridiculous to have survived if they had not been true.[24]

We have done only a part of our diagram but enough to position both the problem and some responses to the so-called Jesus of Nazareth versus the Christ of faith controversy. What has been written so far may seem far removed from the thoughts of the reader. Still, sooner or later, if you continue to read you will meet the controversy. Moreover, the next time you read the scriptures, you will do so with a different sense of what is being written there and perhaps be able to appreciate the interlocking rhythms of fact and interpretation, of event and faith. Finally, having arrived as we did to a conclusion of the existence of the historical Jesus we should see clearly what significance this has for us. The meaning is that indeed Jesus entered into the world of man. The Word was made flesh and lived among us. The God-Man took history seriously by entering it fully. He took with the utmost seriousness the time, place, language, culture and people of this first century Palestine. This Jesus is clearly a man of place, space and history. If we are to imitate him we will do so, not by becoming carpenters, but by taking history seriously also after the example of the historical Jesus.[25]

NOTES FOR CHAPTER 6

1. Ferdinand Hahn, *What Can We Know About Jesus?* (Fortress Press, 1969) p. 20.

2. Gunther Bornkamm in *What Can We Know About Jesus?*, cited above, p. 69.

3. Wolfhart Pannenberg quoted in the *Jerome Biblical Commentary*, edited by Raymond E. Brown (Prentice-Hall, 1969) p. 792. We pause here to remember the language of myth which we described before. The resurrection begged to be interpreted and therefore the resurrection narratives contain various versions and contradictions and no sense can be made out of the time sequence. The late gospel narratives also had to contend with misinterpretations and so additions were added on this account. Such would be the "third day" symbol as a traditional one conveying God's special intervention, the nail marks and eating to underline that he was indeed the very Man of Nazareth whom they saw before the resurrection now risen in glory.

4. Andrew Maloney, "Jesus as the Horizon of Human Hope" in *Does Jesus Make a Difference?*, edited by Thomas M. McFadden (Seabury Press, 1974) p. 106.

5. Raymond E. Brown, *The Virginal Conception and Bodily Resurrection of Jesus* (Paulist Press, 1973) p. 128.

6. Raymond E. Brown, p. 112ff.

7. Reginald H. Fuller, *The Foundations of New Testament Christology* (Charles Scribner's Sons, 1965) p. 148ff.

8. *Jerome Biblical Commentary,* cited above, p. 114.

9. For example, Harnack.

10. As for liturgies it is commonly acknowledged that Matthew in his mandate in his 28th chapter to baptize all nations "has incorporated the baptismal formula already in common use in the Church of his day"; also, "it might be called a piece of liturgical artistry. Luke presents, not an historical account of the institution of the eucharist, but rather what one might almost call an 'impressionist' picture-sequence, portraying the liturgical meaning of the eucharistic sacrifice." David M. Stanley, *The Apostolic Church in the New Testament* (Newman Press, 1967) pp. 128 and 132.

11. Harvey K. McArthur, "From the Historical Jesus to Christology?" in *Theology Digest,* Vol. XVIII, 1 (Spring, 1970) p. 29ff.

12. This is called redaction criticism. See Norman Perrin's, *A Modern Pilgrimage in New Testament Christology* (Fortress Press, 1974) p. 104.
13. Reginald H. Fuller, cited above, p. 17.
14. Ernst Kaseman, *New Testament Questions of Today* (Fortress Press, 1969) p. 63.
15. Gunther Bornkamm, cited above, p. 70.
16. John Ashton, *Why Were the Gospels Written?* (Fides Publishers, 1973) p. 78.
17. John F. O'Grady, *Jesus, Lord and Christ* (Paulist Press, 1972) p. 24ff.
18. Reginald H. Fuller, cited above, p. 106.
19. Hans Kung, quoted in *The Jesus Myth* by Andrew M. Greeley (Doubleday, 1971) p. 19.
20. Norman Perrin, *Rediscovering the Teaching of Jesus* (Harper and Row, 1967) p. 246.
21. Hans Conzelmann, *Jesus* (Fortress Press, 1973) p. 93.
22. Gunther Bornkamm, *The New Testament, a Guide to Its Writings* (Fortress Press, 1973) p. 10.
23. Ferdinand Hahn, cited above, pp. 30 to 75.
24. Avery Dulles, *Apologetics and the Biblical Christ* (Newman Press, 1967) p. 36ff.
25. Carl J. Armbruster, "Through Christology to Christ Centeredness" in *Dimensions in Religious Education,* edited by John R. McCall (CIM Books, 1973) p. 73.

7. Positioning Christ

— 1 —

In the last chapter we saw that the gospels read back into the life of Christ. The resurrection was the impetus. From this impetus it slowly and surely dawned on the first Christians that not only did Jesus do certain things but, as a consequence, he *was* certain things. From his functions, if we want to express it that way, came his identity, his being. In this progression of thought came in due time the various titles which were applied to Jesus: Messiah, Servant, Son of God, Son of Man, Lord. What we call Christology was born, the science of seeing who Jesus was and continued to be for men.

Christology is the doctrine of the person of Jesus Christ. . . . It was because he was who he was that Jesus Christ did what he did. But for the New Testament it was the other way around. In the New Testament men are first confronted by the history of Jesus of Nazareth—by what he said and did—and they respond to it in terms of a Christology, a confession of faith. Through what he does they come to see who he is. . . . Since it is men's response to Jesus, it follows that Christology is not itself a part of the original revelation or action of God in Christ. . . . The church's Christology was a response to its total encounter with Jesus, not only in his earthly history but also in its (the church's) continuing life.[1]

Now this development did not happen all at once but in stages which overlapped. To explore this development we must go back to the diagram of the last chapter and pick up the sections marked 3A, 3B and 3C. The traditions about Jesus went through these stages before surfacing in the written gospels and each stage added its own development.

We must recall many times that Christianity was started in

113

Palestine and that the first Christians were Jews. They were filled with Jewish culture, history, thinking patterns and aspirations. Naturally when these Palestinians reflected on Jesus, a Jew, they would use the terms and concepts of their background. This is the first stage (3A), the first theologizing that took place. Now what did they have at hand? They had the Old Testament, local pre-Christian writings and a lively political situation of rebellion against Rome. They therefore had such concepts as Messiah, a name whose content fluctuated between some kind of priestly and kingly figure who was expected to come and to rule. They had other terms such as "Son of God," "Son of David," "Son of Man" and "Servant of the Lord." All terms were highly overtoned and in one way or another used for some transcendental agent of liberation, redemption and judgment. They were shot through with various notions of leadership, suffering, judging. Such were the terms at hand to help interpret Jesus of Nazareth, his life and his work. Such was the first strata of the traditions about Jesus.

The second stage (3B) the traditions about Jesus went through was one which filtered through the thinking of the Greek-minded Jewish Christians. These were the Jews exposed to Greek culture and thought. Naturally they would have different mental outlooks and titles to use for Jesus. There would therefore have to be a transition and translation from the original Palestinian Jewish reflection on Jesus. It was this tradition which translated Messiah to the Greek "Christos" when that term had been denuded of all nationalism. They introduced "Kyrios," meaning "Lord," indicating that Jesus was not merely passively waiting in heaven to come again soon (as the Palestinian Jews thought) but was there as glorified, as exalted Lord.

Finally, we come to a third stage of reflection and theologizing (3C). This tradition would be among the Gentile Christians outside Palestine and the scattered Jewish settlements. These people were not always familiar with Judaism and the Old Testament, but only with their Greek-cultured world, the world of Greek philosophy. So once more the message and meaning of Jesus would have to be retranslated. (We should be getting the idea now of the quite legitimate process, present from the beginning, of renewal; of making Jesus relevant to every age.) Of course, with this move into a total Gentile world a narrow line had to be walked. The Jewish missionaries (like Paul) tried to steer the course between accommodating the message of Jesus to the Gentiles so they could understand and yet resisting those things which would distort the meaning of Jesus. Unavoidably our first heresies came at this time. In any case, under the influence of Greek philosophy Jesus came to be seen not merely as Messiah, and the reigning Lord, but also as the preexistent redeemer who became incarnate, died, was raised up and was exalted with a name "above every other name."

We have here, in broad strokes, the notion of the message and teachings of Jesus going from the strictly Jewish world to the Jewish-Greek world to the totally Greek, Gentile world. In the process words and concepts have been accommodated to meet the present audience. It is also interesting to note a similar pattern in early Christian writings. As we have seen before, the first literary form of New Testament writings was not the gospel but the epistle. In fact there was no literature at all for the first New Testament generation. There were many reasons for this. The first Jewish Christians were not among the elite and were not a literary community. Besides they looked forward to the imminent coming of Jesus and this was not conducive to literary activity. In addition since they were all Jews, they already had a sacred scripture, the Old Testament. Finally, preaching was more highly valued in those first days. So when they got around to writing anything it was in the form of epistles. Paul's letters may not be the first written but they are the first to be preserved. Significantly the first is a letter to the Gentile Christians in Thessalonica. They had no Old Testament and therefore no competition, so they preserved Paul's letter as the beginning of their own scripture. It was only later, in the desire to know more about Jesus, that the gospels were written, the first one being Mark's. This proved to be more serviceable than the epistles and more durable than the apocalyptic form which was tried (Book of Revelation) and discarded.[2] But again, it is important to remember that by the time of the gospels, the tradition period or, as we might more accurately say, the formation period had gone through roughly three stages (and were still in the process) and this accounts for the shift of emphases and titles. We can quite clearly see how the New Testament writings express one stage of development and later writings a final stage. We can also see how the theologizing progressed and how Jesus became Christ.

— 2 —

When we come to the titles conferred by the first communities upon Jesus we run into an instant irony. The irony is that the one title that we know Jesus rejected is the very one history gave him: Christ (messiah). In the gospels Jesus openly rejects this title and would not claim it on the grounds of current misunderstandings and political overtones. In time, however, the Greek community emptied it of its old Jewish political meanings (and indeed of any meaning) and attached it to Jesus as a title and function.

There were other titles. One was the "Son of God," a title which figures frequently in the gospel stories and one that was put there and into Jesus' mouth by the early Church.[3] Later it was dropped as being too specifically Jewish in origin. Still, even though Jesus never called himself God, no one doubts that he has a unique relationship to God. He was son like no one else was son. "No one knows the Son but the Father and no one knows the Father but the Son and anyone to whom the Son wishes to reveal him" (Matt 11:27). This was the kind of stated relationship added to his life and his "style" which had a great impact on his followers. This relationship and his actions, on reflection, inevitably led his followers to perceive the God in Jesus. So it is here, in Jesus' own sayings and personal life, not specifically in applying any special titles to himself, that Jesus was revealed as God. The earliest tradition did not call Jesus God. The reason is easy to see. The Jewish Old Testament had a very precise content to that word and as such it could not be made to fit the unique status of Jesus. The word God was far too narrow, far too restricted to the Father to include any other notion. Only later would the term God be broadened to include the unique status of Jesus and the Spirit. We see this in the later New Testament writings, for example, in John's gospel when Thomas falls down and makes the unmistakable identification, "My Lord and my God." Or John's opening prologue: "In the beginning was the Word; and the Word was in God's presence, and the Word was God." By this time Gentile concepts were there to help. By this time the community had reflected and come to the realization of Jesus' divinity.

There is more to pause over when we call Jesus God. We have just mentioned that the Jewish Christians could not do this because the term God was so carefully spoken of the Father. There was no way that a Jew could take that holy, centuries-honored term and attach it to a physical body. It would be too much to ask, too much to say. On the other hand we moderns say "Jesus is God" too easily for that phrase does not do justice to either term. It says too little. Jesus is also a man and calling him God preempts that term, preempts his humanity. "To describe Christ as God is to neglect the sense in which he is both less and more, man as well as God within the glory and limitations of his incarnation."[4] Moreover, to say "Jesus is God" can mislead us in thinking that we have a notion of God and then we apply it to Jesus. Hardly. No man has seen God. It is the other way around. We learn first of Jesus, see him in the flesh, what he does and how he acts—and *then* we get a notion of the divine. "We must not read the divine *into* Christ's human life, we must read the divine *off* his human life. . . ."[5] That is why we call Jesus the revelation of the Father. That is why the New Testament states quite clearly and accurately that Jesus did not come to reveal himself but to reveal the Father. So if we are to know anything whatever about the unknown God we must look to Jesus. Therefore Schubert Odgen is right when he says the real question about the divinity is not whether Jesus is an adequate symbol of God but rather whether any God who does not correspond with Jesus' symbols is an adequate God.

— 3 —

In the fourth century of Christianity a devastating heresy called Arianism claimed that Jesus was a mere man indwelt by God but subordinate to him. The Church reacted fiercely to this by asserting once and for all in the Nicene creed that Jesus is really God. This reaction still lingers. So fearful is the Church of the reappearance of this heresy that it has never ceased to stress Jesus' divinity. Among the theologians this is known as the triumph of the Alexandrian school over the Antiochene school. The former stressed the divinity, the latter the humanity of Christ. The Alexandrian school bequeathed to us Jesus as *Pantocrator,* that stern and majestic Zeus-like figure we see in Christian art and this school had dominated till the present time. Now, today, more emphasis is being put on the humanity of Christ. Jesus is no longer seen as a God in human disguise, somehow commuting between divinity and humanity, a man (of sorts) with a divine ace up his human sleeve. The attempt is made to preserve the true humanity of Christ (as the Council of Chalcedon insisted) as well as his divinity. That is why some theologians express the thought that Jesus is God *in* man; or put more emphatically, "Jesus is the Son of God by being man in a unique way."[6] This says that Jesus' humanity is in some way the visible display of the divinity; that the divinity is deep *within* Jesus' being man, his humanity. In this view God is truly immanent in all of creation and in all human beings, but especially he has revealed this fact by being uniquely and specially immanent in Jesus:

> In this perspective it has become impossible to reflect on God as the intelligent agent over and above history, who intervenes at certain moments to save man from blindness and sin. It has become necessary to think of the divine in the deepest dimension of human life, as the matrix out of which we come to be, as the judgment and forgiveness present in our history, and hence to conceive of the divine revelation in Israel and Jesus Christ as the disclosure of this gracious though hidden, dimension of human life.[7]

If God is then the "deepest dimension of human life" then in Jesus he is preeminently present and Jesus' humanity is truly the "Word" of God, God's self-revelation in the flesh. Jesus is the concrete manifestation of the divine immanence, the enfleshment of God.

The danger—and the source of much confusion—is, we may think in terms of Jesus living a double life. . . . But, as the Council of Ephesus said, Jesus is not two sons, but one son. He is the one Son of God. His whole human activity *is* his divine activity . . . Jesus is not someone who leads a completely human life and *as well* a shadow divine life which from time to time intrudes and manifests itself. . . . The incarnation does not mean that God is behind or added to or over-and-above the human: it means the human *is* the very expression (the Word) of God. Jesus' human life is the manifestation of the divine life. . . . Jesus' manhood is the form in which God appears among us. Or to put it more simply and not so misleadingly, Jesus is the form in which God appears among us. He is God-with-us. . . The biblical phrase, "Jesus is God's Word" is splendid precisely because it gives the impression not that he is God's Word *and* man but that he is God's Word by being the man he is.[8]

If we grasp this we will not be caught up in the old problem that Jesus is really a divine person and that the divine "I" was doing all of the reference work. But no; if Jesus is God's Word by being a man, then he is a man with a human personality and reference point; and when he said "I" it was Jesus of Nazareth speaking and experiencing, not some distant divinity. And this will not upset us if we state once more that this man Jesus is the living Word, his *whole* manhood *is* precisely the revelation of God.

As we have had occasion to note before, this kind of thinking reflects the modern dislike for picturing God as "out there" or "up there" somewhere, as someone who suddenly bursts onto the human scene as man and races back home again. On the other hand we need to be cautious lest we reduce Jesus to God's human being who evolved into God's best human expression, who somehow grows into being God's Son. We see this error in Bishop John A. T. Robinson's recent book, *The Human Face of God,* where he says, the incarnation does not mean insertion into the living stream, intervention by

God in the form of man, but the embodiment, the realization of
God in this man." Or again: "That one who was totally and utterly
a man—and had never been anything other than a man or more
than a man—so completely embodied what was from the beginning
the meaning and purpose of God's self-expression . . . that it could
be said of that man, 'He was God's man.' "9 This is not the New
Testament witness. In fact, it is the old adoptionist heresy. No, St.
Paul and the evangelists took up the early hymns and creeds about
Christ and the conclusion these creeds and hymns reached was that
Jesus was the Son of God, one with him from the beginning, equal
to God, God who became man.

It should be evident that since Jesus is God become man or God
in man it is worth repeating our point that Jesus is the revelation of
the Father. If we want to know about God we must look to Christ.
Christ is the center for in him God had done and told everything.
That is why pedagogically it is better to learn about Jesus first (for,
again, who knows God?), see his humanity and from that humanity
God is revealed. "Everything the man of Nazareth says and does is
a revelation of God. God is at work among us in Jesus. He reveals
himself in the living and dying of a member of the human race."10
God truly entered the human condition in Jesus. Now we have one
who is a real inspiration a "man like us in all things but sin"; one
who knew therefore the human condition of hurt, betrayal, ignorance, joy, disappointment, fear, suffering and death.

Moreover, in the light of our previous look at God as immanent
to this world, a "process-God" intimately related to it, we must
position Jesus accordingly. He is not a foreign intrusion of an
absent God but rather the high point, the definitive, in-the-flesh
presence of One already present. "But Jesus is not an isolated
'entrance' or 'intervention' of God into a world which is otherwise
without his presence and action. Rather, he is, as a man, a climactic
and definitive point of God's presence and action among men in a
world in which God is always present and ceaselessly active. Jesus
is not the supreme anomaly: he is the classic instance."11

— 4 —

Years ago Mark Twain wrote his famous book *The Prince and the Pauper*. It was made into a movie and replayed on television many times. You might recall that it is the story of a royal prince who discovers an exact double beggar boy. He decides to switch roles with him, the beggar or pauper pretending that he is the prince and the prince dressing up like the pauper. It takes little imagination to see the excitement, fun and drama the story poses. But let us use the general outline of this story to set forth two possibilities and then we shall relate them to the incarnation and the knowledge of Jesus.

In the first instance, let us say that there was a prince, born, raised and brought up as such. He knew who he was. In the spirit of adventure, as in Twain's story, he sneaks out of the castle, puts on beggar's clothes and goes about in disguise to get a firsthand look at his kingdom. This probably is the mental image most people have in reference to the incarnation. God becomes man. He puts on this humanity as beggar's garments and goes around his earthly kingdom for a firsthand look. He always knows, of course, that he is royalty; that in a pinch he can suddenly reveal himself and get out of any scrape he gets cornered into. Only later on, in his own good time, when his followers are ready for the impact of his self-revelation does he declare that all along he was indeed their prince, the very leader of the realm who shall now reward them all for their loyalty. If this is how we might caricature the average Christian's thoughts about the incarnation, then we can see that the knowledge of Jesus poses no problem at all. He was God—the prince, royalty— and he knew it. He talked the street talk all right and pretended he did not know which fork to use at table, but inside, he really did and could converse with royalty if he wanted to; inside he really knew all things.

But it is not that simple. In fact there was much controversy over what Jesus really knew, a controversy that raged for the first five centuries. However, after the seventh century the generally held position was that characterized in our story: Jesus is God. Therefore he is perfect. Perfection includes the Beatific Vision and infused knowledge. Therefore Jesus did know all things. There was no ignorance whatever in him. We can see once more that this notion is based on the Greek concept of a static, immutable deity. (See chapter 3.) But there was always a stream of thought that saw it differently and modern process theology of which we have written before has picked this up. Perfection, it is said, need not mean something once and for all finished, complete. Perfection consists of movement, process, becoming. If this is so, then Jesus' growing in knowledge would be seen as more perfect than already fully possessing it all. Jesus did have some kind of special knowledge— all theologians concede that—but this does not have to include the Beatific Vision. If Jesus is said to possess the state of the Beatific Vision "the reason—certainly in St. Thomas—is that, being the source of our Beatific Vision, Christ must possess it himself. But this argument applies to Christ only when he has reached his final ful-fillment. That is why, in spite of his unique consciousness of being the only-begotten Son, Christ did not have to enjoy on this earth a vision whose beatific vision quality would make his earthly suf-fering impossible, or whose total comprehension would make any increase in knowledge superfluous."[12] For Jesus to have possessed the Beatific Vision would have robbed him of the precise human suffering he underwent.

On a very practical level, the scriptures certainly seem to bear out the contention that Jesus did not know all things but had to grow in knowledge, was ignorant about certain things. He comes across as no prince pretending to be a pauper. He said outright that he did not know when the end of the world was coming. He asked questions in the Temple. He shared the common misunderstandings of scripture and misquoted it (for example, in Mark 2:26, Abiathar was not the high priest and in Matthew 23:35 Zechariah was not the son of Barachiah but the son of Jehoiada). When he asked "Who touched me?" he asked because he really did not know. He was tempted by the devil and agonized over deliverance from death. So, if Jesus really were ignorant, how do we square this with his status as Son of God?

Perhaps, in search of an answer, we must abandon our Prince

and Pauper imagery and take another. Dickens' *Oliver Twist* will serve as a guide. We might recall that Oliver started out as a poor orphan boy who was eventually restored to his rightful status as heir to his well-to-do relatives. Along this line let us say that there really was a prince who at birth became separated from the royal family. As this child is growing up he does not know that he is the prince of the realm. But as he moves along in life he begins to get intimations here and there, little clues and intuitions that make him realize that he is something more than an ordinary citizen. As he gets older he begins putting two and two together, the feeling gets stronger that he is indeed royalty and after a very traumatic scene it is suddenly revealed to him who he is. *Now,* after the trauma, he is dressed in royal robes, given proper royal titles and his humble followers, overawed, overwhelmed and overjoyed fall at his feet and declare him Lord and Master.

Modern theologians might think along the lines of this analogy. As Jesus of Nazareth grows, as his human consciousness expands, he gets intimations that he is more than man; that somehow royalty (divinity) is his hallmark. His awareness unfolds, his knowledge to express and verbalize this awareness grows, his intimacy with the Father blossoms and after the trauma of the crucifixion the Father raises him up thereby placing his seal on his work and life and indeed on his very person by exalting him as he truly is: Lord and Savior and Messiah. "This Jesus whom you crucified has been proclaimed as Lord and Master . . . ." Notice that there has not really been a change in status. Jesus always was royalty, only this awareness did not come into his full knowledge until later. "Jesus always knew who he was, but just as we need time to express who we are, so he too developed in his self-awareness."[13] Jesus always was God's only Son, but this did not become apparent until God raised him up and affirmed him at the resurrection. No wonder the first Christians and the evangelists, in their enthusiasm, picked up the habit of calling Jesus "Prince" (Lord, Savior, Son of David, etc.) before it was chronologically apparent. It was not unnatural for them to play back the titles that came later.

Now all of this leaves room for ignorance in Jesus. The reason is that all along we have been making a distinction between knowledge and awareness. One can be aware of something and yet not possess the mental capacity to verbalize or express it. One can have certain intuitions about himself, an inner awareness of his uniqueness, an awareness of special gifts he possesses, yet not be able to either understand these gifts or set it down carefully and logically. Only at a later stage of his development can he do this. We think of some famous people who looking back at their childhood express the notions that they always "felt" they had this or that gift, but did not understand it at the time; it was wrapped in obscurity but there. Only later, as they grew and their mental equipment gave them the tools of insight and expression, did the gift come out. So too with Jesus. His awareness of his unique position, his divine Sonship was always there; but his knowledge of it, his understanding of it, his acknowledgment, his expression of it had to unfold, take time. The fact is, taking on his human nature, he took this part too: human nature's laws of slow development of one's mental powers of understanding and expression. So from this point of view, from the point of view of his human knowledge, he was ignorant. Luke is accurate in telling us that he grew in knowledge. So again, "One would then be able to say that his *knowledge* was limited, but such limitation would not at all exclude an intuitive *consciousness* of a unique relationship to God and of a unique mission to men."[14] We must recall that the Council of Chalcedon pronounced definitively that Jesus was truly human and ignorance is a human quality. God gave himself over to our human condition wholly and this included limitations. He had to eat and sleep. He had to walk on the ground and not off the mountain so the law of gravity would not do him in. When he was pierced he bled. When he was given a sorrow, he wept (as over Lazarus his friend's grave). In a word, Chalcedon was right: Jesus came into the human condition of which alienation and ignorance are a part. He emptied himself out into the unredeemed condition of mankind. He took on the slave-condition of mortal men. His agony and pain were living and dying that way, not knowing how it would end, not knowing that he would be made Lord and Christ at the resurrection. So the Son of God deliberately left his omniscience and voluntarily immersed himself for our sakes in a finite mind that had to wrestle with human information and only gradually come to know with this same limited mind what he already felt deeply and unreservedly in his conscious self-awareness: that he was indeed the only Son of the Father. As Raymond Brown concludes:

> A Jesus who walked through the world knowing exactly what the morrow would bring, knowing with certainty that three days after his death his Father would raise him up, is a Jesus who can arouse our admiration, but still a Jesus far from us. He is a Jesus far from a mankind that can only hope in the future and believe in God's goodness, far from a mankind that must face the supreme uncertainty of death with faith but without knowledge of what is beyond. On the other hand, a Jesus for whom the future was as much a mystery, a dread, and a hope as it is for us and yet, at the same time, a Jesus who would say, "Not my will but yours"—this is a Jesus who could effectively teach us how to live, for this is a Jesus who would have gone through life's real trials. . . . In the fourth and fifth centuries the question of Jesus as God and man was not an abstract question debated in the scholar's chambers; it was a question of what God and Christianity were all about. I submit that, if we take the trouble to understand, it remains all of that even in the twentieth century.[15]

— 5 —

Before we give a summary of the last two chapters there are two important points we must make. The first deals with the final section of our diagram: The General Councils of the Church. They are taken last not to imply that they are the ultimate foundation on which everything else rests but rather the other way around. They position, clarify and explicate the everything else. We admitted earlier that the councils are the products of their times and must be retranslated for modern man. Nevertheless, these councils are organic and authentic reflections of all that precedes them in the diagram. Their formulas, however esoteric today, represent genuine developments of the Christian faith. We say this because the councils are sometimes disparaged, dismissed as anachronisms which hinder the faith. But, as Bruce Vawter says, in commenting on Chalcedon (though his words may apply to all the councils), "The New Testament certainly invited the responses Chalcedon gave. It is arguable that other responses could have been offered, but to offer no response at all would have been a betrayal of New Testament faith. Furthermore, that the response was four centuries in coming is as much testimony to the care and concern that went into them as it is to the confusions and bickerings that are more often remembered in their connection . . . . Chalcedon was a genuine development out of the New Testament and . . . its conclusions, therefore, even if not its history, properly concern New Testament theology; and we believe . . . that its conclusions are still more faithful to the New Testament than are the various alternatives more recently proposed in the name of 'biblical relevance . . . .' A decent respect for Chalcedon and its tradition, however, requires imitation rather than reiteration. Or translation rather than recital . . . ."[16] Again, Reginald Fuller adds his thoughts:

> We must recognize the validity of this achievement of the church of the first five centuries within the terms in which it operated. It is sheer biblicism to maintain that the church should merely repeat 'what the Bible says'—about Christology as about everything else. The church has to proclaim the gospel *into* the contemporary situation. And that is precisely what the Nicene Creed and the Chalcedonian formula were trying to do. "The Definition of Chalcedon was the only way in which the fifth-century fathers, in their day, and with their conceptual apparatus, could have faithfully credalized the New Testament witness to Christ. . . ."[17]

None of this implies that we must repeat endlessly the creeds and formulas of these councils. Rather than reciting them we should translate them, update them so that modern man can also be nourished by the truth.

The second point we must make deals with an overview insight on what we have written in this chapter. Recall that we said in the chapter on myth that the early Christians, being children of their times, were forced to use the myths and symbols they knew in order to explain Jesus. It could be no other way for them as for us. We must all use the material at hand. For the first Christians, we saw that they reached into Judaism to come up with Messiah, Son of Man, Savior, Son of God and so on. These were metaphors, current myths, applied to Jesus to explain his uniqueness. They were used to interpret Jesus but the harm came when such metaphors were objectified; that is, when they no longer became symbols to convey an understanding *about* Jesus but became statements *of* Jesus. So the Son of Man symbol which started out to explain Jesus wound up as an objective, transcendental, cosmic figure in its own right. Lord came to mean a preexistent divinity. The New Man came to be cosmic man. In a word, these symbolic interpretations began to be taken literally. Jesus became the preexistent Son of God, the second Person of the Blessed Trinity. The development of this kind of Christology has tended to hide the real Jesus. In moving from Jesus to the Christ something may have been lost.

At this point the reader may be scandalized for we seem to be saying that Jesus is not really divine, not really the Son of God and this is heresy. No, what we are saying is that the reality about Jesus is one thing and possibly the Christological titles such as Son of God and Lord which originally were used as interpretations and which hardened into objective independent statements are another. We are saying that such titles are not the last word, that historically they are provisional metaphors—and metaphors which might inadvertently obscure the real Jesus. We are holding fast to the truth that Jesus is unique and that God is definitively revealed in him. But all that we are asking is this: are titles such as Lord, Son of God and Second Person of the Blessed Trinity the best *interpretations* of this revelation? Have we stopped to realize that such titles which we use so easily are merely descriptive symbols and not objective statements about Jesus? Jesus indeed may be all the things implied in the symbols, but not necessarily the symbols themselves. "The affirmation that Jesus is the Christ, that he is Lord, that he is the Holy One and so on, is not of the historical order, but of the eschatological. It is a judgment about the absolute future."[18]

Let us put it another way. The first Christians and the early Fathers wanted desperately to show the profound truth that the

Father indeed loves us, that he has definitively reached out to us in Jesus, that he has disclosed himself, revealed himself in Jesus. Jesus is indeed the unique communicator of the Father to the world. But, is it not possible—and indeed, as we have seen in our chapter on myth—is it not probable that symbols were used to convey all this? Is not the miraculous birth of Jesus, for example, a symbol indicating the direct outpouring of God's revelation in Jesus? The miraculous birth does not have to be literal: it is symbolic of God's special intervention into history. The use of the title "Lord" need not imply objective, passive divinity as we understand it, but such a title can convey that Jesus uniquely mediated God's authority and therefore that he, Jesus, "transcended the category of ordinary humanity. On the other hand, the idea of Logos attempts to express the incarnation of God's creative self-utterance, the embodiment of his self-communication to the world. The term 'Son of God' has the idea of faithful adherence to the law amid persecution, and of final vindication by God. It could express that in Jesus the messianic expectations have been fulfilled."[19]

You see, what we tend to forget is that the basic thrust of scripture is to declare that God is a God who goes out of himself and who is uniquely present in Jesus Christ. The early Christians and all succeeding generations (especially the great Church councils) have sought to express this divine intimacy in Christ and its meaning for man's redemption and salvation in the most adequate forms possible. "The Christians of the first centuries succeeded by reconfiguring and reinterpreting the religious mythological frameworks and philosophical systems of their era. It is our task to seek out and try to grasp the meaning they sought to embody, and to reformulate it for our time. In pursuing this work, we must reexamine critically those expressions which now may tend to obscure rather than bring to light the reality which is Christ."[20]

Perhaps this will help. Remember Wordsworth's poem in the chapter on myth?

She was a Phantom of delight
When first she gleamed upon my sight;

A lovely Apparition, sent
To be a moment's ornament;
Her eyes as stars of Twilight fair;
Like Twilight's, too, her dusky hair;

We could easily make a creed out of this; that is, take the symbols and make them objective statements: "I believe in Jean (to use a random name) as a phantom and apparition. As phantom she is not confined to space but can pass through corporal elements. As apparition she can appear to men at will but only those who have repented and who have pure hearts shall see her. Her eyes are stars, shining from eternity, co-equal with the moon. Her hair, I confess, is dark, neither blonde nor red but a deep black." We could go on but the point is made. What we have done is to take what was symbolic and make objective statements about it. What was lost in the process is Jean. Exactly who is she and why was she originally described that way? By concentrating too much on the symbols to the point of making them objective realities we have lost the content of the person who was the whole reason for writing the poem to begin with. So too with Jesus. In the process of becoming Christ we have tended to concentrate on his symbolic titles, objectifying him into a preexistent divinity. The result has been to lose the focus of how Jesus originally thought of himself, presented himself and what was the impact on this first audience. We must remember that our creeds, the Nicene and Apostles creed, represent the best possible statements capturing the symbols about Jesus; but they are statements of interpretations, remember (such as "Light of Light"), and may not be the best for our day. They do not pretend to capture or objectify Jesus (as we are apt to assume). They are only the symbols—and ancient ones at that—about his reality.

Still, we are uneasy. It looks like we are trying to downgrade Jesus. On the contrary, the question being asked is whether those Greek terms and creedal statements are still the best expressions of the God who revealed himself in Jesus or whether they ought to be reexamined, stripped away and recast to better get at the revelation of the God who loves us in Jesus. There would be no diminution of Jesus if we did not have to express him as preexistent God or

"Lord" or Second Person of the Blessed Trinity. These expressions, be it recalled, started out as symbols trying to capture the reality. The reality of God's fantastic, loving self-disclosure in Jesus can still be served even if the symbols are rearranged or recast.

In summary we can state these propositions (numbers refer to diagram on page 98):

1. Jesus of Nazareth lived and taught around the years 4 B.C. to 30 A.D. He is a real historical personage (1).
2. He taught and lived, pointing to the revelation of the Father (2). He was executed and was raised from the dead. This was a decisive moment that crystalized his life, message and, later on, his function and identity.
3. Immediately after his resurrection the traditions about Jesus grew. They necessarily began in Palestine (3A) and expanded as they moved among the Jews with Greek mentalities (3B) and finally to the Greek Gentiles (3C). Understandably each phase expanded and brought fresh concepts to Jesus.
4. The gospels (4) were written over three decades later and after most of the letter forms (epistles). They incorporated past and current theologizing about Jesus; his message and his person. He "became" the Christ of faith, not by the community's invention, but by the Spirit's disclosure.
5. The Church councils (5), particularly the early ones, tried to distill into the current idiom (Greek philosophy) the Jewish Jesus who became the Christ. In spite of accusations that they hellenized Jesus, on the contrary these councils preserved the Jewishness of Jesus and his message.[21]
6. Finally, the process of Jesus becoming the Christ is legitimate but we must remember that basically the titles embodied in "Christ" are provisional as are all the derivative titles such as "Son of God" and "Lord." They are highly sophisticated symbols. As symbols the reality behind them is much greater. Therefore it is possible to disturb the symbols and reexpress the reality for modern man.

NOTES FOR CHAPTER 7

1. Reginald H. Fuller, *The Foundations of New Testament Christology* (Charles Scribner's Sons, 1965) p. 15.

2. Raymond F. Collins, "A Witness to Change: the New Testament" in *Theology Digest* (Summer, 1974) p. 16.

3. Norman Perrin, *A Modern Pilgrimage in New Testament Christology* (Fortress Press, 1974) p. 5.

4. Vincent Taylor, quoted in *Jesus God and Man* by Raymond E. Brown (Macmillan, 1967) p. 4.

5. Peter DeRosa, *Jesus Who Became the Christ* (Dimension Books, 1974) p. 56. For further views on Jesus' divinity see Werner George Kummel, *The Theology of the New Testament* (Abingdon, 1973) and R. G. Hammerton-Kelly, *Pre-Existence, Wisdom, and the Son of Man: A Study in the Idea of Pre-Existence in the New Testament* in *Society of New Testament Studies Monograph* Series 21 (Cambridge University Press, 1973).

6. John F. O'Grady, *Jesus, Lord and Christ* (Paulist Press, 1972) p. 106.

7. Gregory Baum, quoted in *The New Agenda* by Andrew M. Greeley (Doubleday, 1973) p. 22.

8. Peter DeRosa, cited above, p. 122.

9. John A. T. Robinson, *The Human Face of God* (Westminster Press, 1973).

10. Peter DeRosa, cited above, p. 29.

11. W. Norman Pittenger, "Process Thought: A Contemporary Trend in Theology" in *Process Theology*, edited by Ewert H. Cousins (Newman Press, 1971) p. 32. See also David R. Griffin's *A Process Christology* (Westminster Press, 1973).

12. Piet Schoonenberg, "He Emptied Himself" in *Concilium* 11 (Paulist Press, 1966) p. 60.

13. John O'Grady, cited above, p. 57.

14. Raymond E. Brown, *Jesus, God and Man* (Macmillan, 1967) p. 95.

15. Raymond E. Brown, p. 104.

16. Bruce Vawter, *This Man Jesus* (Doubleday, 1973) p. 165.

17. Reginald H. Fuller, cited above, p. 250. See also, W. Norman Pittenger in "Meland, Process Thought and Significance of Christ" in *Process Theology,* cited above, pp. 208 and 209.

18. Andrew Maloney, "Jesus as the Horizon of Human Hope" in *Does Jesus Make a Difference?,* edited by Thomas M. McFadden (Seabury Press, 1974) p. 108.

19. Seely Beggiani, "Mythological and Ontological Elements in Christology" in *Does Jesus Make a Difference?,* cited above, p. 39. See also Jaroslav Pelikan's *The Emergence of the Catholic Tradition* (Chicago University Press, 1971) p. 187ff.

20. Seely Beggiani, p. 40.

21. See William J. Bausch, *Pilgrim Church* (Fides Publishers, 1973) pp. 48 and 49.

8. Positioning Redemption

— 1 —

Every Sunday we recite the Creed. In it it says, "For our sake he was crucified under Pontius Pilate." This reflects the ancient belief that we are saved by Jesus' suffering and death. What may surprise the average Catholic is that we are not quite sure how. We believe that we are saved by Jesus and that his cross figures essentially in our salvation, but again, how? How does the death of Jesus some 2000 years ago affect us? How does it save? Are we saved against our will? How can one person's suffering affect another? What change took place on Calvary in reference to God and us? Does Jesus' death on the cross cause God to look more kindly, more forgivingly, on us? If God already loves us even before Jesus' coming (and even, in fact, if Jesus never came) what did Jesus do to make him love us more? If God wills all men to be saved, including men of the Pliocene period (from one to eleven million years ago), the men of the Pleistocene Period (one million years ago) and Paleolithic, Mesolithic and Neolithic man some tens of thousands of years ago, what did Jesus add after such an enormous span of time? So, there are questions here. To position redemption, salvation, satisfaction (whatever term we use) is not easy. In fact, it is a rather complex question. Yet we must take a look at it, however briefly, because in the process of positioning the question we hope to re-emphasize many thoughts we have seen in previous chapters.

First, let us go quickly back to the very beginning of the tradition about redemption. The first thing to strike us is that the thought of Jesus' passion and death as saving us from our sins was not among the earliest explicit beliefs of the pre-gospel times "although there was never a period, not even a very short one, after the resurrection

133

when the saving significance of the cross was not implicitly recognized. It was only gradually, however, that it received explicit formulation."[1] This explicit formulation came surprisingly (to us) when the community reflected, not on what the passion and death did for them, but what it did for Jesus. Only when the faithful reflected on what happened to Jesus and what he became as a result did they take their thoughts further. For remember, Jesus was approved and made Lord and Christ (Acts 2:36) as a result of his life and death. He went through his humiliation into a new life. He was "rewarded" with glory. If his death had ended on the cross, of itself it could not save. Only when it was seen as the prelude to what it did for Jesus—making him Lord and exalted Christ—was it seen as instrumental in what it could do for us. "If Christ be not risen, our faith is in vain and we remain in our sins," said St. Paul.

So the resurrection is an intimate and inseparable part of redemption. To stop at the passion and death is to leave things hanging. It is the resurrection which gives meaning to the death, not the other way around. So we see why at first there was not an explicit consideration of Jesus' passion and death. The first focus rather was on the glorified and exalted Christ. Then the second focus was: what brought this about? And the answer was: his life, passion and death. Then came the final reflection. If the life, passion and death brought about Jesus' exaltation in glory, then, somehow, we too can go the same route. We too can now pass through human suffering and human death and also be "exalted" (saved) into the new life of Christ. Because of Jesus' suffering, human suffering takes on a new meaning. Because of Jesus' death and resurrection, human death is no longer the ultimate human affair; it is the pen-ultimate. Jesus burst the bonds of death. Death could not hold his mighty love. Death lost its power over Jesus and was broken for all men thereafter. So, because of Jesus and through his life, passion, death and resurrection we can be saved. We still have not answered *how* this occurs. We only are pausing to see the force and value for us of Jesus' exaltation:

Once we begin to look on Jesus as truly a man on the march toward the fulfillment of his life, once we accept that his perfection lies not in the absence of struggle but in the ceaseless struggle to understand and to do God's will while surrounded by the forces of evil, then we can begin to identify ourselves in some measure with him. . . . When we provide the full human context for our study of the incarnation, when we read the scriptures to search the face of Jesus the man, we begin to realize that the resurrection was not simply a means of convincing us that Jesus is divine. It is the very consummation of Jesus as a man. It is the end and goal of his human development in this sinful world. He needed to be raised so as to be perfectly one with his Father. When, by the power of the Spirit, God raised him from death he gave to him, as a permanent possession, his own glory and an undying life. That glory and that life is ours to share. This is why without the resurrection we would all perish utterly.[2]

From the consideration of Jesus' resurrection and the life and death that led to it, the early Church began to work several themes. Early hymns celebrating Jesus' death and exaltation began to surface in the New Testament writings. For example, we sense the primitive hymn in St. Paul's famous exclamation that Jesus "took the form of a slave and humbled himself becoming obedient unto death, even to the death on a cross" (Phil 2:6). Other New Testament writings began to talk about redemption, reconciliation and ransom. All these things occur through Christ's death, his free action, his obedience, his service. The results of all this are variously described as "liberation from the slavery of sin, the Law, the devil, and a new rebirth, justification, possession of the Spirit, truth, life, peace and joy."[3] As we have seen already, we are not surprised that the evangelists worked these themes into their material from their own theological and apologetical points of view.[4]

We must not think that these themes were entirely the construct of the first Christian communities. It seems quite apparent that Jesus knew in some way himself that he must face death. It was his own comment that a prophet cannot perish away from Jerusalem. And the violent death awaiting him seems to be a transition into a participation in the divine glory. It was on the basis of just such hints, and in the light of the resurrection, that the first communities began their reflections even though, we repeat, it was never clear just *how* Jesus' death figures as a necessity in his ministry and in our salvation.

> On the basis of these testimonies it may be regarded as certain that Jesus viewed his violent death as the way ordained for him by God, even though we obviously do not know whether he had always had this certainty or had only reached it in the course of his activity. But that poses the crucial question, in what sense then Jesus incorporated this death into his divine commission. . . . Jesus understood the sufferings awaiting him not as fate or a burden, but as part of his divine commission; but it is equally clear that no explanation is given for this divine necessity and no special, independent significance is attributed to Jesus' sufferings as over against his other deeds and his teachings.[5]

This lack of knowledge of just *why* Jesus' death is linked so closely as a necessity for his glory and *how* it saves us has been the basis for various interpretations throughout the centuries. To a few of these interpretations we must now turn.

— 2 —

The first attempt to interpret Jesus' death came, as might be expected, from the Old Testament themes. Here we can find the Suffering Servant of the prophet Isaiah. This Suffering Servant was seen as a prototype of Jesus and applied to him. This meant that someone could suffer for another, could stand in his place. This was the theory of vicarious suffering.[6] "By his bruises we are healed." However, since this interpretation proved to be too Jewish for the Gentiles, other themes were developed. Instead, the notion of ransom came in, that somehow Christ bought us back, ransomed us from sin. But there was difficulty there. To whom was the ransom paid? To Satan? To God? Both had unthinkable ramifications. If to Satan, then Satan had some power over us and over God too. He had to be placated, be bought off. This position tends to make Satan too superior to God, too much the power with the upper hand. If the ransom were paid to God, then did God demand a blood offering? Was he like that? And do we have the spectacle of God buying back from God? Yes, St. Paul said, "You have been bought at a great price" (1 Cor 6:20) but to pay back to either Satan or God had too many difficulties.

In succeeding centuries two main theories about the redemption were prevalent. The first was that of St. Irenaeus (third century). He emphasized the vicarious element by showing that one man's death could benefit many because of the basic cosmic unity of the human race. This meant that representative archetypes could and did affect all who were summed up in their person. St. Paul explores this theme in the symbols of Adam and Christ. "It was through one man that sin entered the whole human race, in as much as all men have sinned. . . . But God's gift of grace is out of all proportion to Adam's wrongdoing. For if the wrongdoing of that one man brought death upon so many, its effect is vastly exceeded by the grace of God and the gift that came to so many by the grace of the one man, Jesus Christ" (Rom 5:15-17). The other theory, the one which we have inherited, was that of St. Anselm of the eleventh century. Because Anselm lived in a feudal system which was very conscious of rank, rights and privileges, he stressed these elements. God, he said, like some feudal lord, has rights and dignity deriving from his innate holiness. If God is offended justice demands satisfaction, a justice, once more rooted in God's holiness, in the very natural order of things. When God was sinned against and this justice was ruptured, only someone equivalent to God's dignity could repay the injustice done. This is why God became man. As man Jesus could do his share in the apology while as God there would be a true equivalent, one equal to make adequate apology stand on its own feet.

At times Anselm's theory has been distorted and God, with all due respect, comes off as a kind of spiritual King Kong who needs his Fay Wray (Christ) to appease his appetite for justice. But Anselm did not imply this. Rather, like Irenaeus, Anselm regards the death of Jesus as

a free act of supreme obedience. This freely-accepted death is not the payment of an extrinsic price for sin, with God binding himself arbitrarily to bestow redemption in exchange. The death of Christ is intrinsically the restoration of the divine order on the human level. The divine order had been violated on the human level by the disobedience of sin. Hence the restoration naturally means free obedience. . . . By fundamental obedience, this inward self-dedication, Jesus attacked the principle of sin, the effort of self-assertion and self-assurance. . . . Thus the actual end of Jesus' life by which he put the seal on his constant self-renunciation was the absolute affirmation of the Other, the Father.[7]

Modern theologians seek other interpretations. For example, some hold that Jesus' sacrifice on the cross essentially means witnessing to the truth to the ultimate end. This, of course, implies a fantastic devotion and love. People who die for their beliefs are to be taken seriously. In this light, sacrifice is labeled "prophetic" sacrifice to distinguish it from that sacrifice which implies blood-letting or material offering. It works like this: the Father's will was Jesus' whole life. To give the Father honor, to preach his message of love, to reveal the Father—this was all that mattered to Jesus. But people and circumstances tried to get him to water down his message, his revelation of the Father, his preaching of the Kingdom. Some people tried to divert his mission. Some put pressure on him to conform. Some merely left him ("Will you also go away?" he said to his Apostles). Finally, there were those who went so far as to plot against him and work for his death. Yet, in spite of all this, the more such people put pressure on Jesus the more Jesus held fast to his mission, to his witnessing to the truth, to revealing his Father. The passion and crucifixion were the ultimate pressure. Jesus' free submission to such torture, preferring it to denying his Father was his great act of devotion. His mighty and unswerving love for his Father would not allow him to compromise that Father's glory even if it meant his own life. So Jesus died, but note that he died, not out of justice, but out of commitment. He made his "prophetic sacrifice."

There are deep conclusions to draw from this; namely, that God did not desire Jesus' death, much less rejoice over it. The Father was not pleased at such terrible suffering and agony. Rather, the Father was pleased that, in the face of such suffering and agony designed to divert or lessen his commitment, Jesus held fast. He held fast because he loved the Father. He witnessed to the bitter end. He was obedient even to the death on the cross. And ever since then, the cross has become, not the shameful instrument of torture, but the ultimate symbol of what it means to love so fully and to lose one's life so completely for God's sake, that one finds it.[8] So the cross saves not only because it is the sign that loving commitment will be rewarded, but also because it is the means by which Jesus loves most fully. Such total love restores all of our possible un-love, puts to right the harmony distorted by our sins.

Another conclusion is that Jesus did not really have to know explicitly from the beginning that he would suffer and die. He did not have a ready-made plan which he set out to pursue. Rather, the suffering and death were derived from what gradually became the inevitable consequences of his dedication to the Father's will. Only when opposition to him grows to large proportions does it dawn on him the significance of the rejection and the consequent death that await him. Moreover, and this is to his credit, as we would express it, he could have chosen a way out, the way of power and political messiahship. But he rejected power. Instead he emptied himself out, that is, made a choice away from human safety and self-preservation and towards obedience to total witnessing.

> Together with the rejection of power, Christ obviously rejected all lust for power and all abuse of power. What we count as "equality with God" he did not pursue as a trophy, but he emptied himself of power and right, and, as Robinson put it so strikingly, of all concentration upon himself. He wanted to be nothing but the totally transparent mediator between the Father and his brothers: to give himself in this was for him nourishment, life and self-affirmation. He was totally himself by being totally given over to God and the many, and if the consequence of this was the death on the cross, he accepted it and suffered it in the fullness of his love.[9]

Finally, Jesus did all this in complete faith and total trust, with the reckless hope against all hope that the Father's love would vindicate him. The Father's love, of course, did and so Jesus was "exalted" on the cross, raised up from the dead and made Lord and Christ.

How does this apply to us? Several ways. First we could say that such total love forever in principle establishes the human race in love with the Father. Jesus' death is the new and eternal covenant between God and man; it says that man need never be afraid: God will conquer and vindicate all because the basic distortion of sin has been, in principle, righted by Christ. Or we could say that Jesus' death saves us in that it is a reminder, powerful and searching, of the already existent and never withdrawn love of the Father. Since Jesus is the revelation of God he forever stirs our faith in such a definite act of love.

There is another point of view that is fruitful. This view says that in one way or another all of the New Testament interpretations of Jesus' saving death are focused on the point that Jesus is giving meaning to all life by what he said and did. The God-Man was showing by his living as well as by his dying what it meant to be truly authentic, truly human. And the sum and substance of his teaching seems to be his words (and actions) that the man who loses his life will save it. That is to say, the man who lives like Jesus as a "man for others," who surrenders himself to the Father's will, who does the works of mercy—such a man is giving of himself. He is therefore dying to self. It is this dying that is the real liberation from the primal sin of self-idolatry. So Jesus' death on the cross saves us, is redemptive, because it models true liberation and says that all self-donating men—all self-donating men from the Pliocene period to the present day—are "attached" to Jesus in the common bond of love and through his mighty thrust they are made worthy of the fullness of eternal life. Jesus' death is the definitive sign of human self-donation, outpouring and therefore of final freedom and salvation. In other words, all of the biblical themes and figures of speech such as suffering servant, ransom, vicarious suffering, etc. are so many variations of the major theme of Jesus' life and teaching: "Unless the grain of wheat falls to the earth and dies, it remains just a grain of wheat. But if it dies it produces much fruit. The man who loves his life loses it, while the man who hates his life in this world preserves it to life eternal" (Jn 12:24ff).

To state it another way: the point of Jesus' death is that he is victorious *in* it. It is not that he died and then lived again as the same Jesus. As we have seen, his new life is not that of a revived corpse, but it is a transformation, a transformation that came in his death. Jesus' life did not resume after death but his new life came *out* of death. He accepted his death as the last total surrender of himself. As in any dying to self, in any reaching out to others and forgetting oneself a man grows, becomes more. He matures. Self-pride has died and maturity has moved a step forward. It is in this sense that Jesus' death on the cross is essential. The cross is his final self-abnegation and by that very fact the cross brings a new maturity, a new growth, a final and unending development by which Jesus is made Lord. Death to self is the precise way in which we all truly live. This is what the cross says. God affirms this truism by raising up Jesus and sealing this as *the* human (and divine) value. This is why we say that God is love. And each time we do this dying to self we live more fully in the Spirit of Jesus. This is why the evangelists separate artificially what we call Easter, Ascension Thursday and Pentecost. These are not real, separate dates; rather they are all aspects of the same motion. Jesus died to self and surrendered himself totally to the Father thereby unleashing a whole new Spirit. The Father approves this life style and tells us that in those moments that we constantly die to self in the service of others we too are raised up (ascension) and given the Spirit (Pentecost). Easter and Pentecost are artificial feasts telling us what is happening to us.

> The asceticism in Christ's death lies in his free embrace of suffering and death not because it followed from his nature but because it conformed to his Father's will. It is for this reason that the resurrection of Christ is not "theologically" a separate event that follows "after" his passion. For the resurrection is simply the manifestation of what actually took place in the death of Jesus. Christ, in an act of total freedom, disposed of his whole life and existence by handing over his whole person to the mystery of a merciful and loving God.

> Because Christ is the designated Victim, the lamb, and the appointed priest this total sacrifice, this emptying of himself is "immediately" acceptable to God. For this reason Good Friday and Easter Sunday must be seen as two aspects of a single and united event. When we

realize this we need no longer think that Good Friday could really retain its saving significance even if no Easter followed. Hence the radical implication of the Passover of Christ from death to life in the resurrection is not an apologetical argument for his divinity but more startlingly it is the foundation and cornerstone for the same transformation of every believer.[10]

So redemption means that life comes out of death. Jesus saves us precisely because he is the definitive statement of that truth. Jesus' being raised up is God's pledge that new life and eternal maturity (transformation, i.e. resurrection) await us. That is why Jesus' death is his glorification: it is his moment of self-surrender, the final decisive "hour" telling the world that this is the way it is with God: life comes out of death. Or, as we may say in a positive sense, God is love and if we too are love we shall live forever. We shall be saved.

— 3 —

Notice that we have skirted around the question of the necessary and intrinsic connection between Jesus' death and our salvation. The reason is twofold. One is that we do not know the answer for sure.[11] We have given several theories but none are definitive. None really explain the necessity of an atoning death or precisely how such a death saves us. And besides, and most profoundly, we may never have a definitive theory because why and how Jesus' death redeems may not be able to be perfectly categorized. It may simply lie too deep in Christian spirituality to lend itself to a definitive dogmatic explanation. Perhaps what the life and death of Jesus ultimately mean must be in the experience of each Christian. Theologian Monika Hellwig catches this nuance when she writes,

> In response to the question as to what then is the meaning of his death, which may also be formulated simply as the question concerning why he died, the answers are no longer as terse or univocal. It is around this question that we have built another whole approach to Christology that has been by no means static or uniform. It is here that Christians have invested the death and person of Jesus

with the meaning that they have learned in their own experience. The explanations have centered on reconciliation, atonement, redemption, and salvation. They have ranged from the ransom paid to the devil to the payment of the just penalty to God. . . . The explanations are important, of course, not because they will ever decipher for us the inner reality of God, or the psychology of Jesus, but because they express our understanding of our own role and task in the work of Jesus yet to be completed, and because they are attempts to understand concretely what that work may be.[12]

Secondly, we wish in any case to get away from the question for it may, in the last analysis, be the wrong question to ask (at least initially). Instead we wish to come back to a better (it seems to us) emphasis. The emphasis is that whatever theory of redemption we hold to—and we are reminded that "even at the present time theologians are divided as to how precisely to interpret the satisfaction performed by Christ"[13]—we must come back to seeing Jesus as the revelation of the Father's love. We must repeat that Jesus' actions of the cross were not an *introduction* of salvation. Rather, what he did there was the definitive, final witness to the *already existing* salvation the Father gives and has given to all men. God wills the salvation of all men of all times. If we hold fast to that we really do not have to "rescue," for example, those people who lived before Christ into salvation by resorting to a "baptism of desire." Such solutions are not necessary. If we believe that God is love and is faithful, then there is, in a very real sense, no need of Jesus to come to forestall his wrath or induce him to love further (atonement, ransom). If God is love, we repeat, and is faithful to man even when man is faithless to him, then he is just that. Jesus need not be savior in the sense that he persuaded, coaxed or induced his Father to re-love mankind after some vague period of un-love. Jesus might be more savior in that he, above all others, is such a definitive sign and witness to God's constant love. He is the one who positions, and defines forever the never ending posture of love from the Father.

What the very adventure of the Son in our man-flesh strives to convey is that there is a welcoming love, an unconditioned acceptance, a relentless and eternal affection in the Father which so far exceeds our own experience that even the selfless career and death of Jesus can only hint at.

Jesus does not come to perform before God; he comes to call us—by revealing to us the character of his Father, and that of ourselves. The actual work of saving men, of purifying them from sin and drawing them into love, has gone on unremittingly as long as there have been men. But our understanding of this was given a jolt of transforming insight in the coming of Jesus Christ. In this sense Jesus is better understood as Revealer, than as Savior.[14]

Maybe that is the proper emphasis: Jesus is revealer of the on-going, saving love of the Father for all men. This would be consistent with seeing Jesus as the revelation of the Father. Moreover, it would rescue him from any appeasement role, from any mediatorship that implied the Father's hatred, anger or disdain. But if Jesus is the Father's self-disclosure, the living Word of love, then salvation means (a) for the believer: knowing, believing and reveling in that fact as well as living a penitential life and celebrating the eucharist and the other sacraments as on-going signs of Jesus' salvation; (b) for the unbeliever: having his life too count for something for whatever sincerity is his, whatever movement of love and concern, it shall be rewarded and he too shall see the God whose name he could not pronounce but whose name he knew in his heart. So in summary we might say this much:

1. Early Christians deduced salvation in terms of what it meant to Jesus himself. He was "saved," raised up. What made this possible was not only his death but his whole devoted life. His death on the cross, however, is a special focusing of his love and as such it is proper to speak of it as causing salvation.

2. The question of just how Jesus' death and resurrection saves us is still open to speculation. As we would put it, something "objective" happened; the distortion of sin was straightened out. Man's posture of true religion was restored. Justice triumphed in Christ. God, in Christ, is reconciling the world to himself (2

Cor 5:19). Redemption is his initiative. But underneath all of this lies, of course, the fantastic love of Jesus for the Father and for us. That is why it was suggested that trying to discover the necessary and intrinsic connection between his death on the cross and our salvation might not be primary (although important). What is primary is the awe and wonderment of the total love of Jesus that led to such an outpouring, a love that once more is but a reflection of the Father's love. Again, the proper emphasis might be on Jesus, not as savior, but as revealer.

3. What he reveals in his mighty act of self-abnegation is the Father's love. He is the Father's revelation of how far God will go to save us, to call us. We are saved by remembering that God's love is bigger than our sin; that his seeking after us has no apparent limitation. The cross proves that.

4. Modern theories tend to stress this movement of the Father's love in Jesus and tell us that our way to salvation is to imitate such self-donation. Ours might be a "prophetic sacrifice"; that is, we too must give our lives out of obedience to the Father's will. We too must embrace the cross as a symbol that decision for God hurts and sometimes brings death. But the man who loses his life for Jesus' sake will find it.

5. Another way to put the same thing is to recall Jesus' own words about the grain of wheat. The necessity here is the necessity of self-death in order that a new and godly life might appear and flourish. The cross once more is the powerful sign of the grain of wheat, of Jesus' self-surrender, of the path we must take to everlasting life.

6. In any case, any theory that repositions our thinking of the Father as capricious and wrathful is welcome. Any theory that weans us away from a too literal vicarious approach, a too literal buying-back notion, a too angry God who demands blood to be appeased is an improvement.

7. Finally, whatever way we look at it, we come back to the fact that the work of redemption is trinitarian. It is the Father's love that sends Jesus. It is under the impulse of the Spirit that we see Jesus as the Father's self-disclosure. It is by the Spirit that we cry "Abba" and take the risks of self-death. Therefore it is in virtue of the whole on-going relationship and activity of the Trinity that we are saved.

NOTES FOR CHAPTER 8

1. Reginald H. Fuller, *The Foundations of New Testament Christology* (Charles Scribner's Sons, 1965) p. 153.
2. Peter DeRosa, *Christ and Original Sin* (Bruce, 1967) p. 12.
3. Karl Rahner in *Sacramentum Mundi* Vol. 5 (Herder and Herder, 1970) p. 428.
4. An example of the apologetic thrust is the evangelists' portraying Pilate as a disinterested party, one who desired to leave local religious matters to work themselves out. This was precisely the point that the early persecuted Christians wanted to convey to Rome: imitate Pilate, leave us alone.
5. Werner Georg Kummel, *The Theology of the New Testament* (Abingdon Press, 1973) pp. 88 and 90.
6. As John Mackenzie says in *Dictionary of the Bible* (Bruce, 1965) p. 793. "It is not too much to say that the conception of the atoning and redeeming death in the New Testament is a development of the idea of the Servant."
7. Boniface Willems, *The Reality of Redemption* (Herder and Herder, 1970) p. 59.
8. Richard McBrien, *What Do We Really Believe?* (Pflaum/Standard, 1969).
9. Piet Schoonenberg, "He Emptied Himself" in *Concilium* 11 (Paulist Press, 1966) p. 62.
10. Edward Braxton in *Liturgy 70*, Vol. 2, nos. 1-2. See also Karl Rahner, *On the Theology of Death* (Herder and Herder, 1972) pp. 70 and 71.
11. Michael Schmaus, *Dogma: God and His Christ* (Sheed and Ward, 1971) p. 75 says, "Why God ordained that sacrifice on a cross would be the means of salvation remains, of course, a difficult question, wrapped in impenetrable mystery."
12. Monika K. Hellwig, "The Uniqueness of Jesus in Christian Tradition" in *Does Jesus Make a Difference?*, edited by Thomas McFadden (Seabury Press, 1974) p. 92. See also in the same book the essay by Barbara Agnew, "The Meaning of Jesus' Sacrifice."
13. Karl Rahner, cited above, p. 329.
14. James Tunstead Burtchaell, *Philemon's Problem* (ACTA, 1973) pp. 37 and 38.

9. Positioning Church

— 1 —

It is evident that Vatican II has drastically repositioned the usual understanding of the Church, the concept most of us inherited in our catechisms. To appreciate this dramatic shift we must examine two causes, one which we might call the literary cause and the other the geographical cause.

The literary cause derives from what we said in the chapter on myth. It bears repeating. We acknowledged that myth arose from the fundamental human need to find an explanation for the world, for suffering, for death, for existence itself. So symbols and myths sprang up spontaneously from the instincts of man. In fact some symbols and myths are so basic that we can call them archetypal; that is, they are the common property of people all over the world. Among such archetypal myths we find the themes of a life after death, god-men, virgin births, gods dying and rising again, etc. Again, such myths are to be found everywhere on the planet simply because they spring from man's universal subconsciousness.

In due time, what happened was that when the Church came on the scene it necessarily adopted the ancient symbols and myths to explain Jesus much the same way we fall back on current metaphors or examples to interpret people and events. This was most natural and expected. What eventually happened, however, was that the Church began to take these common-property myths and make them exclusive. It began to make them its own and made them refer exclusively in reference to its own message and members. What should have happened, of course, was that since it had appropriated the ancient myths from humanity, the Church should have returned them, but now informed (in the old scholastic sense), revitalized and definitively brought to fulfillment in Christ. But the Church did not do this. Instead it took the common symbols and myths, made them esoteric and personal and pulled them into a closed system. We can see what eventually happened. Under the impetus of new scientific discoveries, especially anthropology and comparative religions, Catholics (particularly the college students) were shocked and some suffered a loss of faith when they found out that ideas like the virgin birth, and the god-man and resurrection, etc. existed long before Jesus and the Church. They did not know that the Church appropriated these myths to interpret Jesus. They did not know that the gospels were woven out of the common mythological fare shared with many ancient peoples and religions. They should not have been scandalized to find out that their Church had myths that pertain to the deepest longings of mankind.

The upshot of all this was that by the time this discovery was made, the Church had become a rather closed system, self-defined, shut off from the world and very centered on the difference between the sacred and the profane. But now everyone saw that the Church's symbols and myths were not exclusive property, that they were deeply rooted in humanity, that indeed the whole Church message and language were inevitably related to all of mankind. Yes, the Church was certainly correct in holding that Jesus was unique but wrong in thinking that its process of interpreting him was unique. Rather its language, symbols and myths of interpretation were part and parcel of mankind. So it was no longer tenable to keep apart from the world, no longer tenable to hold such a narrow definition of itself, no longer tenable to keep in splendid isolation. The Church was forced to take a new look at itself and acknowledge its indebtedness, commitment to service and intrinsic relationship to all of humanity for deep down both Church and world spoke the same language.[1]

The geographical cause of the Church's new self-understanding is both easier to see and more dramatic in its impact. More dramatic because what was involved was the direct collision of two age-old principles within the Church itself. The first principle is "God wills all men to be saved" and the second is "outside the Church there is no salvation." For many centuries these two principles were not seen to be in basic conflict. The reason is easy to see. Everyone, for all practical purposes, was in the Church. There were, of course, the "faithless" Jews and the "perverse" Muslims, but most men belonged to that mythical kingdom called Christendom. To be a member of society was to be a Christian and to be a Christian was to be a member of society. In fact, if there is one figure of speech that could well describe the Catholic Church in the era before the seventeenth century it is the Bark of Peter. This figure conjures up a vast fishing boat with Peter and his Apostles at the helm (the hierarchy) plowing through turbulent waters. The Apostles and those aboard are engaged in two tasks. One is to minister to and strengthen those already on board. The other is to reach out and grab to safety those in the waters outside. There is an urgency in the air because obviously drowning and eternal death await those in the waters. Safety and salvation can only be had by being in or climbing aboard Peter's Bark. The missionary enterprise is to pull as many out of the waters as possible. "Outside the Bark (Church) there is no salvation," to quote the inscription on the masthead. In fact, it was a staff meeting on board (the Council of Florence in 1442) which declared most precisely and severely, "The holy Roman Church firmly believes, professes and proclaims that no one who lives outside the Church—not only pagans, but also Jews, heretics, and schismatics—can share in eternal life. They will go into the eternal fire prepared for the devil and his angels unless they reunite with the Church before they die."[2] In this the meeting was only repeating one of the former admirals (Boniface VIII) who had declared, "We therefore declare, say, affirm and announce that for every human creature to be submissive to the Roman Pontiff is absolutely necessary for salvation."[3]

We can leave our maritime metaphors and observe that these sayings, as harsh as they may sound to our ears, were mitigated if we recall once more that to the men who wrote such words, the whole world, as they understood it, was quite small. Besides most of this small world was Christian anyway and so there was no great friction with the other principle that God wills all men—at least

most of them, that is, the Christians—to be saved. But then, came
the sixteenth century. Slowly, through rapid and multiple discoveries it began to dawn on everyone just how small Christendom
was, just how tiny the Church was in relationship to all the "new"
peoples in the Americas and Asia and the far-flung islands. Soon
the sciences of geology and anthropology were demonstrating that
man was hundreds of thousands of years old, maybe millions of
years old. Were all these people lost? All of a sudden, to return
to our figure of speech, Peter's Bark was no mighty warship dominat-
ing the Mediterranean Sea. It turned out in this new perspective
to be but a small rowboat bobbing like a cork on the world's oceans!
The Church, after all, was a minority grouping! Compared to all
the people in the world and all the people who have ever lived the
Church is but a fleeting speck. Most of the human race have lived
and continues to live and die outside of it. And yet—yet, God wills
all men to be saved. Now the two principles (as commonly understood) were in genuine conflict. Clearly, the Church would have
to take a second look at itself. Clearly, there would have to be new
definitions, new self understandings.

So, as we said at the beginning, both literary and geographical
causes forced the Church to drop its isolationist image. Before and
after Vatican II theologians would search for definitions more in
accord with the facts and the Church's mission. Following contemporary theologian Avery Dulles' book, *Models of the Church,* we
shall list five definitions of the Church and pick out one that we
shall explore for the rest of this chapter. (1) There is the institutional model which has dominated, as we have seen, Church thinking for the last several centuries. Dulles rightly sees the Church as
an institution, but also realizes that the emphasis has been far too
weighted on the institutional features to the exclusion of others.
Of all the models this is the one most under attack and the one most
rejected. (2) The Church as a Mystical Community. This model
has the advantage over the institutional one since it does recognize
something more than the visible organization. It reaches out for
more people. It is a good model although it leaves somewhat vague
the relationship between the visible and invisible elements and tends

to denigrate authority and structure. (3) The Church as Herald. This is the Church which exists to proclaim the Word of God. It is there primarily to preach, to tell everyone the good news. Protestants are apt to favor this model. (4) The Church as Servant. This is the model of the activists. They see the Church like Jesus washing the feet of the world. The Church in this view is not out to gain members but to help all men wherever and whatever they are. At times it is difficult to distinguish this kind of a church from secular humanism. (5) Finally, there is the Church as Sacrament. This sees the Church as something that points to a greater reality, that is a definitive sign of something greater. This model comes to terms with the problem of the Church as a minority community and this is the one we shall use.[4]

— 2 —

We start with the now accepted notion that the Church is a minority grouping. To help us over the shock of that recognition let us take a look at Jesus. St. Paul positions his place well: "To me, who am less than the least of all God's people, he has granted of his grace the privilege of proclaiming to the Gentiles the good news of the unfathomable riches of Christ. . . . *It was hidden for long ages in God*. . . . This is in accord with his *age-long purpose,* which he achieved in Christ Jesus our Lord. . . ." (Eph 1:1ff). So what is Paul saying? He is saying clearly to all that Jesus is a late-comer, that Jesus is a minority of one. Furthermore, God became incarnate which means that this Jesus is circumscribed in a particular place, country, race, background, vocabulary and time period. He entered limited human history as do we all. He was born, lived and died at specific moments. Not only that but he came after eons of human beings had lived and died and it has been two thousand years since he walked the out-of-the-way country of Palestine. The majority of the human race past and present have never heard of him and will never hear of him.

Reviewing such facts we come to the conclusion that since Jesus came into incarnate humanity and geography he obviously did not feel the compulsion to be universal. He was content to be particular, to be limited. Not everyone had to join his band or become his disciples (Mark 9:38). Jesus did not come to form an exclusive group or, as we have mentioned before, to reveal himself. He came to reveal the Father's love. He came to be, in his life and cross, the definitive and final indication of the Father's love for all mankind. God came in Jesus, in all of his limitations, to be the forever-sign that he loves us. He came to put the divine seal on anyone who died to himself ("took up his cross") and *out* of such a self-death discover life. He came to say once and for all that whenever men do works of charity and justice, they would be encountering him and receiving his rewards without even knowing it. Such is the force of Matthew 25 where the good say in surprise, "When did we feed you or give you drink?" and receive the reply that as long as they did such things to any human being they did it unknowingly for Christ. So Jesus is the definitive revealer that such life styles as kindness, self-surrender, charity and justice—that "grain of wheat" experience —are what God approves of and rewards. And this in contrast to self-aggrandizement, greed, wealth, ambition, independence and all those values which the world holds so dearly. So Jesus could afford to come late on the scene because men were being saved long before he arrived (although saved in view of the righteousness and harmony between God and man Jesus established to counteract the evil and disharmony of sin). He was now revealing in a special way the truth that already existed from the very beginning: God wills all men to be saved and that love, givingness, self-surrender is the way it happens.

When we understand this about Jesus, we can understand a great deal about the Church.[5] The Church is "a faith community which receives and expresses its identity in the breaking of the bread."[6] What is that identity? That identity is to be a sacrament, that is, to be a sign of Jesus' universal revelation that God loves all men. The Church is the visible sign of the presence of Christ, the visible proclamation of Jesus' own proclamation. The Church exists to communicate "the unfathomable riches of Christ" (Eph 3:8). The Church, like Jesus, has no need of being physically universal nor even any need that all men join it. The Church has a duty to fulfill, namely, that of proclamation, of being the sacrament of Jesus.

All this, we admit, is a far cry from the concept of the Church we are used to. But what we are used to came at the end of a long bit of history. At first the Church was indeed the summoner to conversion and proclaimer of Jesus. Gradually as people were born into the Church the emphasis switched from proclaiming the message to the world to teaching the faith to those already of its numbers. In the process the institutional elements, always an essential part of the Church, tended to grow stronger. After all, someone had to regulate the teaching and the vast numbers and control the organizational structure. This was all right until the fourth century when Theodosius made Christianity the state religion and it got tied in with the civil institution of power. The Church became identified with Roman culture and over-anxious about stability. As a Christian society came into existence, the Church became a part of the established order. As the Church spread and soon became almost one with Europe it began to think of itself almost in quantitative terms. One was a Christian who was baptized into a Christian society which, it was believed, was almost the whole world. Only a few perverse outsiders remained. Also, by this time, the Church had elaborated a whole system of rules, laws, rituals and penalties to bolster the external structure. Gone was the concept of proclamation of witnessing the good news. The thrust was now the self-preservation and stability of the organization. When the Protestant Reformation and the Enlightenment and the French Revolution occurred, whole countries were torn from the Catholic structure. The shrunken Church reacted by insisting more and more on obedience, discipline and authority. A new definition of the Church, designed to bolster these three virtues, was put forth.

The one true Church is a group of men bound together by the profession of the same Christian faith and by the communion of the same sacraments, under the rule of the legitimate pastors, and especially of the one vicar of Christ on earth, the Roman Pontiff. From this definition it can easily be gathered which men belong to the Church and which do not. . . . For the Church is a group of men, as visible and palatable as that of the Roman people, or the Kingdom of France or the Republic of Venice.

The Church, in this popular definition (the one which guided our catechisms) is seen as a juridical body with clear indications who are in and who are out. It was this Church, we saw in the beginning, which had to come to terms with its minority status. It was this Church that was too narrow, too institutional to survive the ramifications of a new global view of the world. But if the Church is not basically an institution outside of whose physical borders no one can be saved, but is, like Jesus, a particular minority sign of the Father's merciful love, then the Church as sacrament is vindicated. Then we do not have to be embarrassed at the Church's being a minority assembly, gathered around the eucharist and nourished by the sacraments. The Church becomes the sacrament of the encounter with Christ as Christ is called "the sacrament of the encounter with God" (Schillebeeckx). The Church is an ever present sign of God's love. It does not have to be physically universal any more than Jesus was. Its task must simply be that of Jesus himself: to be a sign of and to reveal the Father's love and grace.

However, having said this, there is a derivative question we must deal with. If the Church's new position is that of a sacrament, that of a minority sign outside of whose physical boundaries men are saved, then why join? why be a Christian? The answer to this is both simple and profound. To belong to the Church is to belong to those who know. The Church is a community of those who know. Salvation is had outside of the Church but never apart from it. The Church, we must understand, is God's concrete, historical manifestation of his design in Christ for all men. It is a sacramental sign of the grace that is offered to the world and to history as a whole. From the first Christ and the Church have been God's plan of salvation. We cannot be indifferent to that. To believe in Jesus and to believe in the Church is to accept them both as reminder of God's total salvific plan.

> Unless they fall back through evil intentions, all men travel the same road, and it leads them to salvation: it is the road of self-giving through love. The journey is common to all men, who are turned in the right direction by a law that God has placed in their hearts. The only thing is that some people on the road, through God's revelation, know something that relates to all; they know the mystery of the journey. And what they know, they know in order to make a contribution to the common quest.[7]

Christianity is the unique and absolute religion founded by God through Christ. In the sense that all exists in Christ and all is focused in him then we must hold that in principle all salvation and history is Christian right from the start. The Church of Christ is the essential sign of what God intends for the human race, the sacrament which points to his eternal plan "hidden for long ages" but now "achieved in Christ Jesus our Lord."

This makes sense. However we have one further question. There are many varieties of Christianity. Why should we be a Christian in the Roman Catholic tradition? The Church gives its own answer. It says that the fullness of Christianity is found in Catholicism. It concedes that it has many common elements with all Christians. It says however that the full revelation and full structure are to be found in Catholicism. "Thanks to the efficacious promise of Christ, the Church, in full communion with the Petrine See, will always possess the objective elements of the total Christian patrimony: the saving doctrine of the gospel, the seven sacraments, and a legitimately empowered ministry."[8] Again, while the Catholic Church recognizes elements of Christianity in other Christian churches it continues to insist that there are degrees of apostolicity and that the Catholic Church "at least in the objective order, embodies these realities to the highest degree."[9] "The Catholic," as Father McBrien says, "is one who, while recognizing the bond of unity he has with all other Christians inside the Body of Christ, is convinced that the heart and center of unity in the

Church is the eucharist and that the ministerial or hierarchical foundation of the eucharist is the college of bishops with the pope as its head. There are degrees of incorporation in the Church, but the norm of incorporation is one's proximity to these sacramental and collegial realities."[10]

Still, for all this, the Catholic Church admits that there is some distinction yet between the Church of Christ and itself. The documents of Vatican II curiously and cautiously state that the Church of Christ "subsists" in the Catholic Church. What does this imply?

This implies at least some distinction between the Church of Christ and the Roman Catholic Church, while at the same time asserting a positive relationship between the two. The meaning is presumably that the Church of Christ is truly present in its essential completeness in the Catholic Church, but that there is some discrepancy, so that the Roman Catholic Church, as a sociological entity, remains under an obligation to become more perfectly one, holy, catholic—and thus more perfectly the Church of Christ. The Church of Christ is not a purely ideal being—for it does subsist on earth as an historically tangible reality—but it is not unsurpassably actualized in any given community, not even in the Catholic Church.[11]

So the Catholic Church does not deny its uniqueness, nor that in its fullness the Church of Christ subsists in it. At the same time, it recognizes that the Church of Christ is not confined to it, but rather goes beyond it but not without it. That is, all men are somehow connected with Christ whether they realize it or not. The Church continues to be the explicit, overt sign of precisely what God does in Christ for them. Karl Rahner expresses it this way:

The Christian will regard the non-Christians . . . not as having no part in Christianity or as standing altogether outside salvation because they are not Christians, but rather as anonymous Christians who do not realize what they truly are in virtue of grace in the depths of their own consciences. . . . The Christian will not think of making the Church . . . as one of the numerous 'sects' into which mankind is divided. . . . Instead of this the Christian will think of the Church rather as the visible and apprehensible form of that which already has a unifying force at the interior level, as the historical expression of that which is universal to all men. . . . In short, the Church appears to the Christian as the fundamental *sacrament* of a grace which, precisely because it is offered to all, pressed forward to express its sacramental significance in history even where the individual sacrament of baptism has not yet been conferred. . . . The Catholic Church cannot think of herself as one among many historical manifestations in which *one and the same* God-man Jesus Christ is made present, which are offered by God to man for him to choose whichever he likes. On the contrary she must necessarily think of herself as the one and total presence in history of the one God-man in his truth and grace and as such as having a fundamental relationship to all men.[12]

It is true then that in one sense we cannot escape entirely an elitist position: we are Catholics and the Church of Christ subsists most fully in the Catholic Church. Yet, as we now can deduce, this in no way implies the exclusive triumphalism of the past. It implies more than ever challenge: the challenge to witness, the challenge to live a holy life, the challenge to show the rest of the human race that they are loved and that, even unknowingly, the Spirit has been given to them. "The experience of 'church,' then, should not be the experience of entering the safe harbor, the place of privilege; it should be the experience of wonder, challenge in our own lives and mission to the lives of others. The question for the Christian is not, 'What do I get out of it?' It is rather: 'What can I give from it?' and 'To whom am I sent?' Thus the 'gathering' of the church, the *ekklesia,* is at once the experience of the transformation of one's life in a new vision, experience and pattern of action, but it is, at the same time, an experience of one's value and meaning for others. . . ."[13] Everyone has been offered salvation in Christ, this is our message to mankind. "For since Christ died for all men and since the ultimate vocation of man is in fact one and divine, we ought to believe that the Holy Spirit in a manner known only to God offers to every man the possibility of being associated with this paschal mystery."[14] To be a Catholic is not only to be counted among "those who know," but also to be counted among those who possess more fully the Church of Christ. The challenge, adventure and excitement of all this should be obvious. So also should be the responsibility. The need for personal holiness, the need to constantly reform our Church of its sins and defects, the need to build a community of love and service is urgent. Men indeed will always be saved, but more than ever they need a sign, the Sacrament of God's forgiving mercy in Jesus to tell them and to reassure them even when they are not there to listen.

— 3 —

There is much more to be said about the Church and much more that could be said about collegiality, the hierarchy, the inner structure and so on. But we do not want to deflect from the basic repositioning we have tried to do in this chapter. So perhaps it is time to summarize and draw some practical conclusions from what has been written.

1. First of all, it is evident that we must now look upon the Church in an entirely different light. Gone is the old uncritical stance whereby the Catholic Church assumed that it was right, the sole possessor of truth and the one and only physical means of salvation. Now we know that the Church is that minority grouping of those who know, of those who have the eucharist and the sacraments and a hierarchy to help them to be better revealers of the God in Jesus. If we would go back to our old nautical metaphor we now can look upon the Church not as Peter's Bark outside of which no one is saved (in the physical sense of being externally a member of the Church), but as a lighthouse shining its light as a beacon of love, mercy and proclamation. The Church shares with all mankind its deepest longings and aspirations and is a sign-sacrament that Christ is the answer.

2. Secondly, the whole foundation for ecumenism is based on the understanding of the Church as not exclusively the Church of Christ, but that many elements are found in other Christian bodies, even though "it is through Christ's Catholic Church alone, which is the all-embracing means of salvation, that the fullness of the means of salvation can be obtained."[15] Still the Church enjoys a common

heritage and recognizes such in other Christian bodies for, after all, "all those justified by faith through baptism are incorporated into Christ. They therefore have a right to be honored by the title of Christian, and are properly regarded as brothers in the Lord by the sons of the Catholic Church."[16]

3. Numbers are not essential. From all that we have said it seems evident that not all men are destined to belong to the Catholic Church. From what we have said, it is not even necessary. At various times the Church may shrink in size, become a remnant, but still nevertheless a remnant which embodies all that God has willed for all of mankind in Christ. It likewise follows that the Church's missionary activity is no longer primarily "making converts" at least in the old sense that there was an urgency to get all men into the Church. Certainly gone is the notion that all those outside the Church will perish and we must rescue them from idolatry and eternal damnation. Rather the Church's missionary enterprise may take the tactic of inviting the Christ-goodness already present in "anonymous" Christians, of drawing out the possibilities for grace already there, of proclaiming the good news that God loves them. The procedure missionaries may use may well take the form, not of actively proselyting, but of bearing simple, quiet, and firm witness through the life style, faith, deep charity, and the social concerns for those around them:

> It is quite clear in the tradition of the Church and has been made fully explicit in the teaching of Vatican II, that an individual need not be a confessing member of the visible Church to be saved, but that the Church is necessary in the world so that mankind may be saved. In other words, the vocation of being a Christian is the task of helping Jesus knowingly in the salvation of the world in the way that he has pointed out. This, of course, is a most fruitful way of salvation for the individual himself but it is not the only way an individual can be saved. Therefore, it is most important to offer Church membership in the fullest sense to everyone, but not to attempt to force it on anyone who is not ready to make the commitment of his own free will.[17]

4. There are two closing points to make, but briefly since they

have become commonplace. The Church is not the clergy. The Church is a community which indeed demands its hierarchical leadership and authority, but only in the service of all the Church. In other words, the Church is clergy and laity together, each has its own charism and therefore communication, consultation and cooperation are in order. The second point is that we must recall that the Church is not necessarily tied down to the structure as we know it. The Church, in fact, has had many "styles" in its two-thousand-year history. It has been more flexible than suspected and the present Roman organization form we have now is not necessarily its only form.[18]

5. Finally, to be a Catholic is to be part of an ancient heritage that has served well and has held onto the basic message of Christ through many epochs of history. To be a Catholic is to be among those who know God's eternal plan in Christ. To be a Catholic is to have most fully the Church of Christ. To be a Catholic is to be in basic relationship to all of mankind. To be a Catholic is to stand around the eucharistic table in order better to do what Christ did (Do this in memory of me) : to take up one's cross, to die to self, to serve and love others in his name and so continue the great task and privilege of proclamation. To be a Catholic is to bear Paul's basic message to the world about Jesus and his Father: "For I am convinced that there is nothing in death or life, in the realm of spirits or superhuman powers, in the world as it is or the world as it shall be, in the forces of the universe, in heights or depths—nothing in all creation that can separate us from the love of God in Christ Jesus our Lord" (Rom 8:38).

NOTES FOR CHAPTER 9

1. Tad W. Guzie, *Jesus and the Eucharist* (Paulist Press, 1974) chapter 2.
2. Denzinger, 714.
3. William J. Bausch, *Pilgrim Church* (Fides Publishers, 1973) p. 234.
4. Avery Dulles, *Models of the Church* (Doubleday, 1974).
5. On whether Jesus even intended to found a church at all, see "Foundation of the Church" by Alfred Cody in *Theological Studies,* Vol. 34, no. 1, March, 1973, p. 3ff.
6. Tad W. Guzie, cited above, p. 127.
7. Juan Luis Segundo, *The Community Called Church* (Orbis Books, 1973) p. 32.
8. Avery Dulles, *The Dimensions of the Church* (Newman Press, 1967) p. 28.
9. Richard P. McBrien, *Who Is a Catholic?* (Dimension Books, 1971) p. 17.
10. Richard P. McBrien, p. 21.
11. Avery Dulles, *Models of the Church,* cited above, p. 118.
12. Karl Rahner, *Theological Investigations* Vol. X (Herder and Herder, 1973) pp. 31 to 41.
13. Joseph Powers, *Spirit and Sacrament* (Seabury Press, 1973) pp. 112 and 113.
14. The Church in the Modern World, article 22.
15. Decree on Ecumenism, article 3.
16. Decree on Ecumenism, article 3.
17. Monika K. Hellwig, *The Meaning of the Sacraments* (Pflaum/Standard, 1972) p. 31.
18. William J. Bausch, cited above, chapter II.

10. Positioning Sacraments

— 1 —

At one time the Catholic Church popularly held that each and every one of the seven sacraments was accurately and precisely invented by Jesus Christ as to rite, ritual, ceremony and detail. At one time the Protestant denominations denied that five of the sacraments were not true sacraments because they could not be found in scripture; only baptism and the eucharist could. Neither side is any longer so sure about its position. The Catholics have largely abandoned their simple, historical point of view. They admit they cannot determine that the seven sacraments were exactly and unambiguously established by Jesus himself. The Protestants have largely abandoned their dictum of "scripture alone" because modern scholarship has shown that they cannot demonstrate that even their two cherished sacraments, baptism and the eucharist, were exactly and unambiguously established by Jesus himself, and were not in fact largely developed by the early Church.[1] So both Christian communities are searching for other grounds to justify the two sacraments of baptism and eucharist and, as a consequence, on the same discovered principle, the other five. If a common ground can be discovered then Catholics and Protestants may move the cause of ecumenism a little closer.[2]

What do the biblical and first Christian records show? The records show that from the beginning the sacraments are really not precise, defined objects. They are rather part of that overall "mysterion" (sacramentum=mystery) found among Jews and Greeks. They are among the many rites and objects described as showing forth in some way God's special power and saving presence. The pagans had many rites and rituals akin to our sacraments and

163

theologians speak of Jewish sacraments. "... The sacraments of the old Law ... according to the Church's teaching, truly existed. Since Augustine, with a few evanescent exceptions, theology has held firmly to their existence and the Church presupposes it in many doctrinal pronouncements."[3] We must remember that in Judaism there were the raising and imposition of hands, blessings, oil, bread, water, washing, kisses and greetings, the notion of a symbolic meal (Passover), sacrificial offerings, banquets, all of which the Church inherited and accepted. We often forget that baptism was preached and practiced by John the Baptist for the remission of sins. There was an official confession of sins from Solomon's time. Rabbis wrote of an anointing of the sick with oil. So between the natural drive to express oneself in gestures and signs plus the inherited rituals of paganism and especially Judaism, Christianity has many symbolic motions and words and from these came those great signs we know as the seven sacraments. "There were innumerable other symbolic gestures which bound together the early Christians: blessings of bread and the fields, the hospitable kiss, and the washing of feet, the anointing of rulers and the receptions of monks and consecrated women. All of these formed a part of the primitive sacramental texture; though some were of but passing importance and fell into disuse. Only those great Seven were to survive into the early Middle Ages. ..."[4]

Does this mean that in the course of Christian history some vague gestures evolved into the sacraments, gestures and rites that might have been any one of hundreds? No, it means that among all of the rituals, blessings and gestures these seven became the most important and truly the most authentic because they already had within themselves Christ's own dynamism. The Church, under the Spirit, came to recognize this and so drew out of its tradition those elements which best described and evoked the work of Jesus. Again, this tradition was in no way arbitrary for all of the basic grace-actions, from baptism to the forgiveness of sins, can be found in scripture. Scholars point out for example the symbolism in the miracles at Cana as being a reference to baptism. Jesus' multiplication of the loaves is clearly eucharistic. The anointing at Bethany is a reference to the sacrament of the sick and Mary's being at Cana (Mary is always a scriptural sign of the Church) foreshadows Christian marriage.[5] In short, the sacraments are not inventions but conclusions from what was found in the Church's first tradition and in scripture. The actual specification of rite and ceremony came later and was determined by the Church. Jesus did not invent each sacrament in blueprint form even to the degree that the very number seven is ambiguous for several sacraments arise from one source or can be divided; for example confirmation clearly belongs to baptism and holy orders can admit of several grades. That is why Karl Rahner remarks that even the defined dogma that there are seven sacraments must be interpreted with a certain caution.[6] The point is that Jesus indirectly did give us the sacraments to the degree, as we shall see shortly, that he himself is the Sacrament of the Father and he gave us the Church as Sacrament of himself. It is from this fact that the implications of what we call the seven sacraments arise. The precise sacramental theology is a development of a later analytical age, and especially that of the Middle Ages when the number seven was spelled out and the formulas and rituals more properly defined.[7]

So, what do we have so far? We have the understanding that the seven sacraments were not handed down as-is personally from Jesus himself. Rather they spring from the nature of rite itself, they have an association and derivation from the so-called Jewish sacraments, they are to be found in spirit in the scripture, but their exact numbering and defining were to be left to the Church of another age. But what led the Church to do this and why are the sacraments truly real and powerful and part of Christianity? Why were they the natural unfolding of a growing Church? The answer to this lies in what we saw in the last chapter, in the nature of the Church itself as a sacrament.

— 2 —

In their manual entitled "Basic Teachings for Catholic Religious Education" the United States Bishops sum up concisely the current understanding of the relationship between Christ, the Church and the sacraments. "Sacraments are the principal action through which Christ gives his Spirit to Christians and makes them a holy people. He has entrusted the sacraments to the Church, but they are always to be thought of as actions of Christ himself, from whom they get their power."[8] So, as we must, we start with Christ in our understanding of the sacraments. Christ is called the "primordial" sacrament; that is, he is the sacrament or sign *par excellence* of the Father. This is not new to us. All through this book we have been stressing Christ as the revelation of the Father, the Father's self-disclosure. In Jesus, in the incarnation, this disclosure becomes concrete and physical. The Father chose the human flesh of Jesus to redeem us. It was in Jesus' loving act of surrender that he reconciled us all. Since Jesus is the decisive revelation of the Father's love then he and he alone becomes *the* tangible, outward and everlasting sign (sacrament) of that love. He is the primordial sacrament. But, true to the principle of the incarnation, God continues to choose human signals and human material to be present, nourishing and saving to us. Edward Schillebeeckx stresses this point when he says:

> On Christ's side, the possibility of a human encounter is positively established. Human encounter, however, calls for mutual availability. . . . But we, earthly men, cannot encounter Christ (now glorified) in the living body because his glorification has made him invisible to us. . . .

> But on the other hand, it follows from the dogma of the perpetuity of the incarnation and of Christ's human mediation of grace, that if Christ does not show himself to us in his own flesh, then he can make himself visibly present to us and for us earthbound men only by taking up earthly non-glorified realities into his glorified saving activity. This earthly element replaces for us the invisibility of his bodily life in heaven. This is precisely what the sacraments are: the face of redemption turned visibly towards us, so that in them we are truly able to encounter the living Christ. The heavenly saving activity, invisible to us, becomes visible in the sacraments. . . .

> Sacramentality thus bridges the gap and solves the disproportion between the Christ of heaven and unglorified humanity, and makes

possible a reciprocal human encounter of Christ and men even after the ascension, though in a special manner. . . . From this account of the sacraments as earthly prolongations of Christ's glorified bodiness, it follows immediately that the Church's sacraments are not things but encounters of men on earth with the glorified man Jesus by way of a visible form. . . .[9]

So the sacraments are extensions of the incarnation, true encounters with Christ. As Methodist J. Benjamin Garrison says so well, "The sacraments are the church's way of italicizing the saving Word"[10] which is Christ. In scriptural language, the sacraments are not *chronos* ("time") in that they occur willy nilly to this or that individual who activates the rite. They are rather *karios* ("hour," as in Jesus' "My hour has come"); that is, they are saving moments, encounters, italicized words of the salvation in Christ that are being spoken all the time.

We go one step further. The principle of the incarnation has been extended to the Church. If Christ is the sacrament of the Father, the Church is the sacrament of Christ. That is what we saw in the last chapter. The Church prolongs and extends the incarnation. It is the sign of the Sign, "Light from Light," to snatch a phrase from the creed. The sacraments, then, are "vital actions of the Church whose mysterious essence it is to be 'in Christ' and by virtue of Christ, the 'primordial sacrament.' "[11] The Dutch catechism sums it all up when it says, "When we consider the place taken by these signs in the work of salvation, we may sum up by saying that in Christ God became visible and tangible. That in the Church Christ, and hence God, remains visible and tangible among us. And that the Church in turn becomes visible and tangible in the seven signs. They are Christ's hands which now touch us and Christ's words which now ring in our ears. They are his way of being palpable today."[12] So the sacraments are not seven parallel channels of grace to men but rather they are more of a framework of grace that is inseparable from the life of the Church as a whole. ". . . When the Church in her official, organized, public capacity precisely as the source of redemptive grace meets the individual in the actual ultimate accomplishment of her nature, there we have sacraments in the proper sense, and they can then be seen to be the essential functions that bring into activity the very essence of the Church herself. For in them she herself attains the highest degree of actualization of what she always is: the presence of redemptive grace, historically visible and manifest as the sign of the eschatologically victorious grace of God in the world."[13]

Having drawn a straight line from God to Christ to the Church we can go back to pick up two important points. One, we recall, is that Jesus did not (and need not) institute each and every sacrament individually, but rather that the Church drew on the traditions left by Jesus and from the many rituals and blessings specifies these seven as most characteristic of his saving action. And, again, this was not arbitrary, but rather all seven sacraments have their essence based in scripture. So, "without prejudicing or challenging an immediate historical association of certain sacraments with Jesus in his pre-Easter ministry and teaching, we can state simply that the sacraments in general have been instituted by Christ because, and to the extent that, the Church originates with him."[14] And the Church took what was at hand and used it to interpret the mysteries which Jesus had left it. In other words the Church was content to see the already present ancient rituals *transformed* in their inner meaning and value by the creative actions and words of Christ. The Church saw Jesus' life, death and whole redemptive act forcefully celebrated in, and become the content of, the old rituals. So now it is Christ and the salvation in him which is now the core meaning and power of the *Christian* sacraments as opposed to the Jewish sacraments. ". . . True Christian theology joins the institution of the sacraments by Christ with the natural symbolism of washing and eating, which of itself has religious significance. The words of institution simply gave a new meaning to rites already charged with meaning. And the new meaning was not forced upon the natural meaning but rather amplified and enriched it. In no way were the words thought to infuse a wholly accidental, unprepared meaning into actions that were not predestined to receive it."[15] So Jewish baptism, the Jewish paschal meal, Jewish anointing are now given a new internal dimension by Jesus and in the course of time, specified by the Church as such. This is where we get our sacraments.

The second point flows from the first. We just said that the sacraments are rituals, already laden with religious significance, now given a new spirit by Jesus, the spirit of his saving action. Now we can see why the eucharist is the primary sacrament. Since Jesus is *the* sacrament, since his loving act reconciled us to the Father, then the eucharist is primary because the Last Supper sums all this up. The eucharistic meal is the celebration of what God has done and does do for all in the Spirit. Life, death, salvation, resurrection, Spirit—all are celebrated in the eucharist. We eat and drink the death of the Lord until he comes. So the eucharist is the Church's archetypal sacrament because it says so much, because it contains in miniature as it were, atonement and salvation, the central "mysterion" in which the union between God and man is both symbolized and achieved. Therefore since Jesus is *the* sacrament made present in the eucharist then all the other sacraments must cluster about it. All the other sacraments in some way prepare for and support the eucharist. And indeed, "the study of scripture and the Fathers has more and more revealed the reality of the total sacramental complex, in which all the ritual signs form, as it were, a spiritual galaxy revolving about the two central mysteries, baptism and the eucharist."[16] So the sacraments are really expressions of the single mystery of God's salvation in Jesus, variations on a theme as summed up in the eucharist.

— 3 —

The sacraments are the actions of Christ in his Church. This is a statement we have already made, repeating what Vatican II has said. But, simple as that statement is, it has been forgotten sufficiently to produce in the course of history three abuses which we shall now examine: (1) making the sacraments "things" (2) making them magic and (3) making them exclusive.

Making the sacraments things. This is the result of a tendency we have already observed several times before, the tendency to objectify either God or Christ. Objectifying the sacraments, that is, making them concrete, maneuverable things is the result of thinking about grace in the same terms. If we do such and such a ritual (material thing) we produce the commensurate result, grace. It is a simple production involving cause and effect. The outcome of this outlook is to see the sacraments as things, as levers to be pulled to get the product. This in turn can so mechanize the sacraments that we can push further and further into background the notion of God in Christ, the notion of a personal encounter and the necessity of activating and engaging our faith. The answer is to go back to grace itself and to stop looking at it as an object. We would do much better to think of grace as an action. Like love. When we reduce love to a thing and identify love with its object (card, flowers, kiss, etc.) then it is an easy step to feel that the whole love enterprise is satisfied when one does the proper things. "I've put a roof over your head, money in your purse, food on the table and a car in the garage. What more do you want?" asks the unperceptive husband. He has reduced the whole marriage relationship to a contractual thing-exchange. But married love is an action: a caring, a reaching out, a movement of concern, support, forgiveness. So it is with God. God is in action in Jesus. He discloses himself and loves us in Jesus. He wishes to share his life with us. He takes the initiative. He calls, summons, invites and moves in us. This is grace. It is divine *action*. It is encounter, not a divine product packaged and delivered on demand in the sacraments.[17] On the contrary. The sacraments are signs, "rhythms" by which God "graces" us. They are movements which both signify and cause the action of God in a special way in our lives. The sacraments are sign-acts which convey a reality to a person from a Person. Every sacramental gift is a sign of the Giver. The sacraments express the Father's whole loving action towards us in Christ. So the sacraments are not to be approached as things, in any mechanical sense of bargaining: the ritual for the result (grace). Rather the sacraments are to be approached with the greatest spirit of a sense of encounter as two lovers approach each other. They are actions, not transactions.

Making the sacraments magic. This is the natural result of making the sacraments things and, moreover, things to be treasured for the hereafter. The example here would be to see the sacraments as a kind of checking account. One walks up to the cashier (priest), hands him the check (rite) and gets credit for good hard savings (grace). The focus here is on the hereafter. The more one goes to the sacraments, the more grace he stores up in heaven. In this view the sacraments are not really geared to this life; they are savings accounts to make the next life more secure, more comfortable. The magic consists not only in this simplistic view, but in the naive maneuvering of God. God is somehow forced to give grace if the proper rites are performed. It is this exaggerated view that has led non-Catholics to see superstition in the Catholic sacraments. It is this exaggeration that has triggered the present day reemphasis on the faith of the participant; that says that while God is always faithful (the real meaning of *ex opere operato*) man is not. He bears the responsibility for his free engagement in the encounter with God in the sacraments. There is no automatic holiness.

The sacraments as exclusive. Under this title there are two correctives to be noted. First of all, in keeping with the nature of the Church itself as the sacrament of Christ, that is, as a sign symbol of what God intends for all people, the sacraments also are for the benefit of mankind. They are public statements, affirmations in the concrete of what God can do for all. So, for example, the difference between Christians and other people is not so much that Christians are baptized and the others are not. The difference is that Christians declare, in their special baptismal ceremony, that they know all men have been baptized in the Spirit from the foundation of the world. That is why in the previous chapter we described the Church as a community of those who know. They are, in the words we quoted before, the italicized words of God that are spoken to all. So while Christians do have a monopoly on the sensible, signative sacramental manifestations of grace they do not have a monopoly on grace itself. The sacraments exist precisely to proclaim what is offered to all.[18]

Secondly, the sacraments are not exclusive private acts for the benefit of individuals. They belong to and are to be celebrated by the community as a whole. This is not to deny that the sacraments benefit individuals and are a primary source of holiness. Rather it is to observe that even individual holiness exists to build up the whole body, the whole community. The formation of the Christian community, its strengthening and growth in order better to proclaim the Christ is of prime importance. "A community gathered together around a liberative paschal message needs signs which fashion it and question it, which imbue it with a sense of responsibility and enable it to create its own word about man's history. This is precisely what the sacraments are—and nothing else but that. Through them God grants and signifies to the Church the grace which is to constitute it truly as such within the vast human community. . . ."[19] That is why there is something basically contradictory about the sacraments being ritualized in private or alone. The sacraments are liturgy, which is to say, public affirmations and public praises of the Father's saving action in Jesus. They exist to prolong and evoke a faith-filled community. As a matter of fact, it is historical record which demonstrates that the sacraments were geared for the building up of the Christian family. The "major" sacraments, as they are called, baptism, confirmation and the eucharist, served to introduce one into the community of believers. "Interest in the sacraments was nothing else but interest in the matter of belonging to the community."[20] So there must be community presence and participation. This is the reason that Vatican II was so emphatic when it said, "It is to be stressed that whenever rites, according to their specific nature, make provision for communal celebration, involving the presence and active participation of the faithful, this way of celebrating them is to be preferred, as far as possible, to a celebration that is individual or quasi-private."[21]

Actually, we have witnessed a change in most of the sacramental rituals in the past years precisely to bring out their communal aspect. These revisions have been adequate but at times not altogether suitable. There is still a tendency to work backwards from the previous rituals to the sacrament instead of discovering what the essential Christ event is and working out a ritual to evoke that.

Nevertheless the new rituals do have one thing in common: they are all urged to be done communally and provide for such. Baptism within the community Mass, for instance, is meant to show that the baptism is indeed a sacrament of initiation, that there is a two way responsibility involved; that the community "goes bond" for the infant and promises to create those conditions within which the child can mature in the faith. Communal confessions are meant to show that sin is never private but always public. It vibrates on the Christian family; that reconciliation involves not only peace with God but with God's people; that the community, diminished in its prophetic impact because of the sins of its members, must communally be restored and healed as a community. Celebrating the sacrament of the sick (extreme unction) in a communal setting emphasizes that the whole people are involved in the paschal mystery of life, death and resurrection; that there is a mutual demand for common prayer, a mutual need for common concern.

It is noteworthy also that many people have roles to play in the sacramental celebrations. This is an attempt to get away from the sacraments as private transactions between the holy man (priest) and parishioner. It is an attempt to make us realize that the priest does not "give" the sacraments, but rather that the sacraments are community celebrations over which he presides. The priest merely and importantly orchestrates the community in its common motions of growth and spiritual maturity so that it may be a better witness to the world. All this is not to downgrade personal and individual holiness, but merely to point out that personal and individual holiness does not exist for its own sake but for the sake of the building up of the Body of Christ, the Church. To give out the sacraments indiscriminately where a faith-filled community is absent comes too close to magic.

So in our repositioning of the sacraments we may summarize as follows:

1. The sacraments were not specifically instituted by Christ in the popular sense that he blueprinted each one for posterity. The Christian sacraments have antecedents in the general human

need for gesture and ritual and particularly in the Jewish sacraments.

2. The essence of the sacraments can be found both in scripture and tradition, but it was the Church which added the specific enumeration, details and rites.

3. The sacraments receive their importance and power from Jesus himself as the "primordial sacrament." Jesus in turn is sacramentalized in the Church. So the Church's concrete seven sacraments are aspects of *the* sacrament, Christ—continued incarnations of him as it were.

4. Of all the sacraments the eucharist sums up Christ's whole redemptive work of grace; that is why it is preeminent and why it is the central force towards which the other six sacraments are orientated.

5. Sacraments have been abused, at times being reduced either to things or magic or partisan elite terms. But the sacraments, like Christ himself, cannot be reduced to things; they are actions, encounters and ones which celebrate what God has in mind for all mankind. They belong to the Church, to the Christian community for its building up so that it may witness better.

6. Any of the individual sacraments[22] must be seen in the context of the above five summary statements.

NOTES FOR CHAPTER 10

1. John Macquarrie, *Principles of Christian Theology* (Charles Scribner's Sons, 1966) p. 401.

2. See Karl Rahner's suggestion in "What Is a Sacrament?" in *Worship*, Vol. 47, no. 5, May, 1973. Besides the foundation of the sacraments Catholics and Protestants disagree as to their efficacy or power. If like the Protestants we stress only the faith of the recipient, that leaves God's initiative and action out of the picture; if like the Catholics we stress God's automatic power, that leaves the sacraments open to magic.

3. Karl Rahner, *Inquiries* (Herder and Herder, 1964) p. 211.

4. Herbert Mursurillo, "The Sacraments in Early Christian Tradition" in *A Theology Reader,* edited by Robert W. Gleason (Macmillan, 1966).

5. David M. Stanley, *The Apostolic Church in the New Testament* (Newman Press, 1967) p. 128ff.

6. Karl Rahner, *Inquiries,* cited above, p. 238. Father Rahner also reminds us that "The precise meaning of the expression 'institution by Jesus Christ' is to this day a controverted question in theology." This from the *Worship* article cited above, p. 282.

7. For example, by Abelard and especially by Peter Lombard in his book, *Sentences,* written in 1148.

8. "Basic Teachings for Catholic Religious Education" put out by the United States Catholic Conference, Washington, D.C., 1973, p. 11. This manual reflects, of course, the worldwide Catechetical Directory.

9. E. Schillebeeckx, *Christ the Sacrament of the Encounter with God* (Sheed and Ward, 1963) pp. 43 and 44.

10. Ernest J. Fiedler and R. Benjamin Garrison, *The Sacraments: An Experiment in Ecumenical Honesty* (Fides Publishers, 1969).

11. Raphael Schulte in *Sacramentum Mundi,* Vol. 5 (Herder and Herder, 1970) p. 381.

12. *A New Catechism* (Seabury Press, 1969) p. 253.

13. Karl Rahner, *Inquiries,* cited above, p. 204. See also the *Dictionary of Thelogy* by Louis Bouyer (Desclee, 1965) p. 393.

14. Karl Rahner in *Worship,* cited above, p. 282.

15. Louis Bouyer, *Rite and Man: Natural Sacredness and Christian Liturgy* (University of Notre Dame Press, 1963) p. 64.

16. Herbert Mursurillo, cited above, p. 253.

17. Joseph M. Powers, *Eucharistic Theology* (Herder and Herder, 1967) p. 80ff.

18. Juan Luis Segundo, *The Sacraments Today* (Orbis Books, 1974) p. 77.

19. Juan Luis Segundo, p. 99.

20. Juan Luis Segundo, p. 43.

21. Constitution of the Sacred Liturgy, article 27.

22. It is beyond the scope of this book to go into the individual sacraments and their revised rites. Two popular books will help here. One is *The Meaning of the Sacraments* by Monika Hellwig (Pflaum/Standard, 1972) and *The Sacraments in a World of Change* by Joseph M. Champlin (Ave Maria Press, 1973).